John Lasseter |

Contemporary Film Directors

Edited by Justus Nieland and Jennifer Fay

The Contemporary Film Directors series provides concise, well-written introductions to directors from around the world and from every level of the film industry. Its chief aims are to broaden our awareness of important artists, to give serious critical attention to their work, and to illustrate the variety and vitality of contemporary cinema. Contributors to the series include an array of internationally respected critics and academics. Each volume contains an incisive critical commentary, an informative interview with the director, and a detailed filmography.

*A list of books in the series
appears at the end of this book.*

John Lasseter |

Richard Neupert

**UNIVERSITY
OF
ILLINOIS
PRESS**
URBANA,
CHICAGO,
AND
SPRINGFIELD

Frontispiece: John Lasseter, 2002. Photo by Eric Charbonneau.

Library of Congress Cataloging-in-Publication Data
Names: Neupert, Richard John.
Title: John Lasseter / Richard Neupert.
Description: Urbana : University of Illinois Press, 2016. | Series: Contemporary
    film directors | Includes bibliographical references and index. | Includes
    filmography.
Identifiers: LCCN 2015037526 | ISBN 9780252040153 (hardcover : alk. paper) |
    ISBN 9780252081644 (pbk. : alk. paper) | ISBN 9780252098352 (e-book)
Subjects: LCSH: Lasseter, John. | Motion picture producers and directors—United
    States—Biography. | Animators—United States—Biography. | Pixar (Firm)
Classification: LCC PN1998.3.L3925 N48 2016 | DDC 791.4302/33092—dc23
    LC record available at http://lccn.loc.gov/2015037526

Contents

Color images follow page 100

This project began thanks to a casual conversation with my good friend Kelley Conway, who was writing on Agnès Varda for this Contemporary Film Directors series. The editors for the series, Jennifer Fay and Justus Nieland, were welcoming and receptive to a study of the animator-director John Lasseter. From the start, Daniel Nasset, Marika Christofides, Tad Ringo, Matt Mitchell, and the staff at the University of Illinois Press have all been wonderfully supportive and helpful. The result is this introduction to John Lasseter and his role in shaping the narrative, stylistic, and ultimately emotional trajectories of Pixar films.

Mike Hussey, my computer-animation colleague at the University of Georgia, deserves very special thanks. He was always willing to field questions and explain technical terms, no matter how naive. I would also like to express my appreciation to UGA's Nate Kohn, Christopher Sieving, Rielle Navitski, Josh Marsh, and Joelle Arp-Dunham. Holly Gallagher did me a great service by reading and commenting on early portions of the book. Clay Chastain assisted with many practical details, and the students in my History of Animation course proved most inspiring. I am also very fortunate to have the kind support of the UGA Franklin College and especially my good friend, Senior Associate Dean Hugh Ruppersburg; my department head, David Saltz; and Nicholas Allen, director of the Willson Center for Humanities and Arts. My Willson Center research-cluster colleagues Tianming Liu and L. Stephen Miller also provided many new insights into perception, emotion, and mental processing that made their way into this book. The reference librarian Kristin Nielsen and the rest of the staff of the UGA libraries were consistently helpful. Crucial research and travel funding came from the generous Charles H. Wheatley professorship as well as the

University of Georgia Foundation and Franklin College for the Arts and Humanities.

I am incredibly lucky to have a cohort of very good friends and colleagues who offer continuing encouragement and advice, including Matthew Bernstein, Jim Peterson, Kelley Conway, J. J. Murphy, Marc Vernet, David Bordwell, Kristin Thompson, and Eric Smoodin. Along the way, I have been aided by valuable information from a great many people, including B. Z. Petroff, Michel Ocelot, Pixar cofounder Alvy Ray Smith, and David A. Price, whose marvelous book *The Pixar Touch* is essential reading for all Pixar fans and scholars alike.

My wife Catherine Jones continues to amaze me with her cheerful encouragement, thoughtful advice, and impeccable critical insights. And I thank our daughter Sophie for her patience and for always finding the humor in *Tin Toy*, even though the baby cries. But most of all I thank the fine folks at Pixar for these great movies. In fact, I would like to dedicate this book to one of my favorite characters, the often overlooked Luxo Sr.

John Lasseter |

John Lasseter and the Rise of Pixar Style |

Lasseter and company work from the Wes Anderson/Tarantino/
Aardman template, in that their films seem to take place in
neither the past nor the present but in a fondly recalled time.

—Kent Jones, "Beyond Disbelief"

An Apprenticeship in Animation

John Lasseter (b. 1957) is the much-celebrated chief creative officer for Pixar Animation Studios, Walt Disney Animation Studios, and Disneytoon Studios. He is also one of the best known and most successful animators in the world. In fact, his closest peer today may be Hayao Miyazaki. Both men have brought new attention and critical respect to cartoon stories and styles. Lasseter has also proven instrumental in Pixar's meteoric rise as the most recognized animation brand on the planet. Movies directed by Lasseter, from *Luxo Jr.* (1986) to *Toy Story* (1995) to *Cars 2* (2011), helped launch computer animation as a viable commercial medium and guide its subsequent technical and aesthetic development. Further, his Luxo lamp character became an immediate icon, recognized for high-quality, engaging animation. Equally significant is Lasseter's rare ability to adapt and update traditional two-dimensional character-animation principles for a clever synthesis with the 3D computer-generated imagery of the digital era.

Clearly, John Lasseter is one of the most important figures in American cinema today. He has contributed to the revival of character animation and helped propel a return to feature-length animation in Hollywood and beyond. Moreover, Lasseter may have done more to foster thinking, embodied computer-generated characters than anyone else. This Contemporary Film Director series book investigates the individual aesthetic and storytelling strategies that distinguish John Lasseter's films and explains how his personal style grew into a studio style for Pixar. Primary emphasis will be placed on the first several stages of Lasseter's career and his collaborative mode of production within Pixar Studios. By the time of *Cars* and Disney's purchase of Pixar, both in 2006, John Lasseter was firmly positioned as the single most important individual behind Pixar's productions and a new source of optimism for Disney's future animation output. This book chronicles the rise of Lasseter's career and the groundbreaking animated films he directed, revealing ways he and his colleagues at Pixar changed the direction of commercial animation forever.

Admittedly, discussing auteur traits in a commercial animator, director, and producer raises concerns for some contemporary critics. During an era with media products such as director commentaries, online interviews, and "making of" bonuses, auteurs are marketed in ever more complex ways via media saturation, commercial tie-ins, and media convergences. As Dana Polan points out, such marketing of the auteur's brand "is not only imposed on the director by external forces in the business but can come from his own savvy self-promotional tactics" (4). Art cinema and independent directors have always relied upon appeals to their auteur status to garner support and close attention. Hollywood studios have long exploited the auteur as a means for product differentiation. As a producer and studio namesake, Walt Disney famously "performed authorship of his studio's output," positioning himself as the benevolent, responsible patriarch for his family of films and characters (Griffin 140–41). Film historians and theorists routinely acknowledge the potential pitfalls of concentrating on auteurs, yet there remains a persistent faith in the value of studying the contributions of particularly significant individuals for what they can tell us about film culture but also the media industries in which they function. Fan culture typically perceives few of the critical traps. As Adrian Martin points out,

"Auteurism in cinema has always been about an intimate, often secret complicity—we in the audience feel ourselves privileged if we hear or receive the silent 'voice' of the auteur, as if we have received a special gift" (98). Lasseter's employers, Pixar and Disney, have clearly exploited Lasseter's auteurist fame to great effect. Just prior to the release of *Toy Story*, for instance, *Wired* had already pronounced Lasseter one of animation's "authentic, trailblazing stars. . . . If, as they say, whimsy is coded into the genes of animators, Lasseter was definitely born with it" (Snider 149). Lasseter became one of Pixar's biggest assets very early on, and his valuable cultural currency has grown exponentially ever since.

Directors such as John Lasseter, operating in digital, global, mainstream cinema, may be said to offer special hurdles for critics. Andrew Darley points out that digital effects-driven filmmaking, and especially what he calls the "spectacle cinema" of high-budget computer animation, has shifted some of the attention away from creative individual filmmakers and onto their companies and even technologies. Thus, "whilst not exactly displacing director names, it could be argued that [companies such as Pixar and Industrial Light and Magic] have tended to vie with them as a way of accounting for or measuring creative worth within the popular aesthetic imagination" (137). Darley mentions that only two animation and digital-effects directors manage to survive as auteurs in the popular press today. John Lasseter is one of them, though Darley only refers to him by name within a footnote (203). Yet somewhat paradoxically, the highly capitalized mode of computer animation also repositions the animator-artist at the core of production. As Thomas Elsaesser points out, the digital turn in cinema "requires a new kind of individual input, indeed manual application of craft and skill, which is to say, it marks the return of the 'artist' as source and origin of the image" (192). Pixar manages to counter some of the resistance to their corporate clout and commercialism by emphasizing the insight, artistry, and hard work of John Lasseter whenever possible. His highly innovative skill sets and career moves are closely tied to Pixar's successful trajectory: "It is only because Pixar, under the tutelage of Lasseter, struck upon its own way of *integrating* the new capacities of CGI with the traditions of feature animation that it has been able to create characters consistently capable of supporting a globally integrated marketing success" (Schaffer 77). John Lasseter warrants close study on many levels.

As with the other books in this series, *John Lasseter* remains committed to the notion that explaining the work habits and creative choices of an influential filmmaker can teach us much about the craft of cinematic storytelling and, in Lasseter's case, the development of computer animation and the Pixar style. Kristin Thompson argues that Pixar has remained a world leader precisely because they learned quickly how to market their films just like mainstream live-action cinema, including their exploitation of Lasseter: "John Lasseter is sort of the Steven Spielberg of animation—one of the few directors with wide popular name-recognition" (Bordwell and Thompson 163). It is precisely Lasseter's author-function that concerns us here. We are primarily interested in the degree to which he put his mark on Pixar stories and styles in a division of the film industry known for expansive teams with specialized divisions of labor and constant, highly capitalized, technological change and development. Further, Lasseter's career path and eventual creative choices were greatly shaped by the era in which he grew up. An increasingly global entertainment industry was undergoing fundamental changes during the 1970s and 1980s, just at the moment when Lasseter and his new generation of computer-savvy young artists and entrepreneurs were building on and modifying the past models of commercial cinema.

While there was always a vibrant subset of American animation that involved experimentation, the studio system and then generic commercial-television norms shaped and eventually dominated mainstream practices. Early advocates for computer animation included John and James Whitney, who used computers to generate intricate visual patterns equivalent to precise musical compositions. After working in other media, John Whitney came to regard the computer as a new sort of cinematic piano, the ultimate instrument for visual research that helped him defy conventional representational codes (Russett and Starr 180). By 1971, John Whitney's *Matrix* films exploited x, y, and z coordinates to explore three-dimensional space and complex series of visual harmonies. While this sort of avant-garde work proved incredibly influential with computer-graphics pioneers and spurred a whole new field of digital graphics for video logos, TV commercials, and games, its applications for mainstream narrative animation remained relatively tangential. With the acceleration of digital technologies by the 1980s and 1990s, many CGI applications were increasingly aimed at serving or mimicking the conventions of photographic realism and live-action cinema. While a rich array of experimental animation options exist within the wide, pervasive field of digital cinema, Suzanne Buchan explains that "CGI digital tools are enabling filmmakers to create a whole new experience of on-screen 'realism' that is increasingly gaining on photo-indexicality, until now the exclusive domain of photochemical celluloid" (2). Hyperrealism became a dominant goal of new digital developments.

Thus, theatrical cinema provided many of the fundamental models for new digital software, hardware, and their uses. As D. N. Rodowick observes, "Curiously, for an industry driven by innovation and market differentiation, the qualities of the 'photographic' and the 'cinematic' remain resolutely the touchstones for creative achievement in digital imaging entertainment" (101). Photographic and cinematic credibility, or what Stephen Prince labels "perceptual correspondence," in the form of photorealism remained the guiding principle of many technological developments and their applications (Prince, "True Lies," 36). As we will see, Pixar and Lasseter were driven to update existing cinematic-representational and narrative codes from the beginning. One of Lasseter's lasting legacies is his ability to bridge the worlds of the Disney aesthetic and the digital realm. To a very real extent, the resulting hybrid cinema evident in films like *Toy Story* ends up taming the radical potential of 3D computer graphics. Disney's *Bambi* proved more pertinent for their path than Whitney's *Matrix*. Lasseter and Pixar struggled to fit within classical Hollywood cinema's norms, forging new technological and industrial options that reinforced the conventions of past and contemporary film practice. Lasseter and Pixar's significance for shaping and even focusing the direction of commercial computer animation, in its technical and narrative developments, cannot be overstated.

Almost everyone will agree that John Lasseter's life story sounds as though it were fabricated by Pixar's marketing department. Even *Fortune* magazine's 2006 profile of Lasseter called it a "storybook life" that resembled "nothing so much as a Pixar plot line: Protagonist follows his heart, perseveres, gets the happy ending" (Schlender and Tkacyzk 140). However, it is worth noting that Lasseter, like all those Pixar protagonists, required valuable assistance from a community of equally fascinating groups and visionary individuals. Ed Catmull and Alvy Ray Smith first laid the foundations for what would become Pixar Animation

Studios, along with their friends and colleagues from the beginning, Ralph Guggenheim and David DiFrancesco. Both Catmull and Smith earned Ph.D.s before relentlessly pursuing their passion for combining computer graphics and animation into a viable new medium, eventually founding Pixar. Yet it is John Lasseter who has become the public face of Pixar. He is just as much an icon for Pixar as is Luxo Jr. Pixar as an institution has carefully controlled and shaped its image and its history, setting John Lasseter at its nucleus. Many of Lasseter's biographical details and anecdotes have been carefully honed in publicity releases and interviews into a nearly seamless tale of daunting challenges, comical encounters, and amazing triumphs.

Like Walt Disney Studios before it, Pixar has helped make real-life events sound as if they were the stuff of myth and destiny. Routinely portrayed in casual poses, sporting Hawaiian shirts, and surrounded by toys and figures from his movies, Lasseter is consistently presented as a friendly, jovial fellow who, fortunately for all of us, never quite grew up. The parallels between the "creative geniuses" John Lasseter and Walt Disney are regularly emphasized in the popular press as well. For instance, prior to the release of *A Bug's Life* in 1997, *Wired* already declared John Lasseter "the next Walt Disney" and one of the twenty-five most important people who were "bringing 21st-century Hollywood to life" (Daly, "Hollywood 2.0," 201, 212). Even Steve Jobs often stated that "John Lasseter is the closest thing we have to Walt Disney today" (qtd. in Booth 100). Lasseter and Disney are typically presented as "fated" for their immense roles as the two most powerful figures in American animation. The Academy Awards reinforced their reputations, bestowing a string of Oscars on them and their studios. Beyond Disney and Lasseter's famed monumental vision and success, there are indeed many similarities between these two renowned men. Lasseter even shares Disney's passion for trains, installing one on his property. John Lasseter always looked up to Walt Disney as a role model and inspiration, even during an era when others were quite wary of Disney's image and legacy. Yet, as we shall see, it took a great many industrial and cultural forces, as well as individual personality traits and skills, for Lasseter and his colleagues to build the Pixar style. Walt Disney's road map was no longer adequate for the new marketplace and technological realities of Pixar's era.

John Lasseter grew up in the Los Angeles suburb of Whittier, California, with a brother and twin sister. His mother, Jewell Lasseter, was a high-school art teacher who is said to have constantly supported and encouraged her children in the creative arts. His father, Paul Lasseter, was a parts manager for a Chevrolet dealership. As his biographer Jeff Lenburg explains, "Growing up, John learned to draw and take apart cars. He loved doing both. 'Scratch one vein, and it's Disney blood,' he later said. 'Scratch a second and it's motor oil'" (12). John Lasseter has indeed been equally fascinated with animation and automobiles throughout his life. Eventually, *Cars* (2006) and *Cars 2* (2011) resulted from merging these two passions. Already during his high-school years, Lasseter became nearly obsessed with animation, from Saturday-morning cartoons to Bugs Bunny TV shows after school. Early on he decided to become a professional animator. As he explains, "I was a freshman in high school and I had to do a book report. I was rummaging around in the Whittier High School library and I found this book called *The Art of Animation* by Bob Thomas. It dawned on me when I opened this book that people got paid to make cartoons. So I decided that's what I wanted to do" (Lasseter, "Tribute"). He also saw *The Sword in the Stone* (dir. Wolfgang Reitherman, 1963) playing at a local revival movie house during high school and announced to his mother that he was going to work for Disney one day. Lasseter's youthful ambition recalls that of François Truffaut and other impatient French New Wave directors who became resolved in their teens to open doors for themselves and get into the industry. Lasseter even began writing letters to Disney Studios, inserting examples of his drawings as evidence of his talent and determination.

Fortunately for John Lasseter, Ed Hansen, manager of the animation department at Disney, responded to the eager teenager's correspondence. Hansen suggested that Lasseter pursue a solid art education to learn the fundamentals of figure drawing, design techniques, and color theory as preparation for eventually pursuing animation. Hansen even invited him to tour the studio. As Lasseter explains, "Then in my senior year I got a letter from Disney saying they were starting a Character Animation Program at the California Institute of the Arts film school and that it would be taught by these artists from the heyday of Disney" (qtd. in Schlender and Tkacyzk 142). Lasseter submitted his portfolio and was the second person admitted into the cohort of twenty students for this new BFA pilot program in 1975. Moreover, he was offered a summer internship with the program's director Jack Hannah. The unique opportunity to participate in a brand-new and flexible program within the venerable California Institute of the Arts provided a rich, collaborative experience for all involved. Among that initial class were Brad Bird and John Musker. Tim Burton was admitted the following year. They were all quite lucky to find one another in this time and place. Later, Lasseter acknowledged that "we probably learned as much from each other as we did from the teachers, just because we were all into it, and spent so much time together" (qtd. in Paik 32).

The CalArts Character Animation Program, which continues to this day, was begun by two famed veteran animators, Jack Hannah and T. (Thornton) Hee. Both men had worked at Disney since the 1930s and had experience in film and television. Moreover, Hannah and Hee became the first in a long line of major influences and mentors for Lasseter. Hannah had begun as an in-betweener before moving up to animator, story writer, and finally director. Initially, Hannah worked on several key Silly Symphonies, including *The Country Cousin* (1936) and *The Old Mill* (1937), in which he animated the highly expressive bats as they woke up, headed out on their nightly mission, and finally returned home to sleep in the morning. Beginning in 1937, Hannah was assigned to Donald Duck cartoons, and from the 1940s on he became responsible for much of the Donald Duck franchise, directing scores of those short cartoons and even designing the comic books. Given that Donald's dialogue is often incomprehensible, Hannah's challenge was to communicate the duck's thoughts and outbursts visually. He also launched the Chip 'n' Dale series. According to Leonard Maltin, Hannah displayed "a fondness for fast pacing and vigorous gags" (Maltin, *Of Mice*, 70). During the 1950s, he directed live-action portions of Disney's television series before moving over to Walter Lantz Productions, where he directed a number of Woody Woodpecker cartoons.

T. Hee began at Warner Bros., working on the celebrated *Coo-Coo Nut Grove* (1936), and then joined Disney from 1938 to 1946 as a "story man," animation supervisor, and director on high-profile sequences in *Pinocchio* (1940) and *Fantasia* (1940), including the latter's famed "Dance of the Hours" ballet, complete with Ben Ali Gator, Hyacinth

Hippo, and ostrich ballerinas. Next, at UPA, Hee worked alongside Bobe Cannon. He even pitched the idea of making *The Oompahs* from cutout figures rather than cel animation, expanding the options within UPA's modern style. Other CalArts instructors included Elmer Plummer, character animator for *Fantasia* and *Dumbo* (1941), and Kendall O'Connor, who had begun on the Silly Symphonies and worked on *Snow White and the Seven Dwarfs* (1937). All these famous classical-era Disney artists had a great deal to teach this new generation of ambitious young animators, and Lasseter in particular benefitted from their inspiring lessons, their casual, even anecdotal teaching style, and their extensive industry connections. As Lasseter explains, "It was amazing. I had these incredible teachers, and not only were they teaching us great skills, but we were hearing their stories of working with Walt Disney. Walt and those guys took animation from its infancy and created the art form that we know, and now these guys were handing the information to us, this group of unbelievably excited kids. . . . And all of us had the same dream: to work at Disney one day" (qtd. in Schlender and Tkacyzk, 143). It is worth pointing out that by the 1970s, there was a tendency within youth culture and film studies to privilege the brash UPA cartoons or the perceived auteurism of Tex Avery and Chuck Jones over the more bland and corporate Disney products (White 41–46). But John Lasseter never seems to have shared in this popular "critical shift." His goal was to follow the Disney model.

During the summer of 1975, Lasseter's job as Hannah's assistant allowed him a rare access to instructors at the school, as well as several Disney animators. Moreover, part of his responsibility was to go to the archives in search of materials for Hannah's courses. Lasseter was thus in a privileged position right from the start; he immediately became one of the bridges between the students, faculty, and Disney veterans. By fall, after a brief stint at Pepperdine University, Lasseter became a full-time CalArts student. Not only did he work with the talented regular instructors; he also struck up valuable relationships with Frank Thomas, Ollie Johnston, and Eric Larson, three of the legendary animators from Disney's past. Thomas in particular would give talks at CalArts and evaluate student work. During the period of Lasseter's studies, Thomas and Johnston were also beginning to document their time at Disney, pulling together drawings and other materials from the Disney archive.

Their eventual book, *Disney Animation: The Illusion of Life,* became an impressive, landmark history of character animation at Disney from their "inside perspective." Lasseter grew especially close to these legendary animators, and years later, when Frank Thomas died in 2004, Lasseter spoke at his memorial, acknowledging how deeply Thomas had influenced his life and career (Lasseter, "Tribute").

Thomas and Johnston proved particularly inspiring mentors to Lasseter and his cohort. They had begun with Disney in the 1930s and worked their way up within the studio. They were a key duo in Walt Disney's Animation Board of trusted veterans during the 1940s, advising him on personnel, training, stories, and project development. Disney jokingly referred to that group as his "nine old men," in reference to Franklin Roosevelt's unflattering label for the Supreme Court. According to the Disney historian Steven Watts, Frank Thomas was known for exacting research and detail but also a concern for character motivation that "added complexity to his characters." Meanwhile, "Ollie Johnston's drawing possessed a natural appeal, focusing on acting, and he had a feel for emotion that practically defined character animation" (Watts 267). These nine animators, including Larson, helped switch Disney's mode of production away from its piecemeal division of labor. Instead, individual animators would be responsible for every character in key scenes, which lent unity and consistency to each figure while simultaneously helping develop clearer personalities and relationships among the characters. Previously, each separate character in a given sequence may have been assigned to a different animator. Disney's shift to a single designated animator helped guarantee a unified rhythm with more convincing interactions between all characters and even with their settings.

It was this new, concerted attention to character design, personality, and motivation that helped define "character" animation at Disney. Even the simple action of a chicken laying an egg might involve expressing a whole range of emotions in a Disney cartoon. Beyond carefully drawn evidence of the physical strain on the chicken, there should be emotion cues for anxiety, resolve, relief, and finally pride, as the nameless bird becomes a "mother." If the same animator then drew all the surrounding figures, many of whom expressed surprise, sympathy, and even jealousy, the scene could more successfully build an effective microcosm of characters intricately aware of one another and their various "feelings" and reactions. Allowing animators to be dedicated wholly to each scene and/or character helped delineate and develop character traits, while also allowing for subtle shifts in personality. Characters learned and made decisions over the course of an entire film, which would prove especially valuable in features. Eventually, Pixar would also have to go through several different production models for animation teams as they changed over from creating short, personal films with tiny crews to designing much more ambitious features employing large teams of contributing animators and graphic artists for the scores of characters and settings.

Beyond offering a fascinating array of anecdotes and insights into the classical era, Thomas and Johnston in *Disney Animation* clarified and explained their principal strategies, including the twelve "fundamentals of animation," technical processes, and even philosophies that helped distinguish Disney character animation. Importantly, character animation would prove central to Lasseter's education and eventual cartooning goals at Pixar. According to Thomas and Johnston, the overarching challenge of 1930s Disney animation was to communicate clearly developed personality traits for each character and action. Many silent cartoon characters, following in the tradition of standard comic strips, were built around figures who were formulaic types with only a few concisely defined goals and expressions. With the coming of sound, Disney animators wanted to create more complex narratives with characters who could prove more engaging with audiences. As they point out, early Mickey Mouse cartoons had Mickey doing pretty much the same sorts of actions as previous cartoon characters. "Prior to 1930, none of the characters showed any real thought process" (Thomas and Johnston 74). For fairy tales and other stories to really "work," the audience should feel empathy for characters and identify with their fears, goals, and decisions.

Given that Walt Disney was already planning to expand into feature-length animation by the mid-1930s, such character development would be crucial to justifying the longer-duration stories. Thomas and Johnston also point out that Disney Studios' increasingly realistic cues in drawings and sound reinforced the characters' presence and personalities for the audience. Thus, Thomas and Johnston, first in their own animation and then in their mentorship of Lasseter and the CalArts students, helped establish visual and narrative guidelines for successful models of emotionally engaging character animation. And Lasseter became their most vocal disciple, helping disseminate their core concepts: "Character animation isn't the fact that an object looks like a character or has a face or hands. Character animation is when an object moves like it is alive, when it looks like it is thinking and all of its movements are generated by its own thought process" (Lasseter, "Tricks," 47).

The combination of a new, creative CalArts curriculum plus advice from veteran Disney animators who respected the energy and curiosity of their first cluster of students provided a fertile setting for learning and experimentation. Students were given a great deal of independence, which fueled their spontaneity, exploration, and ultimately their personal styles. In addition to access to priceless drawings and scripts from the Disney archives, they analyzed 16mm prints of the major features, including *Snow White, Pinocchio,* and *Bambi.* Lasseter points out the value of these analytical screenings: "We looked at those [prints] again and again and again, all night. For four years we studied those films" (Lasseter, "Tribute"). The CalArts students built upon the fundamental principles and practice of Disney character animation from the classical era. But they also updated their work environment with an open, collaborative spirit between teachers and fellow students. Lasseter is repeatedly credited with being at the heart of this ambitious cohort. "John became a master of creative teaming, sharing story and project ideas, and playing critical evaluator with fellow students . . . a gift that would ultimately help him become a professional animator and an inspirational leader" (Capodagli and Jackson 32). Moreover, this group was so talented that it became routine for Disney's animation department to approach students who had not yet graduated, offering them jobs. Tim Burton and John Musker were hired away before they completed the program.

Disney Studios offered Lasseter a job during his junior year as well. Despite his eagerness to become a Disney animator, Lasseter remained at CalArts, where he thrived in the art-school environment and continued to hone his animation skills and expand his storytelling experience. Meanwhile, another possible career path presented itself to Lasseter and his cohort. Some students turned more toward special-effects work, especially in the wake of *Star Wars* (dir George Lucas, 1977), which had greatly impressed them all. Special effects and new digital postproduction techniques provided exciting opportunities for experimentation by combining animation and live action. *Star Wars* offered a new horizon of possibilities for young, ambitious animators. However, Lasseter chose to remain focused on cartoons: "It made me rededicate myself to animation. I believed that animation could be entertaining on that level" (qtd. in Lenburg 18). Thanks to this intensified resolve, Lasseter's CalArts apprenticeship and collaboration allowed him to establish some of his own narrative traits and aesthetic interests early on. Entering the job market right away would not necessarily guarantee such experimentation and personal development. When he graduated with his Bachelor of Fine Arts in 1979, however, Lasseter would enter an industry that was undergoing some fundamental changes and reorganization.

Outside of the formal courses, Lasseter seemed to see everything as a potential learning experience. His tenure at Disney included summer jobs at Disneyland, where he began sweeping in Tomorrowland during 1977 before being promoted to a ride operator for the Jungle Cruise. "No one really believes this, but the Jungle Cruise taught me a lot of what I know about comedy and comic timing," Lasseter has remarked (qtd. in Schlender and Tkacyzk 143). Pixar's Karen Paik also credits this job with teaching Lasseter about storytelling in ways that working in isolation as an animation student, poring over frame-by-frame drawings, could not: "He played with pacing and delivery, learning to tweak the material to its best effect. He learned how to read an audience's mood and roll with the punches when things weren't going well" (Paik 33). Thus, whether he was scanning the amazed faces at the premiere of *Star Wars* or studying the reactions from yet another boatload of jaded tourists on the Jungle Cruise, Lasseter became unabashedly fascinated with what pleased spectators. Right from the beginning he seems to have dedicated himself to winning over audiences. But he also recognized that manipulating people's reactions involves coordinated collaboration with everyone involved in the process. As Brad Bird explains, "As well as having his own great ideas, John was very talented at provoking ideas from other people, then picking and choosing which suggestions to use and how to use them" (qtd. in Paik 34). Early on, Lasseter possessed a producer's keen awareness of the importance of testing a wide variety of material and options. The selection and ordering of individual story bits and gestures would be crucial to engineering successful responses from a broad range of spectators. Later in his career, Lasseter would repeatedly mention that he believes "you have a responsibility to entertain your audience" (qtd. in Furniss, "Art and Industry," 202). It is no surprise that Walt Disney should have been Lasseter's biggest role model, as opposed to some more personal auteur animator or director.

During his CalArts years, Lasseter also distinguished himself by winning two consecutive student Academy Awards for short animation. His 1979 project was *Lady and the Lamp,* a lively pencil-drawn cartoon composed of just over forty varied shots, including high angles on the action and even the drawn equivalent of a rapid swish pan, all in just under four busy minutes. The cartoon begins as a kindly old fellow awakens the lamps in his store, promising a special day and a visit from a new customer. However, as he starts cleaning up the store, the shopkeeper carelessly slides some lamps down the shelf, unknowingly knocking a sleepy, struggling, smaller lamp off onto the floor. The short lamp's bulb shatters from the fall, which seems to blind it. The lamp initially panics, frantically pulling its own on/off chain and unscrewing the broken bulb base before carefully crawling off in search of a replacement bulb in the cupboard. At precisely the halfway point through the cartoon, there is a cut to black and a clever reverse shot from inside the cupboard revealing the lamp opening the doors and blindly reaching for a gin bottle among the spare light bulbs (figure 1). The sparse dialogue comes from the old Geppeto-like shop keeper (voiced by Jack Hannah), who urges on the lamps: "Hurry boys, get ready, she'll be here any minute." The man's announcement increases the lamp's urgency, as it mistakenly swings the bottle up and screws it in place, pulling the cord to unleash the liquor down into his quaking body (figure 2). The last third of the cartoon then follows the clumsily drunk lamp as it meanders between the bigger lamps, accidentally wrapping its trailing cord around their bases. As another lamp is tripped, it falls onto the little lamp, bumping it out of the frame. The stumbling little drunken lamp finally becomes entwined in the cluster of wires by the electric outlet, pulling more lamps down until the whole shelf falls to the floor. The shopkeeper returns in shock: "Oh no, my lamps, my shop, my gin!" He is ready to toss out the drunken little lamp when the woman customer (voiced by fellow CalArts student Nancy Beiman) bursts in the door and exclaims that the shaken little lamp is just what she needs, and the cartoon ends.

Figure 1: Inside a cupboard;
The Lady and the Lamp.

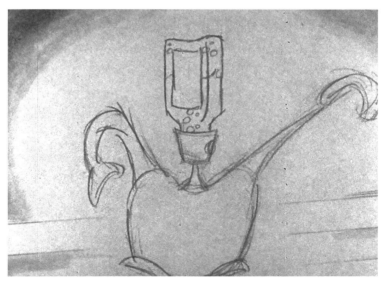

Figure 2: The straining lamp;
The Lady and the Lamp.

While the small lamp's personality is not extensively developed, Lasseter's fluid drawing style allows the normally inanimate object to breathe, stretch, stumble, and even feel pain, as its arm handles tentatively reach up to feel the sharp shards of glass where a full bulb, or head, should be. The lamp is never a solid, fixed object. It shivers and slumps and wiggles. Strangely, the lamp seems more evocative and alive than the caricatures of the human figures. It undergoes a rapid trajectory from struggling to regain its footing on the shelf to accidentally screwing on the gin bottle and innocently bringing about the shop's destruction, all of which provides a broad situational-comedy arc. When he falls over, the lamp even has tiny stars and light bulbs circling above his head to signal his confusion. The restrained sound effects prove effective in evoking a sense of space while simultaneously lending economical audio cues to reinforce the minimal pencil sketches, helping to distinguish represented materials such as glass, wood, and liquid. Further, the image shakes violently when the lamp is pushed off the shelf and out of the frame, providing evidence of offscreen action and space. One of the key moments, the little lamp's fall from the shelf, is exemplary of Lasseter's trial and error for effective sound. He explains that initially he cued up several sample loud crashes to accompany the fall: "I accidentally synched up the wrong sound to it, which was this little tiny minute little 'tink.' . . . I just cracked up because it gave it a completely different feeling. And in a way, it was that moment that I realized how important good sound effects were" (McCracken 14). Later, music arrives right at the "suspenseful" moment when the hurried lamp screws on the gin bottle, and then slow, mournful bass notes accompany the confused lamp as it bumps along blind and drunk before falling onto its "face." The visual and audio style lends the little lamp specific traits while evoking a functional cinematic surrounding space from fairly minimal cues.

Lady and the Lamp stands as a convincing application of many core Disney aesthetic strategies despite the constraints of a student film production. Many of the twelve "fundamentals of animation" from Thomas and Johnston are visible here, including squash and stretch drawings and exaggeration of the figures, as the visual style and storytelling all serve the focused action of a lamp comically stumbling from one misfortune to the next. As Karen Paik points out, "*Lady and the Lamp* was [Lasseter's] first project to display what would become one of his signature talents—the ability to bring inanimate objects to life in a sympathetic and entertaining way" (33). This short student film also began to establish many of the traits that would develop into Lasseter's eventual personal style.

During his final year at CalArts in 1979, Lasseter created a polished and developed three-minute film, *Nitemare*, which won him a second Student Academy Award. For this project, he wanted to construct a cartoon with no spoken words, in part to distinguish it from other student films that were often overly dependent upon dialogue or voiceover narration. The carefully crafted characters and settings are delicately rendered in pencil, with an engaging, professional attention to detail and especially gesture. This short cartoon already displays Lasseter's flair for succinct storytelling. *Nitemare* is a tale about a toddler's fears of monsters in his room as he tries to fall asleep. It was inspired in part by Mercer Mayer's children's book *There's a Nightmare in My Closet*. The general situation also anticipates somewhat the comical bedtime frights and ironic reversals of Pixar's *Monsters, Inc.* (2001). One desperate monster even tries pulling a door open but runs into the wall, unable to escape, in a gag that seems right out of a Tex Avery cartoon.

Nitemare begins with a stark, abstract image of a huge distorted shadow entering a doorway, until the source turns out to be a small, almost ape-like boy pausing on the threshold of his room, on his way to bed. In a closer shot, he hesitates, scanning the room warily. His highly malleable body bends and pulsates as he shivers and leaps fearfully back around the corner. The poor boy's little head, in particular, is in constant flux as it signals his alternating apprehension and relief. His arm returns in the shot, reaching for the light switch, which illuminates his cluttered room. He then confidently strides over to the bed with his water glass. The boy's features include a swirl of pencil loops for hair, large sorrowful eyes near the bottom of his face, and big shuffling feet. From the very first frames, Lasseter establishes that the little boy is highly sensitive and keenly perceptive. His every glance and gesture, including the constant reshaping of his head, efficiently deliver the basic character information. Moreover, subtle piano music loosely accompanies the child, without being rigorously synchronized to his actions. Due to the lack of dialogue, most of the personality and mood cues come from the visual style. For instance, the boy joyously tosses his teddy bear up into the bed before bounding in himself. But each time he turns out the light and tries to sleep, some noise startles him. The covers, which he pulls up around him, are often rendered as undulating, wavelike shapes. Moreover, the entire room is painstakingly sketched and shaded, right down to the minimally drawn water glass and lamp on the bedside table. Much like in *Lady and the Lamp,* the pulling of the lamp cord becomes a highly significant action, and sound, as the boy tugs the chain with alternating panic and reassurance, turning the light on and off repeatedly (figure 3). The boy's emotions set the pacing for the cartoon just as his furtive looks around the room, cued by suspicious sounds, help establish the increasingly frenetic editing rhythm.

As the night wears on, an armlike branch scratches at the window, the mirror seems to become a gaping, toothy mouth, and he imagines a monster lurking in his toy box. Everyday objects like his little rocking chair are animated into frightening, moving shapes. Eventually, the boy becomes reduced to a pair of shaking white eyeballs staring into the terrifying darkness as multiple monsters pop out at him (figure 4). One floor lamp even transforms into a creepy figure in silhouette, just white lines on a black background, that resembles a creature from an Emile Cohl cartoon crossed with a distorted Daffy Duck (figure 5). After an

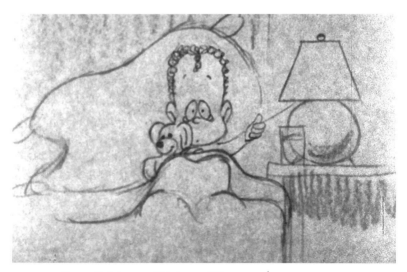

Figure 3: A boy and his lamp; *Nitemare.*

Figure 4: Monsters in *Nitemare*.

Figure 5: Boy versus monster in *Nitemare*.

accelerating montage of the various ghouls appearing and disappearing as the boy pulls the bedside lamp on and off, that floor-lamp monster becomes the only ghost that remains somehow caught in the lit room. It frantically tries to change itself back into the lamp shape, but to no avail. The tables now turn as the boy dons his army helmet, grabs his toy pop-gun, and attacks, while the previously scary monster trembles and cowers in the corner until it cries in pain and fright. Suddenly, a new shot reveals the monster comfortably perched in the bed, but when the lights go out one last time, the scary branch sound returns and frightens the whole batch of monsters into bed with the boy. In the end, one of them turns out the light for the final cut to black, and it is as if the boy has now become a comforting teddy bear for the frightened monsters.

Nitemare is more than a highly accomplished student calling-card production. It provides a rich array of carefully crafted animation techniques, including stark black-and-white compositions for some shots and soft pencil sketches for others. It could serve as an exemplary primer for expressionist drawings as well as cartoony, comic-book images. The boy is just an outline sketch in some shots and a fully embodied figure in others. At one point, the bond paper's watermark even shows, so the cartoon is as much about stylistic options and materials as it is about a frightened little boy. And Lasseter expands dramatically on *Lady and the Lamp*'s use of black frames for bold punctuation of the story's rhythm. In *Nitemare,* the pulsating screen finally comes to resemble an animated flicker film, as the speed of the boy's light-switch maneuvers accelerates faster and faster. Thus, the overall length of four and a half minutes is broken into roughly one hundred shots, some only a few frames long, for a rapid-fire average shot length of under three seconds. The number of drawings, many from extremely different angles and in varying shot scales, is truly impressive for an individual student's film. The meticulously storyboarded narrative unfolds much like a live-action short comedy and avoids the frontal staging of many comic strip–inspired student cartoons. Moreover, Lasseter's penchant for making normally static objects, like chairs and lamps, move and burst forth as animated cartoon characters is already firmly on display here. *Nitemare* convincingly reveals the young Lasseter's talent at creating entertaining cartoons with a sense of rhythm and an artistic style that is as compelling as the story being told.

It is no surprise that John Lasseter was quickly hired by Walt Disney Studios the moment he graduated from CalArts. In fact, he and Disney animation really needed one another at that point. Disney had recently completed *The Rescuers* (1977), with *The Fox and the Hound* (1981) currently in production. However, the animation staff had become increasingly divided by this point, with some of the younger and more creative animators feeling increasingly alienated from the management's decisions. Under Ron Miller's recent leadership, the film division failed to generate adequate revenue, and even the Sunday-night television show's ratings during the 1970s were in a steady decline before it was cancelled in 1981. There were severe pressures to economize and streamline the production departments. According to Leonard Maltin, "The late 1970s and early 1980s were tumultuous years for the Disney studio, with changes of management and philosophy taking their toll on every department" (*Of Mice* 78). In September 1979, one of Disney's most talented animators, Don Bluth, broke away, quitting publicly and taking seven animators and four assistants along with him to form his own company, Don Bluth Productions, with partners Gary Goldman and John Pomeroy. As Bluth explains, "I think it was mainly because my fixation with those early Disney classics was so strong—the production values, the beautiful things that I saw on the screen when I was a child, the stories themselves. . . . All of those things were not there by the time I got to the studio" (Duchovnay 145). Many of Bluth's concerns would later be echoed by Lasseter, who also found himself motivated by Disney's past but underwhelmed by its current output.

Bluth and a number of his colleagues were frustrated with many aspects of 1970s Disney animation. "We felt like we were animating the same picture over and over again with just the faces changed a little. For example, they've gutted all of the meaning from *The Fox and the Hound.* It's become a cute story instead of a meaningful one" (qtd. in Maltin, *Disney Films,* 275). Bluth considered himself to be upholding the spirit of Walt Disney and complained that many other animators were taking too many short cuts, churning out predictable, mediocre work. However, the studio head Ron Miller called Bluth and his friends "a cancer" (Price 51). Michael Barrier even claims that Bluth "was like the leader of a sect—in its own eyes the repository of the true faith—that was peeling away from some mainstream domination" (Barrier 570).

However, while the first feature from Bluth's new studio, *The Secret of NIMH* (1983), was celebrated as visually rich and appealing, its story failed to generate much excitement. It proved financially disappointing, grossing just under eleven million dollars in its first run. Disney's safe and cute *The Fox and the Hound* earned four times that much when it premiered in 1981.

During the fall of 1979, the atmosphere within Disney's animation wing was highly politicized, with many of the veteran animators feeling defensive, having dug in their heels in the face of resistance from Bluth and other demanding animators. They needed the young talent from the new CalArts class of character animators to fill the gaps left by Bluth and his colleagues. However, they were also suspicious of new perspectives and perhaps overly sensitive to any perceived criticism of their work and methods. The animator Tom Sito points out that the young CalArts employees were "brassy, bell-bottomed, long-haired and iconoclastic. They rode bicycles through the hallways. . . . For a sleepy studio whose policy forbidding women to wear pants only expired in 1977, they were a breath of fresh air" (Sito, "Disney's *The Fox*," 13). There were several distinct camps, with clear differences in the studio. Moreover, Disney's remaining animators were under increased pressure, since *The Fox and the Hound* would not be ready for its scheduled holiday release in December 1980. The cost-cutting and cautious approach within the animation division had damaged morale and led to the exodus of talent at a time when the larger Disney corporation desperately needed the animation studio to provide predictable revenue. "They hadn't had a live-action hit since *Herbie the Love Bug* in 1960—Disney entered the 1980s in deep, deep trouble" (Lewis 98). The new recruits had to buckle down immediately and take up where the departed animators had left off.

It would not take long for John Lasseter, the ambitious young animator fresh out of school, to experience the tension of the situation. He also immediately felt frustrations of his own and soon identified with some of Bluth's concerns: "It was the same stories being told with the same level of technology. The only thing new that had been developed since the late 1950s was when they started to use Xeroxing" (qtd. in French, "*Toy Story*," 21). Further, within Disney's carefully controlled pipeline process, every creative decision had to be made and/or approved by the established cohort of senior-level Disney animators, many of whom were opposed to any suggestions or proposed changes to business as usual. They had resisted Bluth's attempts to vary procedures and were apparently in no mood to welcome any new alternatives to their entrenched, institutional practices. As Lasseter explains, "The animation studio wasn't being run by these great Disney artists like our teachers, but lesser businesspeople who rose through attrition as the grand old men retired. . . . The people running animation seemed to resent us. One of the directors told me, 'You put in your time for 20 years and do what you're told, and then you can be in charge'" (Schlender and Tkacyzk 143). Rather than encountering the sort of encouragement and camaraderie he had long imagined at Disney, Lasseter was cautioned and made to feel like a young, undisciplined recruit, which to a certain extent he was.

Ironically, however, Lasseter was initially celebrated by some at Disney Studios as the fresh face of animation there. "Publicly he was made to seem like a rising star. Soon after he arrived the studio sent him on a circuit of campus and television appearances to project a more youthful image for the company; his articulate and approachable manner made him a natural" (Price 50). Lasseter was offered as a sort of antidote to Bluth's complaints and very public departure. He was also meant to counteract the recurring doubts in the trade press over the future direction of Disney animation. Yet, the veteran animators working on *The Fox and the Hound* assumed that there would be a long period of apprenticeship awaiting Lasseter and the other recent CalArts grads. Disney's institutional practices among the animation department did not necessarily match up with the publicity department's campaign to spotlight the new, youthful talent. The rigid, top-down system then in place offended Lasseter's sense of collective creativity and ran counter to the CalArts model and his cooperative interactions with the veteran Disney mentors.

Lasseter's first tasks were to work on *The Fox and the Hound,* as well as the short *Mickey's Christmas Carol* (1983). Though he was apparently not thrilled with these projects, the Mickey Mouse cartoon was released in theaters and went on to be nominated for an Academy Award. Importantly, however, the young Lasseter did not simply accept the standard trajectory and instructions at Disney. He and his friend Glen Keane productively suggested some revisions in *The Fox and the Hound* "to add more tension and excitement to the film's finale, which later wound up in the movie though they were first turned down" (Lenburg 27). Frustrated, Lasseter even took a break early on and worked in London for nearly a year at Richard Williams Animation Studio, which made the Pink Panther title sequences, among other projects. However, he returned to Disney and *Mickey's Christmas Carol*. While working on that Mickey Mouse cartoon in 1981, Lasseter discovered a whole new potential direction for animation. His CalArts friends Jerry Rees and Bill Kroyer were working on Disney's *Tron* (1982) and showed him some of the light-cycles footage on a 35mm movieola. As Lasseter explained on a roundtable in 1988, "I had never seen anything like that before in my life. I was so excited. I wasn't excited because of what I was seeing, but I was looking beyond that, excited at the potential for applying character animation to it" (Furniss, *Animation,* 203). The possibilities for inserting characters into a convincing 3D environment immediately intrigued him: "If this technology could be melded with Disney animation, he thought, he would have the makings of a revolution" (Price 52).

Tron proved an important influence on Lasseter and helped motivate his sudden interest in the future potential for computer-assisted animation. His entire conception of the possibilities of commercial animation changed. He was at the right age and place in his career to become readily excited by new trends in technology and special effects. Just as his attending *Star Wars* with several CalArts friends in 1977 had opened his eyes to new options for popular genre cinema's storytelling, Lasseter's exposure to *Tron* presented him with a new range of opportunities in the creation of animated space. Lasseter had never lost his admiration for Walt Disney's lifelong search for new techniques, from sound to color to the multiplane camera and even Xerox technology. Computers seemed like the logical next tool in the Disney arsenal. Computer graphics provided a timely step forward that would help continue and revitalize the Disney aesthetic. It is worth noting that *Star Trek II: The Wrath of Khan* had just premiered one month before *Tron,* and it contains the famous computer-generated "Genesis Effect" sequence, demonstrating how the fictional Genesis Device could be fired into a dead planet to revitalize the planet into a lush, habitable world. The *Wrath of Khan* scene was created by a small computer-graphics team within Lucasfilm led by Ed Catmull and Alvy Ray Smith. Their ultimate goal was to produce computer-animated motion pictures, which of course they would later accomplish thanks to Lasseter and many others who eventually helped them create Pixar.

The "Genesis Effect," like many early computer-graphics experiments, showed off an impressive mobile camera flying over the planet's surface, following the blast as it rings the planet, transforming its geography. Lasseter, however, preferred to concentrate on the value that such 3D graphics might have for creating a setting into which he could insert more traditionally animated characters. Thus, while companies like MAGI, Triple-I, and Digital Effects foregrounded their ability to simulate spinning geometric objects and flying-camera perspectives sweeping past digitally generated landscapes, Lasseter was more interested in whether computer imagery could provide a highly functional space in which to anchor a story. He saw computer animation as a radical extension of the idea of the multiplane camera with its arrangement of several levels of drawings to create real perceptual depth cues. For instance, during the classical Disney era, Bambi could stroll through a deep forest of convincingly overlapping stands of trees thanks to the multiplane camera. Lasseter began to wonder how the age of 3D computer graphics could update those traditional depth cues for more convincing animated settings. Lasseter and Glen Keane decided that they wanted to experiment with this new toolbox of techniques and apply their findings to character animation and surrounding visual environments at Disney.

Keane and Lasseter went to Tom Wilhite, *Tron*'s twenty-nine-year-old supervising executive, to express their interest in combining animation with computer graphics. Wilhite was eager to help and mentioned that his division owned development rights to Maurice Sendak's *Where the Wild Things Are.* Lasseter and Keane could make a thirty-second test reel. Lasseter would also begin learning to model the environment, thanks to a special arrangement with Chris Wedge of MAGI/Synthavision. Keane's task was to animate the characters, Max and his dog, by hand. Wedge, who had worked on *Tron*, was the same age as Lasseter, twenty-five years old, and, like Lasseter, Wedge had the artistic skills and technological curiosity necessary to see the creative applications of computer graphics. Chris Wedge would later go on to be among the most important directors of early computer-animated features, cofounding Blue Sky Animation Studios in 1987 and eventually directing their hit *Ice Age* (2002). Lasseter built a model of Max's bedroom and hallway, and they calculated the characters' locations in each frame. Keane animated the characters in 2D, using computer printouts as guides. "When his drawings were entered into the computer and colored, the characters were placed in the computer-generated environment" (Solomon 295). Their experiments combined intricate digital camera work with conventionally animated characters and gestures, producing a successfully composited cartoon format.

However, as Lasseter and Keane moved forward with their tests, *Tron* opened to controversial reviews, spurred in part by a vocal and cynical financial advisor who attended the premiere and immediately suggested that investors should consider selling their Disney stock. Puzzled, Roger Ebert, who had given *Tron* his top four-star rating, interviewed Wilhite. The Disney executive remained defensive of *Tron,* but he also seemed happy to report positive news for the future of computer animation at Disney. In the interview, he seems to refer to the project then barely under way by Lasseter, Keane, and Wedge: "'What we're experimenting with now,' he said, 'is a combination of hand-drawn principal animated characters, set down in a computer-generated background. That gives us the best of both worlds: the warmth of hand-drawn animation, and the three-dimensional environments and complete freedom of camera moves of computer animation'" (Ebert, "Interview Wilhite"). Not everyone at Disney would turn out to be as optimistic or supportive of computer animation or the *Where the Wild Things Are* experiments.

John Lasseter was regularly credited with a tendency to establish a daring, even impractical goal and then gather talented colleagues around him to solve the task at hand cooperatively. He is famous for an infectious sense of confidence and excitement. Even the veteran animator Frank Thomas recalled that there were few people who would actually admit to seeing any future in computer animation at that point: "The potential was there, but at the time nobody wanted to do it except for Lasseter and the people he was working with" (qtd. in Paik 39). According to the historian Philippe Lemieux, Lasseter and this project finally helped move computer animation beyond replicating 2D traditions; the *Where the Wild Things Are* tests, "with their dynamic camera movements and the harmonious marriage of the two animation techniques," were vital in suggesting the future direction of CGI. "Simply put, it is equivalent to

Edison's first cinematic experiments or Steven Spielberg's initial digital dinosaur tests during the pre-production of *Jurassic Park*" (Lemieux 109–10). The *Where the Wild Things Are* test footage offered a valuable model for early hybrid 2D and 3D animation. "Their unfinished film demonstrated how hand-drawn animation could be successfully combined with computerized camera movements and environments. The techniques they used were essentially the same as those used nine years later to create the scene of the Beast dancing with his Belle in a virtual ballroom in Disney's *Beauty and the Beast*" (Lenburg 30). As their project progressed, Lasseter gained confidence that this hybrid 2D plus 3D would change the future for animation production at Disney and beyond.

After being encouraged by their *Where the Wild Things Are* footage, Lasseter and Keane decided to combine their tests with a pitch for their ultimate project, a feature-length animated movie. They believed that Thomas Disch's recent short story "The Brave Little Toaster" would be the perfect property for Disney. Wilhite agreed with its potential value and pursued an option on the story. Disch's version went on to become an award-winning children's book and featured a number of appliances and household items as characters, including yet another lamp. While other key figures in Disney's animation department remained resistant to fundamental changes in production techniques in 1983, Wilhite understood the importance of new technology for Disney's future. He and Lasseter pursued the notion of building *The Brave Little Toaster*'s spatial environment in a computer, while retaining 2D animation for its characters. However, they had many practical questions and needed more computer expertise if they were to design and create a convincing CGI setting.

Lasseter and Wilhite decided to visit Lucasfilm, where Ed Catmull and Alvy Ray Smith directed the computer-graphics group within the Computer Development Division. Importantly, Catmull and Smith were firmly dedicated to developing computer animation rather than just pioneering digital special effects for live-action movies at Lucasfilm. Thus they were already open to considering potential creative and business collaboration with professional animators, and especially talent from Disney. "Having a Disney employee try to sell *them* on using the computer for animation was unusual, to say the least. But the *Wild Things* work

Lasseter shared with them was one of the most novel uses of computer graphics they'd ever seen" (Paik 39). However, despite their mutual long-term interests, Catmull declined the offer to forge a partnership at that point.

Soon after Lasseter and Wilhite returned from Lucasfilm, the Disney executives were required to make a decision about whether to pursue computer-assisted animation. Lasseter was called in to show his progress so far and pitch his proposed *Brave Little Toaster* project. Clearly, this was a highly significant decision at Disney since it was Ron Miller, the studio head, and Ed Hansen, manager of the animation department, who met with Lasseter to assess his plans. Miller quickly asked how much a feature-length film incorporating such three-dimensional computer graphics would cost. Lasseter's rather optimistic reply was that it should not cost any more than a conventionally animated film. With this response, the decisive meeting was suddenly all but over. "Miller replied that there was no point in using computer animation unless they could make everything 'cheaper and faster.' With that, he walked out of the room" (Paik 40). That same day, Hansen, who had encouraged and advised the teenaged Lasseter, now called him into his office to fire him. "Since it's not going to be made, your project at Disney is now complete. . . . Your position at Disney is terminated, and your employment with Disney is now ended" (qtd. in Price 53). Lasseter had built a reputation since CalArts of being ambitious, but also incredibly cooperative and even selfless when working with others. However, within the Disney production hierarchy, he instead become known as a loose cannon and an impatient troublemaker. Luckily, the more appreciative Tom Wilhite managed successfully to keep Lasseter on at Disney a bit longer during the fall of 1983 to help wrap up the *Where the Wild Things Are* footage.

Bitter and stunned at his pending banishment from Disney, Lasseter nonetheless retained his commitment to advancing the synthesis of animation with computer graphics. If anything, he became even more determined to prove that CGI could help revitalize contemporary animation. He apparently also continued his faith in the legendary version of Walt Disney as a key role model, especially Disney's fundamental belief in pursuing new technical innovations. Lasseter also kept in touch with his old mentors, such as Frank Thomas, who remained encouraging. Nonetheless, he had just begun to establish himself within the hybrid niche of 2D and computer graphics, a field that necessitated access to vast resources beyond the reach of an isolated, individual animator. To continue, he would need an environment rich in creativity and computer technology. In the meantime, he continued his interest in computer graphics, even attending a conference late in 1983, rather than back-pedaling and pursuing 2D animation options alone. Fortunately, the next major figure in his life, Ed Catmull, would help Lasseter combine his talent for character animation with the newest digital software and hardware available.

John Lasseter at Lucasfilm:
Animation versus Special Effects

Ed Catmull (Ph.D., Utah) and his colleague Alvy Ray Smith (Ph.D., Stanford), both talented artist-scientists driven to combine computer graphics and animation, had assembled a team of visionary digital-graphics technicians over the past few years, including Bill Reeves (Ph.D., Toronto), Ralph Guggenheim, and David DiFrancesco. Cat-mull managed to bring them all together within Lucasfilm's Computer Development Division in 1980. Their ultimate goal was to create a variety of software programs and rendering procedures necessary for computer-animated cinema. The perceived potential value of the computer-graphics group within Lucasfilm, however, was much more focused and practical. This division was charged with devising new video-editing hardware and software as well as developing digital-printing technology to scan computer-generated images directly onto 35mm film stock. Lucasfilm was particularly interested in a technique to help composite computer-generated images with live-action footage. But these processes would also have to allow for digital color correction and increasingly photorealistic graphics to ensure convincing special effects for live-action filmmaking. Catmull was hired to head up this graphics unit because of his initial team's cutting-edge research into rendering and digital compositing. These talented young digital specialists helped establish Lucasfilm as the top commercial venue for experimentation in computer-generated imagery and graphics.

In addition to confronting the daunting research and development assignments in digital effects, the computer division helped solve specific problems for Lucasfilm and Industrial Light and Magic (ILM) productions. With their "Genesis Effect" scene in *The Wrath of Khan*, the team got to put many of their most recent innovations on display, including dramatic virtual camera movements, complex settings built from new fractal geometry algorithms, and a particle system that allowed them to create and render impressive smoke, fire, and other challenging materials and textures. Their sixty-seven-second sequence was packed with spinning planets, rings of fire, shifting colors, bodies of water, and even natural-looking cloud layers. As Stephen Prince points out, previous digital graphics were much more schematic and limited, but this scene, in which a dead planet regenerates immediately thanks to a healing missile blast, unfolded in a much more realistic, cinematic fashion: "The Genesis sequence is cinema's first attempt to simulate properties of organic matter in a photographically convincing manner, one not intended to look like a computer graphic, as did the applications in earlier films" (Prince, *Digital Visual*, 22). Thanks to the success of their Genesis scene and a steady string of in-house technical innovations, Catmull, Smith, and their digital team began to plan for animating stand-alone CGI short film projects, even if such ventures did not fit comfortably within Lucasfilm's overall agenda. Their brief special-effects projects for ILM, including rotating phantom planets for *The Return of the Jedi* (dir. Richard Marquand, 1983), did not adequately satisfy Catmull and Smith, who had more substantial and daring digital filmmaking goals. They were determined to pursue their long-term objective of producing computer-animated filmmaking and eventually a feature-length film.

It was during this period of the Lucasfilm computer group's experimentation and expansion that Catmull and Lasseter crossed paths again. During the fall of 1983, Lasseter attended the Pratt Institute Symposium on Computer Graphics in Long Beach, at which Catmull was a scheduled speaker. Catmull reportedly asked Lasseter how *The Brave Little Toaster* was progressing, and Lasseter explained that Disney was not going to pursue that project and also admitted that he was not sure exactly what he would be working on next. After this meeting, Catmull called Smith to tell him he had run into an apparently unemployed Lasseter, and Smith gave the green light to hire him temporarily for their new project. Lasseter's version of that day almost resembles a scene from a Warner

Bros. cartoon: "[Catmull] was lurking behind a column at the back of the ballroom whispering, 'John, John, c'mere, c'mere . . .'" (Schlender and Tkacyzk 145). As Catmull recalls, "To have a Disney animator on our team, even temporarily, would be a huge leap forward. For the first time, a true storyteller would be joining our ranks" (Catmull 34). In December, Lasseter spent a week at Lucasfilm. Catmull, Smith, and their team had already decided that they wanted to present a short computer-animated film at the 1984 SIGGRAPH computer-graphics conference. However, while such a project could bring some welcome visibility for their group within the industry, a short film seemed peripheral to their official functions and duties at Lucasfilm.

Smith camouflaged Lasseter's role as animator by listing him in the budget as a computer-interface designer. Lasseter would bring his knowledge of character animation and efficient storytelling to the project, but he knew little about actually animating digitally. From the beginning he realized that he would have to adapt and rethink his usual mode of production. He was determined to work closely with these specialists to figure out how best to synthesize their two very different skill sets for a unified project whose every element would be built in a computer. Previously, he had assumed it best for the computer to generate the backgrounds only, while the animator should design and draw conventionally hand-animated characters to insert into the computer's spatial setting. Instead, a new, necessarily open collaborative arrangement, with technicians and Lasseter working side by side, launched a creative new phase for the computer-graphics group and Lasseter alike.

The usual commercial-animation division of labor was discarded. Catmull claims that Lasseter "was the first animator we had ever met who wasn't scared of us" (Amidi, *Art of Pixar Shorts*, 12). The resulting camaraderie and shared problem solving among this small team of graphic engineers and designers established a creative working relationship that echoed back to Catmull and Smith's early days in university computer labs as much as it paralleled the stimulating environment of Lasseter's CalArts studies. As Smith explains, "The right way to think of our group was that it was an academic department" ("Re: Questions"). Everyone was hired for his or her talents and granted considerable respect and freedom. The results would also prove instrumental to their innovative mode of production in the long run: "This collaborative spirit between art and technology would become one of the founding philosophies of Pixar" (Amidi, *Art of Pixar Shorts,* 14).

Lasseter's arrival at Lucasfilm came at a convenient moment, just as the computer-graphics team was beginning to plan their film. Smith and Catmull had decided to establish a strong presence at that next SIGGRAPH convention, displaying their advances in digital compositing hardware, but also showing off some of their new proprietary software innovations to demonstrate that they could construct a complete and convincing animated world, all in a computer. Moreover, they wanted to present engaging character animation, not only moving objects (Smith, "Re: Questions"). Before Lasseter joined the division, they had already designated Bill Reeves and Tom Duff to work on modeling and animation, with Rob Cook and Loren Carpenter in charge of rendering. Unlike any other sort of project, a stand-alone film would allow everyone on their team to showcase their work, including unique breakthrough algorithms, for a very specialized audience of their peers. "The goal as stated in the meeting notes of July 31, 1983, was 'to render a showable sequence of 3-D articulated animation, with edits, in a rich setting. Motion blur very desirable, texture/bump mapping mandatory.' The piece was meant to be symbolic: A computer-animated 3-D character wakes up and sees the world" (Smith, "Adventures," 1). The particle system developed by Reeves for the planet fires in *The Wrath of Khan* would be applied to building a detailed 3D forest set. Lasseter and Wilhite's earlier visit to Lucasfilm, in which they asked whether a computer-generated forest background would be possible, had intrigued Smith and his team. In part because they had not entered into any arrangement with Disney for *The Brave Little Toaster,* the team now wanted to try to build that environment on their own. Thus, even before Catmull and Smith learned that Lasseter was no longer at Disney and was available, they had already been discussing him and confronting the challenging questions he had posed.

Alvy Ray Smith served as director of the project, initially titled *My Breakfast with André,* in playful reference to Louis Malle's recent *My Dinner with André* (1981). It was planned as an in-house production to demonstrate and advertise their skills to the industry. At this point, the computer-graphics group was aware of their need to justify their existence and expense at Lucasfilm. Even the title sequence would show off the first scans from the new Lucasfilm laser scanner. But their overarching intention was to prove that computer-generated animation could tell stories and present characters. The new medium should not be limited to special effects only. In addition to foregrounding their particle system's ability to construct an intricate "natural" forest setting, another priority was to apply their motion-blur program to represent fast-moving actions, mirroring the look of rapid gestures recorded by conventional motion-picture cameras. Without motion blur, fast movements often appeared as quick, staccato little bursts, with a strobe effect that calls attention to the artificial nature of the image. Their overall goal was to demonstrate relatively photorealistic movements, actions, and settings. Appropriately, Smith's initial nine-panel storyboard began with a shaft of sunlight piercing the forest, in which a partially hidden android is sleeping. Gradually, as the film cuts in, isolating the character in closer shot scales, the lighting would shift, revealing him and his skin more and more as he yawns, stretches, rises to his feet, and smiles to meet the day. The demonstration piece would end with a reestablishing shot of André the android standing convincingly in the detailed landscape setting.

Smith was pleased to hand the character design over to Lasseter for his input, since at this point André was merely a storyboard stick figure. However, this is also the moment when the limitations of early 3D software placed narrow restrictions on Lasseter's options. Smith instructed him to build the figure from basic geometric shapes such as cones, cylinders, and spheres, since that was what the computers handled best. Lasseter took the challenge home to southern California and sent back a surprisingly cartoonlike design for André that was quite far removed from the usual gleaming, imposing robotic figures so common in early CGI. Lasseter's André had nothing of the futuristic electronic supermen found in *Tron* or science-fiction graphic novels. This André was more clownish and not at all the sort of android they had expected. As Smith explains, despite the team's initial shock, they came to appreciate Lasseter's version of André: "One of the things we wanted to stress to people was that the new medium of computer imagery carried the 'look' of the artist using it, not that of the computer" (Smith, "Adventures," 4). Lasseter's comical character reveals as much about his own emotionally driven and whimsical aesthetic as it does about the working environment forged by Smith and Catmull. From the beginning, Smith and Catmull encouraged each of their talented colleagues to pursue their own paths and defend their choices if necessary. Their mode of production resembled that of an academic cluster of colleagues debating and ultimately supporting each other's efforts. They did not want a top-down business structure. According to Smith, the André film quickly went through "a massive improvement" as the young newcomer Lasseter "softened André into a lovable little character" and added a second figure, the determined bee, Wally (Smith, "Re: Questions"). Both of these figures would be typical of later Lasseter characters, who are comical, emotionally engaging, and vulnerable.

Building on his CalArts training, Lasseter had returned to Disney's roots and especially Ub Iwerks's original Mickey Mouse designs for motivation, instead of looking to more modern cyborgs or robots as models. As Paik explains, "After all, the early versions of Mickey Mouse . . . had been almost entirely of geometric forms. Taking those early Mickey Mouse designs as an inspiration, Lasseter built a cartoony, soft-looking character, with ellipsoid fingers, tube arms, a spherical head, and a cylindrical hat" (42). Smith began modeling the figure, and Catmull managed to come up with a solution to André's body that pleased Lasseter, who wanted his character to be as flexible as possible. A malleable teardrop body was constructed from melding a cone onto a sphere, then adding some stretch and distortion. Increasing requests from Lasseter led Catmull and others to devise further controls, allowing Lasseter to design an André who could shift his weight, bend, and even shiver. Such ongoing give and take among the Lucasfilm crew helped them all find a creative middle ground, allowing techniques and traits from 2D to be updated or synthesized into the 3D realm. Rather than generating friction between their competing traditions, the 3D process inspired Lasseter to solve his animation problems in new ways, while his expectations and queries motivated his computer-graphics colleagues to rethink their procedures and develop new fixes and techniques within their Motion Doctor program.

These creative collaborations help reveal the productive working relationships that were forged early on between the core management, technical, and animation personnel that would eventually form Pixar. Unlike the fixed, hierarchical environment at Disney, the computer-graphics division at Lucasfilm resembled a small club of devoted researchers. Their mode of production was fairly unique in that they retained some autonomy as a well-funded research-and-development wing within Lucasfilm. Catmull had also managed to establish a truly creative work environment based in part on his experiences at Utah working in Ivan Sutherland's graphics lab. Lasseter's artistic skills, as well as his outgoing personality and technical curiosity, fit well within this ambitious group and their interpersonal dynamics. He began to thrive there and is credited with acting as a catalyst, helping accelerate the team's progress in digital as well as artistic advances. For instance, Lasseter began learning their Motion Doctor software and made suggestions to encourage a more flexible, user-friendly interface for animators. In addition to a new frame-to-frame numbering system that began on the number one like in animation rather than the zero of computer programs, Lasseter pushed for additional controls for moving parts of André's body, which would allow more flexibility in building gestures, including facial expressions. André was eventually built with 547 controls. Early on in the scripting process, Lasseter also complicated the short plot by adding a second character, the bee, to pester André. Wally B (based on Wally Shawn from *My Dinner with André,* and later of *Toy Story*) would have 252 specific controls. Lasseter regularly requested extra fine-tuned controls from Catmull, Loren Carpenter, Tom Duff, and David Sales, who worked out intricate new programs for a more expressive set of eyelids for André and funny, droopy feet for Wally B, among other things. The android project was quickly becoming more than a demonstration of the team's existing digital abilities. The animation group was launching a new stage in their development of a 3D computer-generated filmmaking process, from storyboarding to modeling to rendering of an entertaining, standalone short movie. Lasseter was now serving as a prototype CGI director as well as an animator working within a computer-graphics lab.

The active collaboration among team members also demanded creative mise-en-scène choices. From the start, Lasseter wanted a painterly look for the cartoon, to escape the often cold, crisp, flat lighting of many computer graphics. After looking over various nature photographs, the team decided to build their woods with aspens and red spruces. Lasseter's suggestions for pastel background colors in the forest setting, including contrasting purples, were initially rejected. He countered that the popular illustrator Maxfield Parrish's work could provide a beneficial guide for the color and lighting schemes and then set about convincing his colleagues in an unconventional manner. As Smith recalls, "The production staff trooped down to San Francisco to see an exhibit of Parrish's works to understand his colorful backlighting. Rob Cook helped Bill [Reeves] design a method for simulating the internal shadowing so important to effective plant rendering and also a method for mutual shadowing of the trees" (Smith, "Adventures," 3). This desire for research into real-world referents—constructing aspens and red spruces rather than generic trees, combined with museum field trips to see artistic exemplars firsthand—would become routine practice at Pixar. For instance, animators would later rush to the shore to crawl inside a dead beached whale for real-world inspiration while working on *Finding Nemo* (dir. Andrew Stanton and Lee Unkrich, 2003), and key personnel went on a long Route 66 road trip for *Cars*. But the whole crew also routinely watched canonical movies and explored art history to enrich the digital visual palette for Pixar productions. Lasseter saw the value in balancing real-world cues with the artistry of visual representation, including the highly stylized universe of popular artists such as Parrish.

During preproduction for *The Adventures of André and Wally B*, the computer-graphics division was continually upgrading programs for such things as motion blur, lighting, texturing, and rendering. Eventually, every movement by André and Wally was blurred to some extent, thanks to the new REYES (Renders Everything You've Ever Seen) program, which reportedly used forty-five thousand lines of computer code to operate. The new algorithms employed for *The Adventures of André and Wally B* were also crucial for the development and application of their imaging computer and laser printer. Lucasfilm only allowed the computer-graphics department to make their prototype CGI film as a necessary experiment to help in the functional design and production of a viable, high-resolution computer for visual effects. The graphics team argued that the computer needed some dramatic content to demonstrate its representational and compositing abilities. Thus, the opening traveling shot, with its 46,254 distinct trees, provided a colorful, dense setting for the figures as well as convincing proof of the capabilities for their computer software and hardware in what would become the Pixar Imaging Computer. Smith, Catmull, and Lasseter were still secretly concentrating on applications for making computer animation, while

George Lucas and company were fixated on digital postproduction, creating and selling realistic special effects.

As the project progressed, Smith decided to include a soundtrack, something that would not be necessary were this truly just a visual demonstration of new 3D software. Smith and Catmull were hoping for a polished CGI cartoon to bolster their own agenda for computer-animated cinema. Fortunately for them, Lucasfilm held immense resources beyond computer power, and Catmull and Smith took full advantage of its rare pool of talent. Ben Burtt, the famed sound designer for *Star Wars* and *Raiders of the Lost Ark* (dir. Steven Spielberg, 1981) had an office on the lot and agreed to participate in the project. This partnership began a Pixar tradition of employing efficient, evocative soundtracks that are central to the cartoon's ultimate unity and effect. Lasseter and Smith drew up and filmed their storyboard and pencil sketches of the action as a guide for Burtt, since the finished computer animation would take a great deal of work and then a long period of rendering time before it was viewable. Burtt apparently also gave input on the story's action, including some possible revisions for the ending. This sort of open process, welcoming suggestions from everyone involved, became a trademark of Lasseter and Pixar's mode of operation. They all saw their work as interdependent, recognizing that computer animation was a cooperative venture as well as a newly evolving form. This young computer-graphics unit thrived on new ideas and prided itself on a high degree of shared creativity and camaraderie in the workplace. That someone like Ben Burtt would take the time to help also reflects how unusual and even exciting this film project had become for some at Lucasfilm.

When *The Adventures of André and Wally B* premiered at the 1984 SIGGRAPH in Minneapolis, it proved an immense success, despite several small portions still being shown as pencil tests. Lasseter had designed André and Wally t-shirts, turning the post-conference celebration into a festive promotional party. Beyond the film, the Lucasfilm graphics group presented seven technical papers at SIGGRAPH that year, many of them based on new work accomplished as part of the making of *The Adventures of André and Wally B*. Alvy Ray Smith's presentation involved plants and fractals, Ed Catmull discussed algorithms for complex surface calculations, Rob Cook addressed shading and modeling trees, and Loren Carpenter explained the anti-aliasing of an A-buffer and the REYES 3D system, as well as their team's method of ray tracing. Despite these professional credentials, and the immediate praise for *The Adventures of André and Wally B* within the high-tech world, many traditional animators during this era remained wary of just where computer-generated imagery was leading their medium. However, Lasseter's mix of a cartoony pair of lead characters and a surprisingly fresh soundtrack by one of the top figures in the world gradually helped attract increased attention within the press and industry. As Paul Wells explains, "A high degree of skepticism and mistrust greeted the emergence of computer generated work in the animation industry itself. The potential of Lasseter's animation in the film was elevated with the soundtrack by Burtt, insisting on the notion of 'believability' through recognition of seemingly taken-for-granted everyday sounds" (Wells, "To Sonicity," 26). The names Lucasfilm and Ben Burtt lent a great deal of cultural capital to Smith, Catmull, and Lasseter's project.

The resulting film has a quirky, almost tongue-in-cheek tone and fast-paced rhythm that still stands as a primer for short-format computer animation. Its soundtrack, with its evocative effects and whimsical music, efficiently reinforces and punctuates the action. The initial thirteen-second shot opens on an idyllic hilly setting dotted with green and yellow-orange trees and a sun that "flares" as if it were creating glare on a real, glass camera lens. This bright, shining sun also resembles the flickering light from a movie projector. Clearly, the decision had been made from the start to avoid typical rigid CGI shapes when possible, since a simple fixed round yellow disc in the sky would have satisfied most computer animators at this point. Moreover, the low morning sun provides highlights on one of the ridges, lending additional spatial cues to the complicated geography of tree-covered hills. As the camera travels right and cranes down, a new line of trees rises into the foreground, lending an additional plane of action that begins like a flat row of trees but quickly reasserts volume and depth cues as the camera approaches the ground. A surprisingly intricate visual environment is established with no clear vanishing point and only a vague horizon line. Reeves managed to avoid a routine computer-generated geometric setting, as well as the flashy flyovers seen so often in computer-graphics demonstrations. This is an elegant establishing shot recalling somewhat the three-dimensional sets used in 1930s Fleischer and 1940s George Pal productions. For the

1984 SIGGRAPH premiere audience, the complicated array of textures, colors, and shapes in this first shot of *The Adventures of André and Wally B*, including the chaotic, wild-looking grasses and seemingly endless stands of trees, must have appeared truly remarkable.

Following the big opening shot, there is a dissolve in on a closer view that helps isolate the body of André lying in a clearing. By the third shot, André's colorful surroundings are so detailed that they nearly become distracting. There are dappled brown, gray, and green rocks in the middle ground and on the earth floor of the forest, complete with glowing fallen leaves and uneven ground cover. Fragments of the distant forest canopy are packed into the frame's top corners. Centered in this cluttered frame, filled with organic shapes and colors, the round, red-and-white André seems to hover slightly above the ground as he wakes, stretches, and shakes himself awake. Atop his head is a short usher's cap, made from a slice of a cylinder with a rounded end. While his arms and legs are clearly simple tubes, and his shoe soles are fixed ovals, the addition of diegetic sounds, motion blur, and shaking body parts lend André a lifelike quality. He is suddenly as awake and as alive as any cartoon character might be (figure 6). One of the strengths of

Figure 6: André awakens in *The Adventures of André and Wally B.*

Lasseter's André is that within a matter of seconds the figure goes from a cluster of resting geometric shapes to a "breathing" character who suddenly stares toward the camera with unmatched, off-kilter pupils, registering panic. Only in the next shot, a ninety-degree cut to André in profile, staring nervously into the left side of the frame, do we perceive Wally the bee, who flies, or rather slides, into the frame to confront André nose to nose. Importantly, Wally B arrives precisely at the middle point, forty seconds into the eighty-second cartoon.

The face-off between André and Wally reveals the care that Lasseter, Smith, and the team took to create a composite scene that synthesizes conventional live-action filmmaking practices with the cartoony characters. In the foreground, André and Wally each have three-point lighting, with hot spots from the offscreen sun's key light on André's eye and nose, while the background maintains a complex three-dimensional spatial setting, complete with overlapping trees, grasses that recede into the distance, and shifting fields of color. The lighting effects alone, with the glowing grasses and leaves and the pink-purple sky, provide a stunning environment, especially within the context of early 1980s technology. Lasseter's characters, including the frightened, immobile André leaning back cautiously in the frame, and the sadistic Wally, punching André's rubbery nose, quickly enter into a duel, which is reinforced by Burtt's music. Lasseter's first computer-generated characters are already performing a wide range of thoughts and emotions without recourse to any dialogue. Moreover, Wally, who is also made from variations on basic predefined shapes, especially ovals, cylinders, cones, and spheres, is more abstract than André. His wings are nearly always a blur, but his feet follow below the body with no visible connecting legs. This sort of abstract representation of a body from disconnected parts turns up later in a more extreme example, Chris Wedge's bouncy *Tuber's Two Step,* shown at the 1985 SIGGRAPH. Lasseter not only wanted André's body to be flexible; he developed the flying Wally B to move with marked fluidity. His dangling feet resemble water balloons that add comical weight cues to this bumbling bee.

One of the keys to the anthropomorphism of these characters, however, was Lasseter's concentration on their eyes. He has often explained that the eyes must be windows into the characters' minds—a strategy that classical Disney exploited as well. Thus, in addition to the squash and stretch and motivated actions of the characters, the enlarged eyes with their stark black pupils quickly reveal to the audience where the character is looking and, more importantly, how they react to what they see. Human perception and comprehension are highly sensitive to identifying the direction and purpose of a character's glance. "Social interaction depends upon the ability to infer beliefs and intentions in the minds of others" (Kilner and Frith R32). Our ability to scan and interpret a figure's interest and intentions is not only a key cognitive action, it is greatly aided by clear cues such as oversized facial features, especially eyes. André's erratic blinking also calls attention to his befuddled state of mind. Even his silly little cap pulsates. André could not say, "Oh my, a pesky bee, I must run away," but the audience understands immediately that he is afraid and plotting to exit the frame. And run he does. André shows some clever initiative as he distracts Wally by shifting his gaze and pointing offscreen. When Wally looks away, André grins victoriously at the camera before flying out of the frame (figure 7).

This brief, confident, direct address tells the audience that André is self-satisfied with his ruse. It also anticipates the snow-globe man's

Figure 7: André versus Wally in *The Adventures of André and Wally B.*

similarly confident glances at the audience in *Knick Knack* (1989). As the fooled Wally turns back around, there is a cut to his point of view of a blurry André running away down a path in the forest. Next, Lasseter cuts back to an angry, determined Wally. Before Wally bursts out of the frame in pursuit of André, Lasseter compresses his body into a squashed ball to communicate his intention and set up the explosive exit, which turns Wally B into an abstract cluster of blurred shapes. "Once Wally starts moving, his appendages follow at different speeds depending on their weight, with this heavy feet dragging behind more than his lightweight antennae—a touch of cartoon-style realism grounded in the classic animation principle of follow-through" (Price 59). Charles Solomon notes that the sequence works well because Lasseter relied on traditional cartoon timing: "When Wally takes off after André, his feet leave four frames after his body" (296). Further, the chase benefits immensely from extreme motion blur that is worthy of a Tex Avery cartoon. It also recalls a Bugs Bunny cartoon in which Bugs has to give poor Elmer Fudd his comeuppance, reasserting his superiority. *The Adventures of André and Wally B* keeps one foot in the Hollywood cartoon tradition while also stepping into the new world of computer graphics (figure 8).

Figure 8: André and motion blur in *The Adventures of André and Wally B.*

Finally, after three pursuit shots from extreme comic book–style angles, Wally catches André just out of the frame, which causes the entire field of vision to shake, as if his stinging and knocking down of André in the offscreen space was so violent that it shook the camera on its tripod. The sun is also distorted again in the final shot, flaring on the lens and overexposing the supposed film stock. Such references to conventional "filmmaking" processes return over and over in subsequent Pixar films. These early examples also point out the extent to which Lasseter was striving from the beginning to bring the cinematic and computer-generated modes of production together for a new product that nonetheless remained familiar to audiences. At the end of *André and Wally B*, as Wally, with a bent stinger, proudly flies back into the shot, André's little cap sails in, knocking him too out of the frame, in a nice topper that is underlined by Burtt's musical accompaniment. Smith encouraged Lasseter to move the violence of the stinging offscreen to create a stronger, more comical effect. As Catmull points out, Lasseter's "genius was in creating an emotional tension, even in this briefest of formats" (36). André and Wally had proven their distinct personality traits, and each acted on some conscious fear or desire, or both. According to Price, Lasseter had, for the first time in a computer-animated film, applied the classic animation principles that had evolved over the decades at the Disney studios. They were tools that animators used to move characters in a natural-looking way, to give characters an appealing look and, above all, to make characters *act* (58).

By contrast, another film at SIGGRAPH that year, the colorful *Snoot and Muttly*, by Susan van Baerle and Douglas Kingsbury of Ohio State University's computer-graphics research group, offered clever CGI effects but ultimately failed to create engaging action. *Snoot and Muttly* featured mobile camera movements, dancing birds, and floating spheres, but the figures remained elaborate graphic and rhythmic experiments. The flamingos were composed of globe heads, drooping cone beaks and tails, bending cylinder necks, and long legs that kicked and hopped rather spastically. They never developed into characters with recognizable intentions or personalities, though the figures did bounce and sway as they wandered about the three-dimensional playing space. Creating walk cycles with the illusion of the figure's feet actually seeming to touch the ground was a major hurdle at the time. *Snoot and Muttly*'s skipping creatures hovered and skated over the ground's surface rather than stepping on it, as if they were not quite composited into the space. In *The Adventures of André and Wally B*, the close-ups, clear, evocative gestures, and expressive soundtrack provided decisive advantages over the competition.

From fade-in to fade-out, the eighty-second *Adventures of André and Wally B* foregrounds repeatedly the wide range of special technical abilities available at Lucasfilm's computer-graphics division. The characters, which were initially geometric, wire-frame models with convincing surfaces mapped onto them, proved flexible and distinct. The settings glow thanks to the lighting cues and a vast number of colors that exceeded the range of most digital coloring packages. And while André in particular seems to float across rather than inhabit the landscape in some shots, the compositing of figures and background proved that computers could generate complete, unified animated cartoon worlds. All this ambitious work was also staggeringly expensive, even from a research-and-development point of view: the final version ended up requiring an unprecedented array of computer power, with five big VAX computers at Lucasfilm, ten more at MIT, and two new Cray supercomputers to complete all the rendering. *The Adventures of André and Wally B* was the product of a small, highly skilled team of individuals working within a highly capitalized and unusually generous high-tech corporation.

George Lucas was still not completely convinced about the future of computer animation after the SIGGRAPH premiere. *The Adventures of André and Wally B* reinforced his opinion that computers were still most useful for automating postproduction tasks (Sito, *Moving Innovation,* 242). However, many people in the digital field now recognized Lucafilm's computer-graphics department as the industry leader, and the former Disney animator John Lasseter as the person best positioned to show the commercial and narrative application of traditional animation storytelling within the new transitional era of digital computer animation. In August 1984, *The Adventures of André and Wally B* was presented at the Toronto Animation Festival in its complete form. Also that summer, however, Lasseter's mentor Frank Thomas, who had seen early portions of *The Adventures of André and Wally B,* published a cautionary article in *Computer Pictures* lamenting that so far, computer animation could not reproduce subtlety or convincing movements. Nonetheless, for his conclusion Thomas advised that in the future, any successful computer characters "must have appeal and good acting and appear to think. . . . The real question now is, who will be the first to do it?" (Thomas, "Can Classic," 26). Thomas's concern was shared by many in the industry, but it also became another personal motivating factor for Lasseter, who aimed to prove decisively to Thomas, Lucas, and the industry that computers could perfect character animation.

Importantly, the intense production experience at Lucasfilm was not only instructional for Lasseter; it transformed his working methods and the horizon of expectations for computer animation. Because the computer division was still officially dedicated to research and development of hardware and software products, Lasseter's position there was not secure. Smith and Catmull had only been able to add him to their budget for the SIGGRAPH project. After the 1984 conference, Tom Wilhite contacted Lasseter with a tempting new job offer. Wilhite had just left Disney and was in the process of forming a new company, Hyperion Studios, with several colleagues. The name tied the upstart studio closely to Disney and animation history, since Walt Disney's first Los Angeles studio was built on Hyperion Avenue in the 1920s. Wilhite followed Don Bluth's example, quitting in frustration at current Disney management, while exploiting his departure to assert that he was closer to the spirit and tradition of Walt Disney than those remaining at the studio. Wilhite took *The Brave Little Toaster* project with him, planning to animate it in conventional 2D. He convinced Lasseter to accept the director position and move back to southern California. But within a few months, the financing for their feature-length project faltered, and preproduction was halted. Lasseter was again about to be out of a job. Disappointed, he contacted Catmull, who worked out a way with Smith to hire him back at Lucasfilm as a full-time employee animating their subsequent short-film projects. Eventually, Whilhite completed *The Brave Little Toaster* (1987). That version was directed by the CalArts graduate Jerry Rees and cowritten by Joe Ranft, with some financial help from Disney and distribution through their Buena Vista Pictures. At that point, Lasseter and Pixar were still eight years away from the release of their own first feature film.

Lasseter was relieved to be hired back at Lucasfilm, and as a regular employee this time, while the computer division also benefitted greatly from his return. He had already proven his significance for their creative team. As Smith explained, "I could make things move [on the computer screen] but couldn't convince you they were alive and thinking. Animators are actors; they make you believe something that is not true. I've watched them for years and don't understand it at all. John was the best hire of my life" (qtd. in Capodagli and Jackson 31). From this point on, the future Pixar's core production talent was in place and would struggle to remain so. It is important to note that for animators of the 1980s, to say nothing of the industry model since, employment often involves temporary, limited-time contracts. This project-to-project business model has become the norm in much of animation, especially for CGI features that need very large numbers of technicians and animators for specific stages of production only. Yet, later, as Pixar grew, Lasseter, Catmull, and Smith were determined to maintain a dedicated crew within a sustainable, innovative work environment, which is not always easy in such a volatile industry marked by sometimes long, slow, even halting preproduction periods and then intense production and postproduction and a series of tight deadlines.

After completing *The Adventures of André and Wally B*, Catmull, Smith, and their computer-graphics group were increasingly determined to pursue computer animation, without getting held back by Lucasfilm's interest in special effects. Reportedly, George Lucas had been disappointed by *The Adventures of André and Wally B*, seeing it as a rather crude, and certainly expensive, exercise. He was still not convinced that computer animation itself was as pertinent for his studio as digital color correction and CGI effects within live-action movies. As Lucas explains, "I put together a computer division because I wanted to get a digital printer. At that point I wasn't as interested in three-dimensional animation as I was at getting at the core issue, which was, 'How do you get in and out of the computer?'" (qtd. in Vaz 108). However, while Catmull and Smith began to sense that they would need to find a new, more welcoming home for their team and goals, Lucasfilm provided the chance for Lasseter and their division to pursue another milestone in computer animation.

Steven Spielberg was producing *Young Sherlock Holmes* (dir. Barry Levinson, 1985) and had contracted with ILM for the special effects. He was open to including some CGI shots, in part because of his earlier admiration for the Genesis Effect scene. Lasseter was put in charge of animating a stained-glass knight who comes alive and leaps from his frame as part of another character's hallucination. This sort of reflexive device of a still image suddenly coming to life has been used in animation since its earliest days and also connects back to magic acts and conjuring in phantasmagoria spectacles. Moreover, one such illusion, "Pepper's Ghost," proves particularly pertinent, since it involved projecting images onto a pane of glass (Gunning 55–57). With *Young Sherlock Holmes,* for the first time a computer-generated figure would jump into the real-world setting, and this CGI character would interact with, and frighten, a live-action character. Thus, this short sequence provided the team an opportunity to showcase many of the strengths of their computer-graphics unit, from animation to software programs to cutting-edge hardware, including the new Pixar Image Computer and the final compositing made possible by David DiFrancesco's digital laser-scanning process.

Bill Reeves, Lasseter, and a few other computer-graphics technicians worked closely with other departments within ILM to plan and complete the *Young Sherlock Holmes* sequence. The digital animation ended up providing just over thirty seconds of screen time, in six brief shots, and took approximately six months to complete, including the compositing. Dennis Muren was the film's in-house visual-effects supervisor. Muren was initially unsure whether Lasseter and his crew could pull off the required realistic effects, and he seemed to resent that much of Lucasfilm's resources had gone into the computer division, with little to show so far beyond the *Wrath of Khan* scene and "a sort of demo," *The Adventures of André and Wally B.* As he explained, "That was about it. So I felt if we were going to have all of this equipment, why not go in and see what we could do with it?" (qtd. in Shay, "*Young Sherlock,*" 42). This suspicion about the real value of the computer division and its interest in animation was apparently quite common at ILM, so the *Young Sherlock Holmes* assignment was also a significant test. "As the first computer effect meant to blend seamlessly into a live-action scene, the project was an opportunity for the graphics group to prove it had been worth Lucas's investment—that computer graphics was a viable option for film effects" (Paik 45). The successful result would grant the computer division a great deal of goodwill within Lucasfilm.

During production, the computer-graphics team was fully aware that the *Young Sherlock Holmes* effects job, as well as all their ultimate goals, relied heavily on a highly capitalized workplace and a great deal of interaction between people with a vast array of specialized talents. They also needed patient, generous bosses. There were few places in the 1980s where such a working environment existed, so they understood how fortunate they were to be at Lucasfilm, with access to their technicians and facilities. It was here that David DiFrancesco and his team could develop and perfect their digital laser scanner for transferring CGI effects directly to film stock, creating cinematic images with resolution far beyond what was possible shooting off of cathode-ray tubes. Moreover, early on in this project, Eric Christiansen, a stained-glass artist who had designed windows for the Lucas Skywalker Ranch, was brought in to create a small knight in glass as well as to explain the physical materials and construction techniques. Lasseter expanded on that two-dimensional frame with some clay to produce a model with more volume. Chris Evans, an ILM matte artist, helped paint the church set's stained-glass window for digitizing. The ILM model shop also filmed the technician Jeff Mann in cardboard armor going through gestures so there would be a rough visual layout of the action. Bill Reeves finally had to enter all the information into the Pixar Image Computer, before Lasseter and the rest of his crew could begin animating the final footage. Eventually, the animated knight would be composited into the live-action setting, which was shot in England. But the live-action footage was shot with a soft, smoky look that they feared would not match up well with the CGI imagery. Lasseter accompanied Muren to the British studio to oversee the visual challenges, including the range of lighting and textures involved. As Muren points out, "At that time, we still weren't sure if a computer image would work out" (qtd. in Mandell 66).

John Lasseter and his team, including Eben Ostby and Bill Reeves, ended up creating a complex series of shots and actions. This haunting figure must appear real to the frightened and drugged clergyman, while remaining recognizable as a mental subjective vision by the audience. They decided that its body could be more like a hologram than like a true creature made of solid glass plates. The final knight retained a mysterious, hazy look, but to prove frightening, it required perceived weight and volume. For the initial shots, the stained-glass window of a knight standing with his bloodied sword over a murdered king begins to pulsate in the dark, smoky church. The swelling, discordant music and loud sound cues for crackling glass further draw attention to the window's vibrations. Suddenly, the knight comes crashing down in a series of distinct fragments as the separate panes drop from the window to the church floor below. The extreme motion blur on the moving sections adds to the fantastic effect, as the bits and pieces fall together into a rather awkward looking knight, facing the Reverend Nesbitt (Donald Eccles) in an unsettling two-shot. But as the pastor examines this haunting figure in a point-of-view shot, the camera centers on the glossy suit of armor and bloody blade, before tilting up to the knight's fractured brown painted-glass face.

Lasseter and the crew avoided having hard-edged, solid surfaces for the knight, which remains a soft-focus figment rather than a photo-realistic glass figure. As the knight advances, his thin body is revealed; like heavy stained glass, the knight was designed to appear roughly one inch thick. He also walks quite clumsily; he is, after all, walking for the first time and is made of glass plates that do not quite line up together. It was apparently Muren's wife, Zara Pinfold, who suggested that the knight would be more frightening if it moved like a suspended mobile, without the usual lead connecting the different panes of glass (Mandell 66). As we will see with his subsequent shorts and *Toy Story*, from the beginning of his career, Lasseter always paid close attention to the connections between a figure's supposed real-world materials and its degree of animated mobility. As Muren explains, for this project, the computer team provided crucial texture cues: "Lasseter did artwork on a lot of bubbles and dirt, and painted it on a computer paint program . . . there were five or six texture mattes going with each piece" (qtd. in Mandell 69). For *Young Sherlock Holmes*, Lasseter, Ostby, and Reeves also manipulated depth of field along with texture on the slightly translucent knight, allowing hot spots from background candles to show through the painted-glass body, which also remains reflective in places (figure 9). Much like the dueling playing cards in Disney's *Mickey thru the Mirror* (1936), the knight is revealed to have two identical sides. Muren wanted the CGI lighting to provide reflections or glints on the Knight's blade as well, to help guide the audience's eyes and undercut any overly clean lines on the

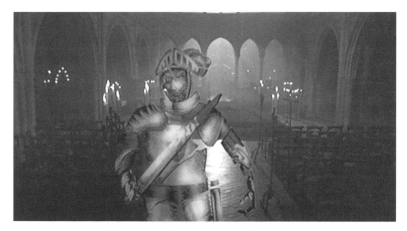

Figure 9: The translucent knight
in *Young Sherlock Holmes.*

sword (Mandell 68). The lighting cues could also be focused and shift across the scene as needed to match better the "real" space of the composited interiors and live actor. Further, while the knight marches threateningly toward Reverend Nesbitt and away from the camera, the knight's second, severe face can be seen on his reverse side, making him more haunting and otherworldly. In the final reestablishing shot, in which the knight prepares in profile to stab the clergyman, there are a few ambiguous depth and overlap cues. It is not quite clear whether the candles, for instance, are in front of or behind his body, or whether we see them through his form. But the knight is concrete enough to scare the shocked, drugged preacher, who runs fatefully out of the church and into the street traffic (figure 10).

The *Young Sherlock Holmes* sequence was Lasseter's final major project at Lucasfilm. For some in the industry, it was also a wake-up call for the potential of CGI effects, since this example avoided the cold, precise, digital sheen demonstrated in *Tron*. The knight sequence was heralded as a "techno-visual breakthrough since it contained the first moving digital character, or 'synthespian,' ever seen in a Hollywood feature" (Venkatasawmy 84). *Young Sherlock Holmes* gained quite a bit of attention within the computer-graphics community as well as praise from critics, including a rather satirical review from Roger Ebert: "The effects

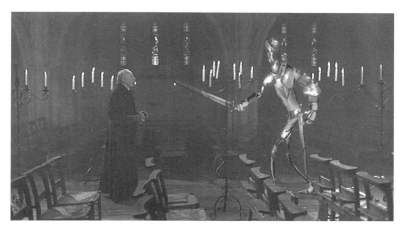

Figure 10: Face-off with the knight
in *Young Sherlock Holmes.*

were supplied by Industrial Light and Magic, the George Lucas brain
trust, and the best one is a computer-animated stained glass window that
fights a duel with Holmes. I liked the effect, but I would have liked it
more if, at the end of the movie, Holmes had drawn Watson aside, and,
using a few elementary observations on the apparent movement of the
stained glass, had deduced the eventual invention of computers" (Ebert,
Rev. of *Young Sherlock*). The movie received a nomination for best
visual effects at the Academy Awards, though *Cocoon* (dir. Ron Howard,
1985) took the top prize. Special-effects historians credit *Young Sherlock
Holmes* as a milestone for digital painting and the use of digital mattes
in feature filmmaking, but also as "the first feature film whose effects
were painted directly on the film with a laser" (Smith, *Industrial Light,*
212). This project entered the history books just as decisively as *The
Adventures of André and Wally B.* Working on this unique special-effects
collaboration was also instructive to Lasseter, who learned to appreciate
Dennis Muren's management style and the mandatory daily meetings
for the entire crew. Lasseter claims that the experience proved a lasting,
positive influence on his own eventual directing process: "The room was
always open for discussion and Dennis really listened to everybody. I
was amazed by that. . . . It molded me as a director in all the good ways"
(qtd. in Paik 46).

Despite the successful effects animation in *Young Sherlock Holmes,* the computer-graphics group was still not assured a solid future at Lucas-film. The company had a new president, and its upper management began to streamline it into more financially sustainable corporate units. The forty-person computer division, which had now fulfilled its basic requirements, providing the means to scan film images into and out of the computer for postproduction effects, seemed increasingly periph-eral. For the sake of job security, Lasseter could have made a transition into the special-effects department at ILM, but he remained committed to computer animation as a stand-alone mode of narrative production. According to George Lucas, "Once we had all the technology that we thought we needed from Pixar, I decided I did not want to stay in the business of just manufacturing hardware and software. . . . I knew that John's ambitions and Ed's ambitions were not in that business either. They wanted to make animated movies" (qtd. in Hearn 170). With the completion of *Young Sherlock Holmes,* Lucasfilm began looking into viable options for spinning off their computer-graphics unit.

Although the ultimate fate of the computer division was more complicated than a simple decision by George Lucas alone, Lucasfilm entered into a string of negotiations during 1985 to sell off the division and their Pixar computer to major medical-equipment, imaging, and engineering firms. The best future applications for this computer group, the Lucasfilm management believed, may lay outside motion pictures, in their potential for CAT scans and fMRIs and designing automobiles. According to David A. Price, the search for new owners took a toll on the group, as Lucasfilm kept wanting to shrink their personnel to make them into a cheaper, more marketable package, while Smith repeatedly countered that the entire creative team was the key of the group's suc-cess: "The real value wasn't in the hardware designs and the software; it was in the collection of extraordinary talent" (71). However, given the computer group's fifteen-million-dollar price tag, with no clear evidence that they could generate adequate profits by themselves, no buyer came forward to take the computer-graphics division off Lucasfilm's books. Further complicating the sale was a general economic uncertainty among digital-visual-effects companies during this era, which culminated with the financial collapse of three well-known computer-effects companies in Hollywood, Digital Productions, Omnibus, and Robert Abel (Sito, *Moving Innovation*, 169).

Steve Jobs, who had met earlier with Smith and Catmull via their mutual friend, the computer pioneer Alan Kay, initially turned down a chance to buy the ILM computer-graphics division. After an increasingly impatient Lucas urged Smith and Catmull to help find buyers, they decided instead to look into how to form their own company, seeking outside investors so they could purchase their department away from Lucasfilm, run it themselves, and remain independent. This new business plan brought them back to Jobs. However, Jobs preferred to buy the controlling interest in Pixar all by himself, while allowing Catmull and Smith to manage the company. As Jobs explained, "They were way ahead of others in combining art and technology, which is what I've always been interested in" (qtd. in Isaacson 239). Steve Jobs eventually offered five million dollars instead of the initial fifteen-million-dollar price. A desperate Lucasfilm accepted, and at the end of January 1986, Pixar Inc. was formed. Jobs retained 70 percent ownership, with cofounders Catmull and Smith and all the other thirty-eight initial employees, including Lasseter as well as the office staff, receiving varying percentages of the company. Jobs also guaranteed five million dollars in new investments to provide Pixar with a steady financial footing. Jobs met regularly with Catmull and Smith and others for board meetings and became increasingly interested in their business, offering a number of suggestions—some welcome, others less so. The significance of this new working arrangement for Lasseter was that once again he was in a creative, collaborative environment. The new Pixar company also provided strong support and economic incentives for pushing forward with computer animation.

Yet, the Pixar personnel would have to continue advocating for their goal of digital filmmaking. It turned out that Steve Jobs put great faith in the Pixar Image Computer as the intended source of Pixar's projected income, rather than recognizing the full value or potential of its animation work. At this point, the computer, which featured Lasseter's design of a beveled-square-with-a-dent front-panel design and distinctive Pixar lettering, cost $125,000 and was not even a stand-alone unit. It required a Sun workstation to operate, and its software was daunting and far from user-friendly. Jobs nonetheless imagined that the Pixar rendering software, Renderman, combined with the image-processing computer, would revolutionize desktop publishing and design, eventually leading to a popular consumer version for generating 3D graphics and photorealistic imagery. "Pixar's small animation department—consisting of Lasseter, plus the part-time supporting efforts of several graphics scientists—was never meant to generate any revenue as far as Jobs was concerned" (Price 89). Steve Jobs had made his fortune selling computer products and planned to continue to do so. He never saw himself as a new brand of movie producer. For him, the central function of Pixar's animation was to demonstrate the amazing capabilities of their computers and Renderman, helping to fire the imaginations of potential clients.

Animation continued to be central to Catmull, Smith, and Lasseter's mission, but they had not presented any new stand-alone cartoon to show at SIGGRAPH in 1985, in large part because of obligations for *Young Sherlock Holmes.* Pixar was determined to signal its debut as an independent company with a new film for SIGGRAPH in August 1986. The 1985 convention had featured a number of important entries, including the ambitious Canadian short, *Tony de Peltrie,* directed by students at the Université de Montréal, Philippe Bergeron, Pierre Lachapelle, Daniel Langlois, and Pierre Robidoux. Their fanciful, melancholy narrative about an aging, leather-faced nightclub performer impressed Lasseter. While *Tony de Peltrie* featured convincing wood-textured flooring and smooth camera movements, it also included the sort of raucous, surreal distortion and floating objects that were far from Lasseter's personal aesthetic. Its mental subjective fantasy structure, however, does anticipate that of *Red's Dream* (1987). But while Lasseter kept track of other innovations in computer animation, he decided after the formation of Pixar that he needed to learn more about modeling, so he began learning the Model Editor program Reeves had designed, which involved typing computer code to construct an object. It was at this point that Lasseter made a complete break from his past 2D animating methods, even as he remained determined to adapt traditional character animation to 3D computer animation. He was shifting from being an animator surrounded by computer-graphics engineers to becoming a computer animator. *Luxo Jr.* would complete that transformation.

Finding Luxo: The Rise of Pixar's Short-Film Style

While Pixar pursued the marketing and upgrading of their image computer in 1986, Catmull and Smith also wanted to keep animation central to their long-term business strategy. Their creative, collaborative work environment allowed for several employees to undertake their own research and animation projects. For instance, one of the new challenges that fascinated Bill Reeves was writing programs for the complex shifting movement of waves and accompanying reflections of light and color. His resulting footage of colorful, nearly transparent, undulating flags and intricate waves breaking on a shoreline, *Flags and Waves*, was shown at SIGGRAPH that summer. Similarly, Eben Ostby explored new techniques for rendering. He devised an impressive short exercise, *Beach Chair*, which also screened at SIGGRAPH. Meanwhile, Lasseter worked on his own project for SIGGRAPH alongside Reeves, Ostby, and Sam Leffler. These four brought valuable individual skills to help forge a productive team that was mutually inspiring and instructive. The adventurous animation work at Pixar was always an active component of their research in software and hardware, and the resulting films cleverly displayed those innovations. That Lasseter's shorts became entertaining mininarratives in their own right helped fuel interest in the new Pixar and their surprising range of striking innovations across the computer-graphics industry. While ILM remained the home of cutting-edge digital special effects at this point, Pixar would rapidly become known as the world's premier site for the research and practice of computer animation.

John Lasseter's experiment, learning to build a character's models from scratch in the computer, began with the Luxo lamp on his desk. This project synthesized the familiar with the unknown, since the lamp was an everyday object that also referred back to *Lady and the Lamp*. However, this time he was creating the figure by typing data into a computer and drawing with an electronic sketch pad. Once he managed to digitize a version of the lamp, add realistic textures, and manipulate its motion with the animation program, Lasseter began fundamentally changing his approach to movement and timing. "When I was able to move an existing model, I stopped thinking about individual frames and starting thinking of time as a whole" (qtd. in Paik 59). The lamp seemed somehow more alive than earlier characters he had animated via distinct, 2D drawings. This Luxo was turning out to be more like an entire physical puppet or toy than a sketch of a lamp to Lasseter. Early on, prior to SIGGRAPH, Lasseter demonstrated his motion study at the 1986 Anima festival in Brussels. There, the filmmaker Raoul Servais encouraged him to expand the Luxo test reel into a little story, no matter how concise and brief it had to be due to the expense and technical limitations. Narrative and humor would really prove its value.

Unlike his own student films, which revolved around a single character, first a lamp on a shelf and then a sleepy boy, both reacting to assorted events and characters around them, this time Lasseter followed the narrative model of *The Adventures of André and Wally B*, building the tale around two characters who play off one another. Lasseter paired the Luxo lamp with a smaller "child" lamp. Tom Porter had brought his baby son in to work, and Lasseter was apparently amused by the toddler's proportions, including his seemingly oversized head and relatively short arms. Lasseter realized anew that a child is not just a shrunken version of an adult, and its toddler-specific movements had comic potential. Given that the initial wire-frame model for the lamp was already constructed in the computer, Lasseter began to manipulate a second, smaller version of his Luxo rig, shortening and distorting it slightly. The "child" lamp would not simply be a smaller, mirror-image version of the Luxo. For instance, its springs and support bars were condensed and placed in slightly different configurations. But to preserve the comic awkwardness of the little lamp, the bulbs in their "heads" were precisely the same size, with only the taller lamp's much larger dome shade seeming to have the correct proportion. Thus, the smaller lamp was a "younger," incomplete version of the larger lamp. It would be shaped in a more juvenile manner and also have more immature, rapid gestures in order to set up quickly the differences in age, attitude, and behavior.

The well-known *Luxo Jr.* film helped establish Lasseter and Pixar's reputations within the computer-graphics community. Further, this was Lasseter's first real directing job. The animation team had a limited amount of time before the August SIGGRAPH deadline, but they also suffered from a lack of equipment, sharing one interactive workstation in their office for their several demanding projects. As Lasseter explains, "We were so limited by the lack of computer power that we couldn't even give the characters a background. We just locked the camera down and had this wood floor that faded off to nothing. . . . For the first time, a computer-animated film focused on the characters and the story" (qtd. in Schlender and Tkacyzk 149). Replicating the background for each frame would have proven too expensive and time-consuming at that point. Thus, in marked contrast to *The Adventures of André and Wally B,* there would be no virtual crane shot and no colorful, detailed landscape or setting. However, for *Luxo Jr.,* Lasseter would again use the offscreen space and an evocative soundtrack to signal a larger space beyond the fixed, shallow framing. As the production progressed and the SIGGRAPH deadline approached, Lasseter famously began taking the night shift at one point so that everyone could find adequate access to the computer. Eben Ostby also developed new procedures for the animation program to help calculate the rotation of the rubber ball, which would become significant for this project and subsequent Pixar shorts. The resulting *Luxo Jr.* lasts just over ninety seconds, not counting the titles, but it also announced the beginning of a new era for John Lasseter and Pixar.

The plot, like the visual space, is pared down to a minimum. Initially, a large static lamp is bumped and perhaps awakened by a colorful rubber ball rolling in from offscreen right. The lamp examines the ball, cueing the audience that the bulb and metal shade function like a face and head. It bats the ball back twice to an unseen partner, then the ball returns, rolling across the frame and disappearing offscreen left just before the smaller lamp leaps into the frame, pauses to look up to the larger lamp, and then seems to shiver with excitement as it continues hopping across and out of the frame, chasing the ball. As the ball and Junior return into the shot, the larger lamp constantly scans the action, guiding our attention and reinforcing its own agency. At the exact midpoint of the cartoon, the small lamp jumps up onto the ball, quickly rocking and bouncing on it until the ball punctures, slowly lowering Junior back down to the floor. Luxo Jr. uses its shade to flop the flattened ball over, gets a disapproving shake of the shade from the larger lamp, and crumples lower, accompanied by the sound of its hinges, which resemble the deflating ball's noises. Once it limps out of the frame, however, a much larger ball rolls into the frame and past the parent lamp, pursued by an ecstatic Junior, leaping higher than ever in the air. Luxo Jr. exits frame left, trailing its undulating cord behind like a flicking tail, as the larger lamp, still centered in the frame, turns to the camera as if to say, "What can you do?" and shakes its head once more.

The absence of distracting details in the background and shallow playing space for the lamps also concentrates the audience's attention. Even without faces, the lamps prompt spectators to center their gaze on the two bulbs, shades, and key gestures (plate 1). This short film prefigures many of Lasseter's subsequent plot points, where characters briefly strive to break out of some routine and experience a brief triumph or moment of joy, before suffering some sort of disappointment prior to their moment of self-realization. *Luxo Jr.*'s world was clearly enhanced and transformed by the CGI: "The computer was Lasseter's tool for achieving moods, character animation, and acting nuances in a pair of gray lamps that 2D animation might have expressed differently" (Sarafian 212). Lasseter's experiment in computer-animated performance proved momentous.

One of the most striking advances in *Luxo Jr.* compared with *The Adventures of André and Wally B* was the addition of shadowing within the virtual setting. Historically, animators who want to add a sense of volume to their cartoon characters have added shadows to help suggest depth cues, separating their figures from the background. Even *Gertie the Dinosaur* (dir. Winsor McCay, 1914) cast shadows on the ground, so when she raised and lowered a foot, an accompanying shadow would expand and contract, providing quick real-world prompts for mass and figure-ground separation. Such cues also help exaggerate the sense of movement. While *The Adventures of André and Wally B* incorporates sophisticated lighting cues to preserve a consistent lighting setup, with directional light providing three-point illumination and some attached shadows to reinforce the direction of the key light, it does not include cast shadows. When André first sits up, his hands do not cast shadows onto the ground or onto his body. This absence of spatial cues furthers the impression that he is hovering over the background rather than really resting embedded in a naturalistic setting.

For *Luxo Jr.,* Bill Reeves worked with Rob Cook and David Salesin to devise a self-shadowing algorithm that could calculate a "depth map" from the point of view of the light sources. As Lasseter explains, "Instead of storing information on the color of the objects in its view, it stored information on the distance to other objects. If one object appeared in the depth map before another, you knew that the former should cast a shadow on the latter" (qtd. in Amidi, *Art of Pixar*, 18). This application was also put to work by Lasseter to construct a number of light sources. Not only does the offscreen key light motivate shadows from a lamp's body and springs onto its own bottom base, but when one Luxo "looks" at the ball or another lamp, it also generates hot spots of light on those objects from its own bulb. Lasseter's simulation of white diegetic electric light lends a convincing naturalism to the film. Even the oscillating cord casts plausible shadows on the floor as it flops up and down. By contrast, the cords in *Lady and the Lamp* can only slide around the screen like thick pieces of string. Thus, the relatively simple, shallow space of a wood-textured floor of *Luxo Jr.* gains immeasurably from the variety of lighting intensities and constantly moving, shifting shadows. A *Positif* article later celebrated the result: "When the lamps turn their bulb toward the audience we can read surprise or deception in the simple circle of light" (Ciment 14) (figure 11).

Significantly, Lasseter's lamps present personality and natural movement, even though they are set in a relatively artificial environment with an empty black space behind the small section of floor on which they perform. But another parameter that helps lend these characters

Figure 11: Luxo lighting and emotion; *Luxo Jr.*

personality is the soundtrack by Gary Rydstrom, who worked with Ben Burtt at Lucasfilm. In his first Pixar film, Rydstrom combined "realistic" sound effects with the more alternative cartoony visual world of computer animation. Paul Wells emphasizes Rydstrom's pivotal role in reinforcing the anthropomorphic traits in Lasseter's characters as well as helping to anchor them in a tactile, physical world. Some of the squeaks, for instance, were the recorded sounds of real light bulbs being screwed in and out of their sockets. "They ultimately sound as if they embody the particular emotional responses of the characters as they encounter their situation" (Wells, "To Sonicity," 27). Rydstrom saw many of the sound effects as "voices" for the CGI figures: they are evocative but also connected to the denoted textures and materials. "When the ball deflates, it is identified with the specific sound of the air being expelled; however it is the interpretive reaction of the characters, who perceive this almost as a last exhalation of breath, a cartoon death gasp, that makes something physical and material into something metaphysical and emotional" (Wells, "To Sonicity," 28). The soundtrack also includes sounds from offscreen, further unifying the image with a larger, unseen spatial realm. Throughout Pixar's history, sounds would lend concrete cues for materiality but also serve as emotional prompts to communicate the central characters' thoughts to the audience.

Luxo Jr., Flags and Waves, and *Beach Chair* were all ready to be screened at SIGGRAPH in August 1986. Steve Jobs decided to attend the conference, as Lucas had for *The Adventures of André and Willy B.* Lasseter traveled with him to Dallas, where *Luxo Jr.* was shown on the program in the large arena accomodating six thousand attendees. The premiere reception was riotous, and *Luxo Jr.* won the best-film prize. Seeing *Luxo Jr.* generate an immediate joyous outburst from thousands of computer-technology fans had a profound effect on Jobs. He later claimed that this was the occasion when he understood Pixar's potential: "Our film was the only one that had art to it, not just good technology. Pixar was about making that combination, just as the Macintosh had been" (qtd. in Isaacson 244). The next year, when *Luxo Jr.* was nominated for the best animated short film at the Academy Awards, Jobs attended the ceremony. It lost to *A Greek Tragedy* (prod. Linda Van Tulden and Willem Thijssen), but "Jobs became committed to making new animated shorts each year, even though there was not much of a business rationale for doing so" (Isaacson 244). *Luxo Jr.* had also certainly surpassed Ed Catmull's initial goal of making a little film for SIGGRAPH "that says who we are." *Luxo Jr.* further demonstrated Lasseter's talent for combining many traditional character-animation tactics—including squash and stretch, anticipation, arcs, and secondary action—with computer animation. The next year he would even present a paper, "Principles of Traditional Animation Applied to 3D Computer Animation," citing *The Adventures of André and Willy B* and *Luxo Jr.* as his test-case examples. He was consciously updating classic Disney and Warner Bros. cartoon styles for the digital age.

Lasseter became an energized advocate for computer animation. Over the next several years, with the premiere of each new Pixar short, he was always ready to explain how his films synthesized past and present. He came to bristle at repetitive skeptical critics: "I don't like it when people come up to me and ask why we did it with computers. . . . I want to create something that looks real—like the lamps in *Luxo Jr.*—but simply can't be. . . . This is character animation'" (qtd. in Lee, "Computer Animation Demystified," 98). Lasseter's task of justifying the time, cost, and astounding technology required for a few minutes of animation recalls the challenges faced by Technicolor's Herbert Kalmus in the 1930s. Kalmus used to show Disney's *Funny Little Bunnies* (1934) to prospective live-action producers and shame them by asking, "How much more did it cost Mr. Disney to produce that entertainment in color than it would have in black and white? The answer is, of course, that it could not be done at any cost in black and white" (Kalmus 578). Lasseter and Catmull were busy trying to prove the same point about computer animation.

Computer animation in 3D was not simply a more expensive version of traditional animation; it was a different mode of production, with a different potential outcome that nonetheless rested on some shared principles from the past. But *Luxo Jr.* would simply not be the same film or experience in conventional 2D animation. For instance, while the little Luxo lamp may jump about, expressing its joy via its gestures and keen sound cues, much like a happy bunny in a 1930s Silly Symphony, Lasseter had to revise or even discard some of his specific training, including the notion of timing, beginning with extreme key poses and then the multiple in-between stages of an action. "I developed a way of layering key frames. I was able to see three or four key frames as if they had been laid on top of each other. It allowed me to make adjustments to each of them. . . . Once I decided where the move would start (in this case a hop), how high it would be and how far Luxo would hop, then I went back and worked on the little things, the nuances'" (qtd. in Lee, "Computer Animation Demystified," 99). Dan Torre points out that much of animation involves compiling layers to composite the image. In CGI, the construction process of building progressively from model to rigged skeleton to surface, coloring, texture, and lighting all mirrors our cognitive perception and working-memory comprehension of images in a series of layers (56). Computer animation required that Lasseter adapt technically as he solved basic animation problems and expanded upon historic techniques. He also had a close-knit team of determined computer researchers surrounding and supporting him. They all increasingly came to function as a small, interdependent artisanal crew within a large, highly capitalized workplace.

The positive reception for *Luxo Jr.* rested in large part on the relationship of the two lamps, as much as on the visual style, clever soundtrack, and fast-paced action. At the SIGGRAPH premiere, the digital pioneer Jim Blinn asked Lasseter whether the parent lamp was a mother or a father, proving convincingly that gender and even family relations are attributes quickly assigned by viewers. Subsequently, Lasseter has explained that he sees it as a father-and-son drama, since a mother lamp would be less tolerant of her child hopping precariously on the ball (McCracken 8). Stephen Prince also praises Lasseter's job of establishing paternity and emotional traits so quickly: "The animation endows these [lamps] with personalities and the roles of father and child. . . . Squash and stretch, timing, and exaggeration delineate the characters and their emotions. Dad moves slowly, with gravitas, Junior with quicker, chippier actions . . . to convey emotion and thought. . . . Dad moves only from neck, head, and shoulders; Junior moves with his entire body" (Prince, *Digital Visual,* 106). As Brad Bird observes, "*Luxo Jr.* to me was very John Lasseter in the sense that the lamps were very simple, seemingly mechanical, emotionless things, but he got a tremendous amount of expression out of them. . . . One of the things I love about John's work is there's absolute joy in it!" (qtd. in Paik 60).

The sparse, effective soundtrack adds affective congruence, as it intensifies the narrative situation, increasing the spectator's empathy for the "child" lamp's temporary shame and disappointment, and then shifts to reflect his sense of euphoria and abandon when he returns with the bigger ball. Thus, *Luxo Jr.* became a hit on every level and a wake-up call to many young would-be animators. "The fun and sensitive Luxo lamps shed light on the possibilities of associating graphic computation with emotional values that, in the 1980s, seemed to be a privilege of traditional animation alone" (Wiedemann, "Pixar," 402).

The historical importance of *Luxo Jr.* and its impact are difficult to overestimate. Many animation students of the 1980s saw it as a compelling reason to pursue computer animation. Meanwhile, the popular press began to grant more attention to Pixar, expanding its visibility beyond the computer-graphics world. During 1990 and 1991, as Pixar was revising its structure and business strategy, Lasseter and Stanton made four variations of *Luxo Jr.* for the PBS *Sesame Street* show, including *Light and Heavy, Surprise, Front and Back*, and *Up and Down*, greatly extending Luxo's audience. *Luxo Jr.* was eventually named a cinematic treasure for preservation by the Library of Congress National Film Registry. Moreover, *Luxo Jr.* was quickly acknowledged as more than Lasseter's calling-card film; it came to represent a new phase in animation within popular culture. It also marked the point when journalists, guided by Pixar's publicity department, began associating Lasseter with the legacy of Walt Disney: "As *Steamboat Willie* was to Walt Disney and his studio, *Luxo Jr.* was to John Lasseter and Pixar: the company's breakthrough animated short. Each film announced to the world its creator's distinct vision" (Amidi, *Art of Pixar Shorts*, 17). Leonard Maltin underscores this parallel between Luxo Jr. and Mickey Mouse: "I like the fact that Luxo still has significance to the people at Pixar, because that's their Mickey Mouse essentially. That lamp that they brought to life started the ball rolling for them. And I think there's a wonderful sense of continuity that is expressed when they use that as their symbol" (qtd. in Paik 62). John Lasseter was rapidly becoming one of the bright spots for industry professionals and critics alike. His personality contributed to his reputation, as he quickly became appreciated for his pleasant, earnest, and entertaining interviews. His positive attitude and collaborative working relationship with everyone around him, all the way up to Steve Jobs, ensured his role as the public face and spokesperson for the up-and-coming Pixar Inc.

Nonetheless, Pixar's financial situation and business model were still uncertain for the first several years with Steve Jobs. Efforts to market and sell the Pixar Image Computer and software continued but proved disappointing. Fortunately, Disney entered into a new deal in which Pixar's Computer Animation Production System (CAPS) would be used to help scan and color drawings and then composite them with other background art before printing the result onto film stock. There was great promise for this hybrid system, merging computer graphics with traditional commercial animation. Pixar was positioned at the center of the newest phase of animation's evolving mode of production just as Disney was about to embark on a renewal of feature-length animation, which would begin in earnest with the release in 1989 of *The Little Mermaid* (dir. Ron Clements and John Musker). Increasingly, however, Jobs became impatient with some of Pixar's top personnel, especially Alvy Ray Smith, and the lack of guaranteed income streams. Smith and Catmull saw themselves as semiautonomous, but Jobs occasionally brought his intense, even erratic management style to bear on Pixar. His interactions with Alvy Ray Smith in particular became so strained and even contentious that Smith eventually left Pixar. By contrast, Jobs and Lasseter formed a productive and creative relationship. Despite strong personality differences, the two ended up working well with one another: "Lasseter was an artist, so Jobs treated him deferentially, and Lasseter viewed Jobs, correctly, as a patron who could appreciate artistry and knew how it could be interwoven with technology and commerce" (Isaacson 243). Even when Jobs would arrive at board meetings determined to cut back his personal expenditure on Pixar, he regularly ended up agreeing to cover the costs of every new short film they proposed. Catmull and Lasseter continued to convince him of the films' significance for Pixar's reputation and future business ventures.

For the next Pixar short, Lasseter again composed a story and style that fit the ongoing technological innovations under way around him. Bill Reeves was expanding the options for particle systems and testing new versions of rain, which typically follows rather chaotic rhythms that defy some of the usual repetitive computerized patterns common during this era. He had also begun constructing a cityscape. His night-time urban setting allowed for the rain to accumulate into puddles that also reflected the light from street lamps and surroundings (Amidi, *Art of Pixar Shorts*, 21). As Philippe Lemieux observes, natural phenomena, such as organic rain and distorted reflections, were quite a challenge during this era. These qualities are directly opposed to the mathematical, structured, binary world of computers (111).

Reeves's experiment with this sort of film-noir environment inspired Lasseter, as did Eben Ostby's current work. Ostby was developing a realistic model for a bicycle with rapidly spinning spokes and gears. Lasseter devised a scenario in which a lonely, unsold unicycle dreams of performing in a circus and upstaging the clown. The cartoon would make full use of the latest texturing advances at Pixar and help put the groundbreaking work by Reeves and Ostby on display. The result, *Red's Dream,* also became their first and last short created with the Pixar Image Computer. By concentrating on the red unicycle and its mental subjective dream sequence, rather than on the humanoid clown figure Lumpy, Lasseter was again lending personality, or at least the human ability to desire, to an everyday object. The team also increased dramatically the lighting cues for the exterior night scenes and interior bike-shop setting, expressively linking the setting to the character's mood.

Red's Dream follows a precise, condensed three-act structure that fits many of the contemporary script manuals of the era, including Syd Field's *Screenplay: The Foundations of Screenwriting.* The opening portion includes five atmospheric shots of rainy nighttime streets dissolving one into another, then three shots inside Eben's bike shop that isolate the unicycle before cutting to a close-up of its saddle, or head. The cut-in could be a reference to the famous bicycle-seat shots in François Truffaut's *Les Mistons* (*The Mischief Makers,* 1957). The circus dream that follows also acts as a cartoon homage to Federico Fellini's *The Clowns* (1970). This introduction, bathed with sad saxophone music composed by David Slusser, lasts fifty seconds. The fade follows a virtual dolly-in on Red's saddle and a cut to black, after which the central section containing the circus act begins with Lumpy the clown appearing in a circle of light for his performance, riding Red.

Backgrounds for the circus space were limited to a black void, much like those for *Luxo Jr.,* as the floor again provided the foundation to anchor the figures. Available memory was limited in the Pixar Image Computer, so the circus dream sequence included little environmental data, and the relatively empty scenographic space helped reduce the rendering time. The circus floor in *Red's Dream* was painted with the red star and yellow and blue circle pattern from the ball of *Luxo Jr.* The bicycle sounds, including a squealing tire as he brakes, were created digitally on the synclavier and call attention to Red beneath the brightly colored clown and its huge red and white sneakers. As a series of shots reveal the tentative clown's juggling act, Red becomes more than a physical support. First, one of the primary-colored balls falls out of the frame and is batted back to the clown, then we see Red pull out from under Lumpy to save another dropped ball.

After Red peels off to rescue yet another wayward ball, he seems to appreciate his independence. He squeaks and repeatedly tosses the green ball up and down on his pedal as the clown, feet still pumping as if on a unicycle, circles nearby. By the cartoon's temporal midpoint, Red has begun to upstage the clown. Lumpy's face displays increasing surprise and then panic, much like a Warner Bros. cartoon character who realizes belatedly that he has walked off a cliff (figures 12 and 13). Only when the full weight of the situation has finally registered with Lumpy, who even looks apprehensively toward the camera, does he fall out of frame. As with all the Pixar shorts, Lasseter communicates a character's shock or extreme emotion with large and subtle physical gestures and especially head and eye cues. He never resorts to placing indexical graphic markers such as "?!" over a character's head, as in more figurative cartoon traditions. Once the clown disappears, Red performs solo, juggling all three balls with his pedals. The crowd roars, and the proud Red begins to bow.

Finally, after one hundred seconds of the circus act, there is a match-on-action cut back to the deserted store, where Red continues to bow. Gradually, just like the clown before him, Red recognizes that something is wrong and slows his bowing, realizing where he is. Back from his fantasy, he bends and then meanders into his corner, his 50-percent-off tag dangling around his neck, beside the bucket catching leaking drops of rain water. This third act, like the opening sequence, lasts fifty seconds. The second act's duration is precisely twice as long as the setup and resolution, suggesting that the storyboards were designed to match Syd Field

Figure 12: Red confronts the Clown
in *Red's Dream.*

Figure 13: The Clown registers panic
in *Red's Dream.*

or similar script-manual formulas. However, the film's structure also fits Lasseter's own tendencies. Like the prototype narratives for André and Luxo, the cartoon begins with one figure who is soon joined by a second, competing character. The soundtrack for *Red's Dream* remains manipulative and highly functional. Its sound design was again created by Rydstrom, who guides our attention toward narrative details while simultaneously reinforcing the environment and narrative by providing emotional as well as textural cues. For instance, when Red performs, those bouncing balls sound springy, reinforcing the squash and stretch as the balls soar and land on his pedals. A highly selective array of sounds reinforce the concrete qualities of Red, his springs and pedals, as well as those solid green, red, and blue balls. Later, the metal squeaks shift from happy, birdlike chirps when Red is performing to mournful, slow squawks when he returns to his corner in the lonely, dark shop. Rydstrom reportedly spent six weeks on sound effects for *Red's Dream,* with twenty different tracks layered one over another (McCracken 15). Paul Wells points out that Rydstrom's sound effects increase the film's pathos and impact by framing the story with Red's "mute isolation" in the bike store, reinforcing the melancholy tone that avoids the usual comforting, secure sounds of a Disney cartoon (Wells, "To Sonicity," 29–30).

For the story development of *Red's Dream,* Lasseter wanted to include the sad ending, despite protests from others at Pixar, in part because he believed it would add more emotion, in the tradition of Frank Thomas and Ollie Johnston's teachings on establishing pathos for character animation. He even jokes that the downbeat ending of *Red's Dream* began Pixar's "blue period" (Young). Lasseter's combination of film-noir traits with the cartoony dream sequence reveals his playful attempt to synthesize cutting-edge CGI with traditions and even conventions from cinema's past. Red is composed of rather simple geometric shapes, though he also bends and twists on occasion when his emotions warrant it. But Lumpy the clown was more complex in terms of surfaces and shape. His head had been sculpted initially in a 3D program and resembles a balloon that has lost air unevenly in different quadrants. Yet his body parts, much like those on André, include cylindrical arms and legs and altered teardrop feet. The gaudy coloring, including the droopy orange and red tie and orange wire squiggles of hair, help distract from some of the geometric shapes and mechanical movements of his construction. As the title suggests, color is central to this cartoon; its bold, saturated hues are motivated more by the Sunday comics than the usual subtle Disney realistic palette.

But *Red's Dream* was also a successful transitional film for Lasseter and his team, as they worked to combine technological advances with their increasing confidence in storytelling. The Pixar Image Computer and the ChapReyes rendering program they were using could not allow for motion blur, so Lasseter, Reeves, and Ostby incorporated more exaggerated squash and stretch on the bouncing balls to grant them increased action cues. Some parts, including the sale tag hanging around Red's neck, were even hand-animated by Lasseter. Nonetheless, the Pixar Image Computer and ChapReyes were vital to completing the animation on time. They could render individual frames of the circus scene in only eight to ten minutes, which was much faster than their competition. "Minicomputers might consume roughly three hours of computation per frame, or almost nine months of computer time for the entire sequence" (*Ars Electronica*). Nevertheless, Lasseter and his crew came to realize that their animation software program, Motion Doctor, was no longer adequate for their increasingly complicated creations. Lasseter, Ostby, and Reeves met with their core colleagues, including Loren Carpenter, Rob Cook, Sam Leffler, and David Salesin, to discuss the possibility of devising a new set of software fixes. They decided that a whole new modeling environment was needed, so the team set to work on a program they abbreviated as "Menv." As Amid Amidi points out, "Menv was designed from the ground up to accommodate the workflow of a traditionally trained animator like Lasseter" (*Art of Pixar Shorts* 22).

The Menv program broke the stages of animation and various parameters, including modeling, animating, and lighting, into various modules that could be readily upgraded. It was initially designed for Silicon Graphics workstations. Animators had more immediate access to a wider array of tools and controls for gesture and body movement, providing options for character animation on an intricately complicated interface that ultimately made animating more efficient and fluid. Unlike the previous modeling software, various animators could now more easily access and update their collective projects. Eventually Menv allowed hundreds of people to work on the same files, streamlining the production process. This sort of collaborative computer-graphics design, in which Lasseter could influence the software controls at his disposal, helped provide important advantages for Pixar. Their company was continually inventing and upgrading procedures that made sense from the creative as well as the managerial perspectives. The presence of top in-house computer engineers available for ongoing research, development, and problem solving gave Pixar distinct creative advantages over potential animation competitors. Subsequently, other 3D animating programs popped up and copied some of Menv's format and interactive menus, but Pixar continued to develop ever newer versions, including Marionette and Presto.

When *Red's Dream* premiered at the SIGGRAPH conference in July 1987, it was actually introduced by Lasseter's mentors, the Disney veterans Thomas and Johnston. Their very public support lent weight to Pixar and especially Lasseter, suggesting that Pixar had come fully into its own now with a film that continued the spirit of Disney character animation, even if in a new 3D CGI mode. At that same SIGGRAPH, Robert Cook, Loren Carpenter, and Ed Catmull presented a paper, "The Reyes Image Rendering Architecture," and Lasseter offered his "Principles of Traditional Animation Applied to 3D Computer Animation" paper. Pixar's presence was decisive that year. Between the screening of *Red's Dream,* the technical presentation on Reyes, and Lasseter's aesthetic advice, Pixar managed to position itself as a leading source for computer-animation production, software, and concepts. Lasseter's talk in particular offered an insightful outline of his own practical guiding principles and narrative strategies, many of them adapted from his CalArts education and his experiences updating Disney traditions.

The "Principles of Traditional Animation" presentation included a thorough lesson plan that drew heavily from the classical-era Disney art instructor Donald Graham, while succinctly summarizing Thomas and Johnston's chapter "The Principles of Animation," from *Illusion of Life.* Though Thomas and Johnston explain twelve principles, from squash and stretch through to "appeal," Lasseter rearranged them slightly and dropped just one category, solid drawing, as he adapted their lessons for computers. Lasseter also replaced the 2D Disney examples with his own illustrations and lessons from *The Adventures of André and Wally B* and *Luxo Jr.* For instance, Lasseter's demonstration of anticipation involves Wally preparing to zoom out of the frame in pursuit of André.

The category of "slow in and out" is updated with spline interpolations for in-betweens and fewer extreme key poses, since different movements in computer animation, including rotations, may have their own temporal structures. As he explained later, setting key frames for various controls on an individual character worked much better and allowed the computer's calculations to generate more appropriate in-betweens (Lasseter, "Tricks," 45).

Lasseter's analysis and real-world problem-solving decisions for *Luxo Jr.* convincingly prove that his techniques are truly rooted in Disney tradition while revamping those strategies for the age of computer animation. Importantly, Lasseter's paper also reinforces his generosity, since it seems to be serving the double duty of explaining his own practice while urging his potential competitors on so they can all improve their mode of animation together. Right from the beginning, he warns that the increased access to computer-animation systems will unfortunately give rise to much "bad animation," since too few people in CGI were familiar with these key principles for generating successful and entertaining animation. As the layout supervisor Craig Good points out, "Many of the artists at Pixar dislike the typical style of computer graphics," with cameras swooping through space (qtd. in French, *"Toy Story,"* 28). Such spectacular and freewheeling shot compositions combined with limited character movement stands in opposition to Lasseter's principles. As further evidence that Lasseter's own work was "good animation," *Red's Dream* won the Golden Nica award at Ars Electronica's new computer-graphics festival in Austria.

During the mid-1980s, John Lasseter was immersed in computer animation, often working around the clock with his core colleagues to meet deadlines, all while struggling constantly to justify the animation unit's expense to Steve Jobs and others within Pixar. His private life also ended up revolving around computer graphics. He met his future wife, Nancy A. Tague, at a SIGGRAPH convention. She worked at Apple, and one of her projects in 1988 was to help design a short animated segment to prove the versatility and potential of the new Macintosh II computers. Tague was in charge of design and also worked as an animator. The recent CalArts graduate Andrew Stanton worked as her illustrator. The result was *Pencil Test,* which features a pencil icon that leaves the flat computer screen, leaping into the "real" 3D animated world to confront an actual solid pencil. However, the bulk of the narrative concerns the attempts by the small flat icon to return into the computer screen after the Mac II has been turned off. Despite its valiant efforts, the icon remains stuck in the 3D world outside the computer. The humorous title sequence allows the icon to continue hurling itself against the screen, only to repeatedly fall back into the offscreen space below. The surprise ending, with the frustrated pencil icon still flinging itself against the screen, to happy music, remains somewhat open and unresolved. *Pencil Test* displays a rapid-fire pacing and is a very polished short film that also functions as a fine advertisement, verifying and even celebrating the Macintosh II's abilities.

The pencil icon itself is composed of five separate components, including the triangular lead point, which serves as a "foot," and the pink eraser, the pencil's "head." Lasseter, credited as coach, seems to have had some influence over the final action, since this simple icon displays a great deal of personality in a bare-bones scenario. Twisting motions of the pencil's flat torso suggest which direction he is "looking," despite his lack of eyes, and when the pencil gets an idea of how to turn the computer back on at the midpoint, all the five sections of its body stretch out, displaying a renewed confidence and excitement. After the pencil desperately catapults itself against the computer's on switch and slides back down, the space between the green "neck" band and the pink eraser head expands to show the strain and effects of falling, and the head becomes increasingly elongated before dropping out of the frame. Many of the early lessons from *The Adventures of André and Wally B* are visible here, including building a character from isolated body parts that clearly are not connected. The pencil's fall also anticipates the snow globe's tumble off the shelf in *Knick Knack.* Tague's Macintosh piece makes excellent use of techniques to compensate for the limitations of technology by forging visually clever solutions that simultaneously suggest emotion and intention, and thus character psychology. Importantly, Tague also helped Lasseter with the write-up of his SIGGRAPH "Principles" paper, and a number of those principles are on display in *Pencil Test.* Their work had quickly become cooperative, with each benefitting from their shared expertise.

While every project and short film at Pixar served as a valuable research-and-development experiment, their next film, *Tin Toy,* proved to be the most significant prototype for their eventual feature-film productions. This cartoon fully displays several of the fundamental traits of Pixar character animation, including ironic reversals to structure the plot and increased cues for a perceptive, thinking central figure. Lasseter and the animation unit had just begun to settle into a schedule of producing one short film each year for SIGGRAPH. However, as David A. Price explains, Pixar was still defined as a company producing and selling computer-imaging hardware. There was a continuing suspicion and resentment from some Pixar employees about the expensive short cartoons. Ed Catmull was routinely forced to justify the animation division's role at Pixar. Thus, when Steve Jobs came to hear Lasseter's pitch for *Tin Toy,* a film about a toy's encounter with its human baby "owner," he needed serious reassurance. Price quotes Ralph Guggenheim, the manager of the animation unit, as claiming, "We knew that [Lasseter] wasn't just pitching for the film, he was pitching for the survival of the unit" (104). *Tin Toy* would prove highly successful at justifying Jobs's faith and continued financial investment in Lasseter and the entire animation group.

John Lasseter has repeatedly mentioned that the initial idea for *Tin Toy* came from watching a home movie of his sister's son Timmy playing with his toys. Bill Reeves also had a toddler at this point, so he too was motivated to pursue a project built around a child and its toys. Moreover, the previous year, in 1987, Lasseter, a toy enthusiast, had visited Japan's Yokohama Tin Toy museum. That experience led to the decision to update a one-man-band toy as the central toy character, pitted against its human child for the cartoon's plot structure. *Tin Toy* would also prove to be another Pixar film with no dialogue. Thus Lasseter and Reeves needed to establish quickly a sense of place and efficient story actions and emotions to provide clear markers of the central toy character's purpose and even personality. Once they began, Reeves regularly brought his daughter Julia in as a sort of live model for the toddler's gestures and body scale. Fortunately, they also had the luxury of a five-minute playing time to allow some visual gags and character interactions to develop more naturally and dramatically as the events unfold in real time. For instance, early in the cartoon the tin toy will use his green accordion as a sort of shield to protect himself from a bombardment by plastic toy balls. Later that same noisy instrument will give away his location. But eventually the accordion returns to its intended function of creating silly, entertaining music for the child. This sort of recurring motif follows the same trajectory as a Buster Keaton gag and reinforces story action and characterization, lending unity and added coherence to the resulting fifty-five separate shots of the tin toy and baby's confrontations.

Tin Toy opens to the chipper theme song from *The Price Is Right*, while the camera travels across the floor to reveal an empty Pixar shopping bag and tin-toy box before craning down to a medium close-up of the brand-new Tinny standing at attention. His eyes guardedly scan the space until a long shot reveals how tiny he and the surrounding plastic ring toys are in the large living room. Once the baby Billy crawls into the room, occupying center space and manhandling the plastic toys as he sneezes and drools, the tin toy tries to step backward unnoticed. At this moment Tinny seems to discover for the first time that he cannot move without creating music, since the drum beats, cymbal crashes, and horns toot in cadence with his gestures. The cartoon then shifts into a fast chase film as Tinny races away in panic, with the delighted ogre of a baby in clumsy pursuit. As he crisscrosses the floor, Tinny gets caught up in his initial box before scurrying under the couch, where he discovers scores of other toys cowering in their secret hiding spot. However, the awkward baby falls down and cries. Tinny, unlike the other toys that simply turn and look to him, displays a sense of guilt. As the child whimpers, Tinny looks down to his accordion and realizes he has the ability and perhaps inherent ethical responsibility to entertain his owner, so he slowly sacrifices himself, leaving the haven under the couch and venturing toward the frightful child. However, by the time Tinny approaches the baby, Billy has already become distracted and amused first with the empty box and next with the Pixar bag. Tinny, offended at the baby's indifference, follows the child, trying to do his duty as a toy, playing his music. The ironic reversal, of the toy initially running from the child but ultimately pursuing him, provides a unified, comic structure to bracket this simple tale of a toy discovering its essence and purpose, only to be ignored by the ungrateful child.

Much of the initial attention to *Tin Toy* was directed at the challenges in representing Pixar's first CGI child Billy, who seemed rather disappointing and even inhuman to some, in contrast to the lively metallic toy.

Just as the old man running the shop in *Lady and the Lamp* seemed less engaging than the young drawn lamp, Lasseter's tin toy got all the best expressions and gestures, making it the central character. From its shot composition to its soundtrack, *Tin Toy* is firmly constructed around the perspective of the toy. Lasseter shaped the story to establish a rapid shift in emotions for the central Tinny, from naive excitement to fear to guilty resignation to open frustration, all communicated with body gestures and sound effects rather than dialogue. While the story is strictly restricted to the toy's plight, the style is also anchored in his point of view as he sizes up the blubbery baby or stares out at him in horror through the wrinkled cellophane window of the box (figure 14). Ralph Guggenheim explains that these point-of-view shots were initially rendered as conventional flat images, then run through warping software by Eric Herrmann "to get that distorted look" (Lee, "Computer Animation Demystified," 102). Moreover, thanks to the complex interior environment, the fumbling humanoid baby, and intricate camera movement and lighting schemes, Lasseter's tale of a toy learning the ropes in his new home exploits the full arsenal of techniques available to deliver a clever, fast-paced comedy that allows Tinny to transcend the world of his geometric shapes and mathematically precise movements.

The tin toy seems more human than the baby in part because of his clear emotions, thanks to his facial gestures and visual prompts that

Figure 14: Tinny's perspective
on the baby in *Tin Toy*.

also suggest he is considering his options. For instance, when initially confronted by the child, there are three reaction shots as Tinny witnesses the baby chewing and drooling on a plastic donut ring. His expressions change quickly from joy to shock to disgust. For the final reaction, just before he decides to flee, the toy even looks directly to the audience for confirmation and sympathy (figure 15). The animation team immediately set up the tin toy as a thinking, motivated being. Gary Rydstrom's clever soundtrack adds much to the lifelike dimension of his character. As Paul Wells points out, when Tinny dashes under the furniture to take cover, "the tin toy actually takes 'breath,' augmenting the sense of its anthropomorphized humanity, at a moment of playful sentiment." Even the toy's attached accordion offers what Wells calls an "'inner wheeze' of sympathy" when the baby falls (Wells, "To Sonicity," 32). Tinny thinks, acts, and breathes in relief and emotes via his instruments, all of which help make him "human," or at least a developed, empathetic character, rather than just a moving series of rigid CGI shapes. The action and characterization also benefit from a fast-paced, classically edited plotline, full of point-of-view shots and shot/reverse shots, with an average shot length of just over five seconds. It is worth noting that, thanks to the unique volumetric qualities of CGI "sets," editing techniques like reverse shots are relatively easy because rather than having to draw the distinct perspectives on the characters and backgrounds in both shots

Figure 15: Tinny looks for sympathy in *Tin Toy*.

from scratch, as in traditional animation, the animator or layout artist may "program in the 'camera angle' and check the resulting shot for continuity" (Pallant 134). CGI brings many fluid upgrades to conventional animation practice. Clearly, Lasseter's synthesis of CGI devices with his training with mentors such as Jack Hannah reinforced the successful creation of this tin toy who communicates his thoughts and emotions with a limited range of gestures, sound effects, and musical rhythms.

In contrast to the very cognizant toy, the baby seems rather incomplete, a sort of prototype human being. While Lasseter, Reeves, and the team had several live models for the child, for the basic shape and proportions they bought a Toys-R-Us doll to digitize. Next, they shaped and digitized a clay head to allow for mapping the muscles onto the face. However, the soft clay surface eventually led to some shifting data points, resulting in a somewhat more lumpy child than was initially intended. Given that the baby's face had to be more flexible but just as expressive as that of the tin toy, Lasseter and Reeves studied facial muscles and how they signify emotions. As part of their research they looked at a SIGGRAPH paper by Keith Waters on muscles and facial expressions that outlined a variation on parameterization techniques for more malleable gestures, including lip movements (Waters 17). They also consulted the *Facial Action Coding System* designed by Paul Ekman and Wallace V. Friesen and published in 1978, which "identified each muscle in the face and examined how contractions of individual and grouped muscles registered expressions and emotions" (Amidi, *Art of Pixar Shorts*, 23).

Reeves then designed controls for allowing intricate adjustments to specific points on the face, visually weighing down the virtual skin, as if pulled by unseen internal muscles. This system pleased Lasseter and fit his animation background, since it allowed more elastic, organic surfaces. As Jennifer Barker points out, *Tin Toy* managed to produce a CGI body that was "a hulking monstrosity of baby fat and flesh, smooth and soft but also wet, soggy, and gooey in a most unpleasant way" (46). Thus, while these increasing digital controls provided for more pliable figures and gestures in the tradition of hand-drawn animation, they also paralleled the more tactile methods associated with clay animation or sculpture. In her description of Pixar's process for *American Cinematographer*, Nora Lee writes that *Tin Toy* approached the norms of stop-motion animation. However, rather than working with adjustable physical material,

"Eben Ostby and Bill Reeves make their puppets out of mathematical algorithms and pixels" (Lee, "Computer Animation Comes of Age," 79). The results were a very mobile metal toy and a fascinating attempt at a human child, complete with a rather comically solid bucket of a diaper.

Philippe Lemieux points out that the animated Billy the baby was initially perceived as unrealistic and even a failure by some. "If Tony de Peltrie had a child it would doubtless resemble this monstrous baby," with its empty eyes and unconvincing movements (Lemieux 112). Yet, Lemieux asserts that Tinny taught computer animators a valuable lesson: "This short film's success, despite the disappointing baby, proves an important point for CGI, which is that absolute verisimilitude is not necessary. As with traditional animation, caricature and exaggeration, coupled with a good scenario and clever direction, suffice for communicating emotion" (112). Even Lasseter and Reeves would admit that *Tin Toy* may not have worked as well with a more realistic or cute baby. From Tinny's point of view, the child is supposed to be a monster that sneezes, cries, and tosses his toys about like an insensitive giant. Only later, with *Toy Story*, will the human owner, Andy, gain a valuable, if limited, set of sympathetic human traits, though the cruel neighbor Sid could be said to remain closer to the frightening, primal aspects of *Tin Toy*'s Billy. Perhaps Sid is the grown-up version of this creepy, drooling toddler. *Tin Toy* premiered at SIGGRAPH, though the film was not yet in its finished form, so only the initial pursuit of Tinny, trapped back in his box, was shown. Nonetheless, *Tin Toy* created a sensation at SIGGRAPH, and subsequent screenings and the finished film went on to win an Academy Award for best animated short film for Lasseter and Reeves.

After earning the Oscar and hearing rave reviews at a host of film festivals, Lasseter could become more confident in the future of Pixar's animation unit, though he was also beginning to weigh more options for himself. As Jeff Lenburg explains, *Tin Toy* changed the animation unit's destiny: "After Pixar burned through around $50 million invested by Jobs in its first decade, producing critically acclaimed but commercially unviable computer-animated cartoon shorts and selling very few computers, *Tin Toy* marked an important turning point for Pixar" (59). The Academy Award inspired Steve Jobs to adopt more fully Catmull and Smith's original vision that Pixar's future lay in computer-animated motion pictures. Thus, this Oscar was not only a significant milestone for Lasseter,

Reeves, and their animation team; it also validated the years of hard work and careful, confident preparation by Smith and Catmull. Further, *Tin Toy* "established Pixar's credibility within the film industry, including at Disney, where executives tried repeatedly (and unsuccessfully) to recruit Lasseter" (Sims 145–46). Michael Eisner and Jeffrey Katzenberg saw the potential in Lasseter's computer animation, as well as the possible franchise value in *Tin Toy*. As Katzenberg explains, "Lasseter's shorts were really breathtaking both in storytelling and in the use of technology. I tried so hard to get him to Disney, but he was loyal to Steve [Jobs] and Pixar" (qtd. in Isaacson 248). Lasseter's decision to stay with Pixar helped solidify Pixar's privileged position within the computer-graphics world. If he had left for Disney, Pixar's trajectory toward an animated feature film could have been seriously delayed, if not scuttled altogether.

Jobs and Pixar managed to retain Lasseter, despite Disney's generous attempts, in large part because of the positive working relations he had forged over the past few years with the creative and supportive Pixar team. Catmull, Smith, and Lasseter had indeed managed to establish their own mini-studio and compete head-on with every other animator in the world by the late 1980s. Yet, they were well aware that their continued existence depended upon the benevolent sponsorship of Steve Jobs. Moving forward to their ultimate goal of a feature-length animated film depended upon their team's consistent progress toward new technological solutions and economic strategies in order to overcome a long line of industrial constraints. Winning the Academy Award for short animation helped reaffirm their master plan, confirm their mode of production, and validate their storytelling principles, all of which helped establish a recognizable Pixar style of character animation. The heightened level of detail made possible with computer graphics was being combined with a playful, childlike world of cartoons inspired by Walt Disney and Chuck Jones. As William Schaffer observes, "The purest form of the 'digital magic' invoked within Pixar films involves the photorealistic animation of banal domestic objects that are transformed by becoming the focus for emotional and/or imaginary investments—lamps, unicycles, toys" (86). By the time of *Tin Toy*, a Pixar style was discernable, and increasingly marketable.

The Pixar animation unit's final short animated film prior to *Toy Story* was *Knick Knack*, which featured another toy figure. This plastic snowman trapped in a glass snow globe became Pixar's most embodied, overtly thinking character so far. According to Amidi, *Who Framed Roger Rabbit* (dir. Robert Zemeckis, 1988) had greatly impressed Lasseter, motivating him to tackle more flexible, "cartoony" characters in a more gag-oriented comedy. Rather than struggling with complicated organic human shapes, Lasseter and his team decided to exploit more directly the geometric shapes that computer animation does so well (Amidi, *Art of Pixar Shorts*, 25). The resulting *Knick Knack* continues the toy-world motif of *Tin Toy*, without the baby, but it also recalls the shelf full of lamps from *Lady and the Lamp*. Here the shelf is populated by cheerful souvenirs, including swaying springy palm trees from Jamaica and Palm Springs, a bouncy pyramid, and a voluptuous bathing beauty from sunny Miami perched on an ashtray shaped like a swimming pool. (For the 2003 rerelease, however, her large spherical breasts were removed.)

The plot structure's first third establishes the characters and space, with the happy-go-lucky souvenirs all clustered in one section of the shelf, joyfully moving to the rhythm of Bobby McFerrin's vocal work. On the far end of the knick-knack shelf is the isolated snowman, Nick, in his "Nome Sweet Nome" globe. However, just before the one-minute mark, the frowning snowman notices Ms. Miami waving to him. He not only perks up, he also apparently realizes for the first time that he is encased in glass; the sound of him rubbing up against the wall of his globe even resembles a whimper. This shot of the surprised snowman echoes the moment of self-realization in *Tin Toy* when Tinny discovers to his horror that he cannot flee from the baby without the loud noises of his attached instruments. From Tinny on, Lasseter's main characters are regularly forced to face up to their physical and/or personal limitations, and only in the features will they be able to overcome those existential challenges.

Once the snowman discovers his predicament, he undertakes a series of increasingly risky attempts to break free. Throughout the middle third of *Knick Knack*, he assaults the glass barrier with his hard Styrofoam igloo, a normal hammer, then a jackhammer, a blow torch, and finally explosives. With each new failure, Lasseter cuts to Ms. Miami, who appears ever more impatient. Moreover, the snowman's facial features, which include the bent-carrot nose and small black coal-like spots for his eyes and mouth, become ever more expressive. Interestingly, *Knick Knack* was later the subject of an experiment in students' recognition of emotions from facial expression, in part because of the clear nonverbal cues in the snowman's wide smile or frown (Vercauteren and Orero 196). Nick even combines that broad smile with glances toward the camera and audience as he makes a confident click-click sound, as if to say, "Watch this!" Paul Wells notes that Gary Rydstrom contributed this clicking sound as "vocal tick of recognition" reinforcing further Nick the snowman's obsessive need to escape and "get the girl" (Wells, "To Sonicity," 33) (plate 2).

Eventually, after all else fails and the final explosion has displaced the globe right up to the shelf's edge, the snowman's final drastic solution is to lean forward, toppling the globe off its perch to fall (and presumably crack open) on the floor below. As the globe tumbles, shifting the snow off the floor, the snowman sees an emergency-exit door and leaves his prison, falling freely but landing in a fish bowl. Initially, his face registers disappointment, but then he notices an attractive mermaid figurine smiling at him. He pauses and looks once again to the camera to acknowledge his good luck, but just then his dreaded old globe falls perfectly around him, trapping him via the same exit door that had saved him seconds earlier. Once more he is entombed in the globe, doubly encased now in the fish bowl, unable to reach his second female object of desire (figure 16). The three-minute *Knick Knack* is composed of

Figure 16: Doubly encased Snowman; *Knick Knack.*

thirty-six shots, for an average shot length of five seconds, punctuated with multiple point-of-view and reaction shots and staged in a limited internal space. Moreover, *Knick Knack*'s representations of the sexually frustrated snowman's determined efforts and imprisoned situation offered convincing evidence that CGI characters could generate just as much empathy and humor as any other sort of animated bodies and without dialogue. Lasseter offered compelling, physically present characters in evocative narrative spaces that just happened to be created in a computer rather than on cels or with clay.

Knick Knack also marked several important shifts in the Pixar animation group's mode of production. For one thing, it was completely animated in a stereoscopic format, so it could ultimately be released in conventional 2D or 3D. Moreover, given the newly expanding staff in the animation unit, Lasseter began to serve as lead animator and director, overseeing the work of the small production team. In *Knick Knack,* "Lasseter still animated all of the major characters, but the animation cycles of the secondary knickknacks were created by the modelers who had designed them" (Amidi, *Art of Pixar Shorts,* 25). To a very real extent, Lasseter was moving into the role of a studio-animation auteur in the tradition of a Chuck Jones or Tex Avery. He served as director and made all final creative decisions, lending *Knick Knack* a unity and humor consistent with all his previous Pixar films, yet he also worked closely with his crew. Further, the story was a collaboration, including suggestions from the entire unit. The end credits signal that it is "a film by" ten different people (Lasseter, Eben Ostby, Bill Reeves, Ralph Guggenheim, Craig Good, Don Conway, Flip Phillips, Yael Milo, Tony Apodaca, and Deirdre Warin). The Pixar animation unit was now equivalent to a team at Warner's Termite Terrace in the classical era, where everyone may have performed quite specialized tasks, yet their close interaction helped fuel the creativity in the resulting films. By the time of *Knick Knack,* this corner of Pixar was already working like a commercial-animation studio.

While one initial goal for Lasseter and his team had been to produce a more cartoonal film built from predefined shapes, *Knick Knack* nonetheless provided opportunities to experiment with new techniques and test out recent software procedures, including constructing underwater shots populated with a moving character and props. Bill Reeves adapted his particle system to the enclosed watery environment of the snow globe. The various movements of the snowman would directly motivate the path of the thousands of plastic flakes inside, which spin at varying speeds, often combined with motion blur. The flakes could also float slowly back down toward the floor, reinforcing naturalistic gravity, friction, and inertia cues. Lasseter used the *Knick Knack* snow cycles as an example of Pixar's ongoing progress in simplifying the animation processes: "I just animated the character, and played with a few parameters, and the computer did all of the snow floating around. So as we go on, more and more tools are being developed" (McCracken 12).

Importantly, however, while Lasseter and the Pixar team seem to have reverted somewhat to the overtly geometric shapes of their earliest animation, with a stark white crescent for Ms. Miami's smile, simple cylindrical tree trunks, and repeated semicircles for the igloo and snowglobe outlines, among others, the shapes flexed and pulsated in ways that could not have been accomplished for Luxo or Red. Further, the snowman's lumpy body takes advantage of some of the sorts of controls developed for Billy the baby, but since the snowman is only meant to be a plastic toy, this shifting, swelling body was never meant to appear as a realistic human. The playing space was also less elaborate than the craning camera and deep space of *Tin Toy. Knick Knack*'s background is a basic wallpaper print, a sort of middle ground between the black empty backgrounds of *Luxo Jr.* and *Red's Dream* and the more cinematic soft-focus walls of *Tin Toy*. Thus, *Knick Knack* offered an impressive synthesis of many of Pixar's accumulating proprietary techniques and storytelling tactics.

Knick Knack ended up as a culminating short film, demonstrating that Lasseter's character animation had reached a highly efficient and entertaining phase. This time, the entire Pixar short was completed in time for the 1989 SIGGRAPH meeting in Boston, where it was screened in 3D to very positive reviews. That Bobby McFerrin, who improvised his vocal track while watching a rough cut of the animation, offered his services for free, "out of a belief that the film was cool to be involved with" (Price 108), further demonstrates the extent to which Pixar animation was already making its mark within contemporary American popular culture. According to a *Sight and Sound* review, Lasseter was "responsible for breathing life into what had previously been a medium controlled by technicians and programmers." They also boasted that *Knick Knack* displayed the sort of pace and humor that few animators, in any format, had accomplished since Tex Avery and Chuck Jones (Swain 65). Maureen Furniss sums up the significance of Lasseter's Pixar shorts and their visual realism for the larger field of animation: "What really seemed to excite the critics was the way in which these CGI works came alive with personality and told stories in a cinematic way. They disproved the general belief that a computer could only produce cold and unengaging imagery" (Furniss, *Art in Motion,* 180).

Lasseter agrees that these shorts offer personality: "With all of my short films, I strived to integrate human characteristics into the objects I chose as my subjects. In *Luxo Jr.,* a little lamp steals the spotlight with his playful antics. *Red's Dream* reveals what a lonely unicycle dreams about. In *Knick Knack*, a glass-domed snowman is undone by his machinations to join a lively crowd" (qtd. in Pintoff 39). Every character had to project some specific desire and cluster of personality traits. Beyond the characters and their motivating emotions, Lasseter argues that everything in the frame, characters, objects, backgrounds, "even the space around the objects" should have a narrative purpose justifying their inclusion (Pintoff 39). *Knick Knack* provides a clear example of this principle in that every other minor knickknack functions to tempt Nick the snowman, or remind him how uncomfortably tense and isolated he is in his Alaskan dome, compared to their liberated bodies swaying to the freewheeling beat of McFerrin's playful, relaxed, friendly vocals. Thanks to his new awareness of the lives of these other knick knacks, the snowman will never again feel at home in his globe.

Though *Knick Knack* did not garner an Academy Award nomination (Nick Park's *Creature Comforts* won that year), it is nonetheless credited with further bolstering Catmull, Smith, and the animation department's confidence and determination to move forward with a feature film. They had overcome many key technical and narrative hurdles. *Knick Knack* delivered engaging digital characters performing convincingly in highly functional, visually appealing environments. The animation team also learned what was and was not yet possible with their software, hardware, and financial resources. By the time of *Knick Knack's* premiere in 1989, a CGI animated feature seemed to be a real possibility. Moreover, they could build upon and adapt many of the models, figures, and programs they had already created. "The kinds of objects, sets and props rendered and animated in the anthropomorphic manner familiar to Disney and the classic cartoon tradition in these accomplished preliminary exercises, all reappear in more developed form in the feature film [*Toy Story*] itself. The technical groundwork of the 1980s is capitalized on in the 1990s" (Darley 83).

However, Pixar as a corporation was facing new challenges that would delay any smooth, linear transition from shorts to features. Further, there were still only ten people in the animation group with Lasseter, which accounted for barely 10 percent of Pixar's staff. The bulk of the company was still focused on selling hardware and software, and the animation group generated no revenue. Chuck Kolstad, now CEO, began studying possible options for the animation unit to develop income and help justify their existence at Pixar. There had already been occasional mention within Pixar of potentially producing television commercials, and several advertisers were known to have been impressed with Lasseter's work and its potential for marketing their products. Television commercials could offer some immediate relief to Pixar's financial predicament while providing more real-world animation experience telling stories within a high-profile short format.

Moving into television commercials, while not initially popular with everyone in the animation division, made sense on a number of levels. Ralph Guggenheim agreed to oversee the production of the advertisements. His plan was to launch thirty-second commercials to bring in much-needed income, but then use that new production experience to move on to an animated TV special of thirty or sixty minutes as an apprenticeship before making the risky transition over to a feature-length movie. Turning to commercials also allowed Pixar to hire more animators. Even after *Knick Knack*, Lasseter was still the only official animator. Ed Catmull agreed that contracts for television commercials would warrant hiring new talent for both short- and long-term goals: "Commercials are like little short stories, and by doing them we would subject ourselves to the real-world deadlines and pressures that you'd have to deal with if you were going to make movies" (qtd. in Paik 64). To find a steady but manageable string of orders, Pixar entered into a production deal with Colossal Pictures of San Francisco. The first contract was for a pair of commercials with Toppan Printing of Japan, followed by a Tropicana orange juice commercial. As the commercial division began making progress, Lasseter and Pixar hired Andrew Stanton and Pete Docter, in part because of their background training in traditional animation and their ongoing interest in computer-generated graphics. Lasseter had already worked with Stanton on Tague's *Pencil Test,* but he met Docter only on the recommendation of Joe Ranft, then a writer at Disney and instructor at CalArts.

In Pixar's first Life Savers commercial, the voiceover narration ironically states that the Life Saver family just got a little smaller, as the visuals introduce a whole passel of little Life Saver "holes" bouncing ecstatically past their slowly rolling full-sized parents and off into a playground. The energy difference between the slower parents and the frenetic little candies recalls the contrast between movements of the father and son in *Luxo Jr.* Further, the commercial's smooth tracking shots help deliver a fluid, efficient, and entertaining fifteen-second introduction to the colorful new candies. The old and new Life Savers are all realistically rendered, and the bright three-point lighting on each translucent little piece of bounding or swinging candy casts a shadow on the ground, reinforcing their volume and motion cues. The miniature Life Savers deliver a cheerful, even playful performance in their rapid-fire introductory commercial. By 1990, such television work brought in $1.3 million in revenue and rose to around $2 million for the next several years thanks to a steady stream of new customers (Sims 146). As Price observes, "Pixar's ability to create photorealistic versions of inanimate objects and turn them into expressive characters was novel to television audiences, and other advertisers quickly took notice" (110). However, according to Catmull, while the animated commercials allowed them to hone their technical and storytelling skills, "we still were taking in significantly less money than we spent" (53).

Pixar's commercials division created forty-nine advertisements and logos between their first job for Toppan Printing of Japan in 1989 and 1995, the year of *Toy Story.* Lasseter is credited as director or codirector on ten of these ads, including the Life Savers "Gummie Savers Conga" (1991), which won Pixar their first Clio Award. This commercial's voiceover points out that the new Gummie Savers may look and taste like traditional Life Savers, "but they don't move like 'em," as the flexible, brightly colored candy bends and leaps around the Conga dance floor. Once again, a frantic pace, with spinning lighting effects and six action-packed shots in thirty seconds, launches the new candy amidst a slickly produced and highly polished commercial. The candies not only "move to a different beat," as the titles point out, but they manage to come alive as swaying physical objects, even characters, for the viewer. Similarly, Pixar's Listerine ads personified the bottles as feisty boxers knocking germs out of the ring and even a Robin Hood archer firing arrows in rapid, noisy succession at targets in the fresh, green forest. Pixar traits such as motion blur, clever point-of-view shots, and dramatic, motivated camera movements certainly help attract and hold the television viewer's attention. They also signal intentionality and personality traits for objects as diverse as plastic bottles, oranges, and straws. As one journalist at the time wrote, Pixar "uses computers to animate—and practically humanize—the inanimate" (Kanner 22).

Each Lasseter commercial is based on a good-humored, tongue-in-cheek tone. Neither the characters nor their animator-narrators seem to have allowed themselves to be taken too seriously. Lasseter and his team also managed to work with a variety of clients, delivering short, effective commercials that were often based on concepts and scenarios from the advertising agencies, including the intertextual references to Hollywood movies for Listerine. Throughout, Lasseter's old rule of never moving a camera without a good justification held, and Pixar also continued to avoid the typical computer-graphics devices such as flyovers and morphing shapes in their television commercials. Even though these advertisements were projects of necessity far removed from the animation unit's ultimate goals, they were designed to reaffirm Pixar's aesthetic style and professional reputation. These commercial experiments also fit perfectly within 1990s digital-graphics contexts. Stephen Prince points to this new generation of CGI commercials, with morphing figures and anthropomorphic products, as exemplary of the industry's shift away from the norms of photographic representation: "Digital imaging can bend, twist, stretch, and contort physical objects in cartoonlike ways that mock indexicalized referentiality" (Prince, "True Lies," 29). Pixar was a leading player in making this digital transition part of the everyday experience of media production and consumption.

Computer animation was generally more expensive than live-action advertisements, but test markets with the Pixar commercials for Tropicana and Life Savers saw marked increases in sales. Every new ad contract was perceived as an opportunity to develop further Pixar-styled character animation. For instance, by 1994, Levi-Strauss and the advertising agency approached Pixar for a commercial on women's jeans, in large part because of Pixar's reputation of "bringing character and emotion to inanimate objects" (Goldrich 12). Jan Pinkava directed the Levi's spot, which featured a wooden female mannequin wearing jeans. As *Shoot* magazine put it, "The mannequin conveys a palette of feelings and attitudes such as enthusiasm, disappointment, surprise, wariness and delight," all without any facial features (Goldrich 12). Lasseter and his team were well aware of their own strengths as well as the value of product differentiation in building their brand and rehearsing the skills they would need before launching a feature-length film populated by a wide variety of characters and environments. The commercials functioned as occasions for research and development while they helped pay some bills and increased the size of Lasseter's animation unit. Pixar's reputation within the industry continued to strengthen as well.

While Pixar's commercials gave Lasseter and the animation team new goals and challenges, the software engineers perfected additional programs to sell to graphic artists and desktop publishers. Thus, 1990 turned out to be an important transitional year for Pixar. The Pixar Image Computer portion of the company was sold off, and everyone remaining moved into new facilities away from ILM's lot. However, Pixar continued to cost Steve Jobs vast amounts of money, with losses of $8.3 million in 1990 alone (Price 113). By the spring of 1991, Jobs reorganized the company, rescinding employees' earlier stock options and laying off thirty of Pixar's seventy-two full-time employees. The animation unit's commercial productions, as well as a few key software product lines, including the developing RenderMan, now became the core of Pixar's business model. The dire financial situation also motivated new deliberations over the animation unit's next stage beyond the commercials.

Before launching into producing a feature film, which still posed enormous economic and technical hurdles, Kolstad's plan all along had been to produce a thirty-minute television special exploiting the Tin Toy character they had already developed. That strategy seemed right on target at this point. Disney's Jeffrey Katzenberg, impressed by Pixar's shorts and commercials, but also the computer-assisted effects in recent Disney features such as the final scene in *The Little Mermaid*, raised the possibility of a joint venture. A group from Pixar, including Jobs, Catmull, Smith, and Lasseter, among others, met with Katzenberg to pitch *A Tin Toy Christmas* for Disney television. Lasseter and his colleagues were relatively optimistic about expanding on *Tin Toy*, their biggest success so far. They explained that they had already built some of the models and that the toys work well as subjects since they are naturally geometric in design. Their shiny plastic surfaces were relatively economical to build, and they fit the crisp CGI aesthetic. Katzenberg, confident in Lasseter's talent and Pixar's infrastructure, surprised them by wanting to enter into a deal for a feature film instead. According to Catmull, Katzenberg would have preferred to hire Lasseter away from Pixar, explaining at the meeting, "'It's clear that the talent here is John Lasseter,' he said, as [Alvy Ray Smith], Steve [Jobs], and I sat there, trying not to be offended. 'And John, since you won't come work for me, I guess I'll have to make it work this way'" (Catmull 55).

As a result of Katzenberg's offer, the Pixar managers decided to enter into the feature-film agreement with Disney and skip their planned intermediate step of a television show completely. Andrew Stanton and Pete Docter went right to work adapting their group's previous *Tin Toy* script, expanding their earlier ideas into a treatment titled "Toy Story," while the two studios undertook detailed contract negotiations. In July 1991, Pixar, which was still exclusively creating television commercials, entered into a deal with the Walt Disney Company, which would provide most of the production budget, approve major creative decisions, and distribute *Toy Story*. Disney also retained an option on two subsequent computer-animated features from Pixar as well. Lasseter, who had left Disney in 1983, now entered into a partnership that finally completed the original goals of Catmull, Smith, and everyone within the Pixar animation unit.

Feature Films, Thinking Characters, and Emotion

> When animating characters, every movement, every action must exist for a reason. . . . All the movements and actions of a character are the result of its thought process.
>
> —John Lasseter

Completing a feature-length CGI motion picture offered many specific, even daunting, challenges beyond those already encountered in the production of the Pixar shorts and television commercials. The shorts had not used any spoken words up to this point, and Lasseter had never really written dialogue beyond the few short statements for his student film *Lady and the Lamp.* The notion of a feature-length script would be new to most of the team. Moreover, *Toy Story* required a wide assortment of characters displaying an extensive range of emotions and actions. Lasseter and Pixar would have to generate their most embodied characters yet, many with competing or overlapping desires and character arcs, all inserted into a compelling story unfolding within an intricate and practical CGI environment. Complicating matters further on the managerial level, Alvy Ray Smith left Pixar just before the Disney contract was finalized, leaving Catmull and Lasseter to negotiate with the two competing corporate and narrative visions of Jobs and Katzenberg. Clearly, Pixar's survival and future were intricately intertwined with the ultimate success of this large-scale commercial production.

Beyond the increased narrative demands, producing a feature film put new pressures on the studio's structure as well. The series of television commercials had justified adding a number of animators to the staff, but now the requirements of telling a story with scores of speaking characters and 3D environments urgently necessitated expanding the company with a wide variety of new positions. During the 1930s, Disney Studios had taken years to increase their hiring and training prior to putting *Snow White and the Seven Dwarfs* into production. Pixar now had to accelerate and update that process. Interestingly, the bulk of the new animators hired during the expansion for television commercials and now *Toy Story,* such as the veteran animator Bud Luckey, came with backgrounds in hand-drawn, 2D character animation rather than computer graphics. Lasseter claims that each of the new animators was selected in part for their acting ability and the performance of their drawings: "That's really what I'm hoping will stand out in the film: the acting" (qtd. in French, *"Toy Story,"* 30). As Tom Sito points out, another of Lasseter's insightful moves was "building one of the strongest storyboard teams ever seen" (Sito, "Moving Innovation," 249). Storyboard artists brought a valuable set of skills beyond those of digital technicians and animators, bridging the productive activities of screenwriting, shot composition, and design. Storyboards allow creative visualizations of the action and offer concrete staging options. *Toy Story* would prove a crucial, transitional moment for Lasseter to build upon the production and storyboarding traditions from classical Disney while adapting them to Pixar's digital mode of production and resulting narrative style.

For the first time, Pixar began implementing the Avid Digital Media Composer for updating the storyboard stage during *Toy Story.* According to Joe Ranft, some scenes were storyboarded as many as five times: "With the Avid, John could say, 'Let's add this drawing into the sequence' and I'd go draw it up, and it would get digitized into the sequence" for more immediate viewing of the changes (French, *"Toy Story,"* 27). The coproducer Bonnie Arnold points out that this system allowed most of the film's editing to be worked out ahead of time during storyboarding: "It's sort of like an assembly line, because as each shot moves through the production pipeline, it gets further refined. Then it can be slugged into our ongoing rough cut, and we can see the changes we've made incredibly fast. We replace the initial storyboards with a crude version of the shot, called rough polys. They just show the action, they aren't lit or rendered yet. Then, when we get our lighting finals, we can drop that into the Avid" (qtd. in French, *"Toy Story,"* 27). Lasseter would provide constant input during these stages, and after he approved them, they could be tested easily by the supervising producers at Disney animation. Pixar also benefitted from the Alias software system, which allowed new options in modeling and digitizing sculptures of the central characters. *Toy Story* thus announced a brand-new era in computer-animation and production processes. As Andrew Darley points out, Pixar's first feature was "the culmination of an intensive research and development program" within the digital domain of new Hollywood, as it helped create "the apparatus necessary for the production of detailed and sustained character-centered storytelling that could rival that produced by established means" (82). *Toy Story* would indeed prove a revolutionary stage in American filmmaking, though it also fit comfortably within many conventions of classical Hollywood storytelling. Lasseter and the Pixar team struggled to balance the new demands of CGI with the core narrative traditions of Pixar and Disney during every aspect of the production.

The first stage of preproduction involved writing a script Lasseter and Catmull liked that could also earn a green light from the Disney executives. The initial idea remained that they would tell a tale from the perspective of a cluster of toys who were all devoted to their young boy "owner" Andy. The protagonist, Tinny of *Tin Toy,* would become separated from Andy at a gas station, eventually meeting up with another lost toy, a ventriloquist's dummy. The two would then share an unsettling and unsuccessful odyssey in search of Andy. Early on, however, the script substituted different sorts of toy protagonists. Tinny was replaced with a shiny new plastic astronaut action figure, eventually called Buzz Lightyear, after Buzz Aldrin. As Lasseter recalled, "If you look at the essence of a buddy picture you have two characters as opposite as you can get. So we thought what would be the most extreme opposite of a space superhero? Bud Luckey, one of the animators, came up with the idea of a cowboy doll" (French, *"Toy Story,"* 36). Thus the dummy was changed to a cowboy, Woody, named as a tribute to the African American western star Woody Strode. These toys, Woody of the Old West and Buzz from the new frontier of outer space, would now compete for the attention of their owner, Andy.

However, Katzenberg pointed out that the bulk of the narrative would follow two central characters with the same basic goal. He suggested that the Pixar team watch successful buddy pictures such as *The Defiant Ones* (dir. Stanley Kramer, 1958) and *48 Hrs.* (dir. Walter Hill, 1982), featuring competitive and antagonistic interracial male characters from different backgrounds who are forced to work together, eventually forming a close bond. Lasseter brought Joe Ranft into the scriptwriting team to join Stanton and Docter. Stanton also cited Buster Keaton's *Steamboat Bill, Jr.* (1928) as a model, since all the humor arose from the various ways Keaton's character dealt with his small stature and physical limitations (Sragow 17). Acknowledging that they knew little about feature-film script structures, Lasseter and Docter even enrolled in a Robert McKee three-day scriptwriting seminar. In addition to hearing McKee's lessons on plot points and timing strategies, they learned the value of creating a series of personal challenges to help define the essence of their central characters. This class was taught in 1992, five years before McKee's influential book *Story: Substance, Structure, Style, and the Principles of Screenwriting* was published.

Disney's executives, including Peter Schneider, the head of Walt Disney Feature Animation, were also quickly made aware of Pixar's lack of storytelling experience. According to Katzenberg, "At first there was no drama, no real story, and no conflict." Katzenberg is credited with suggesting early on that the toys should behave like adults, rather than children, when the humans are not around, which would assure richer and more appealing characterizations and hopefully attract a wider audience (French, *"Toy Story,"* 22). Further, he suggested they make the earnest old Woody more "edgy," even jealous and belligerent toward his new competition, Buzz (Isaacson 286). The plot would now revolve more around how Woody tries to outsmart the confident though naive Buzz, pitting the other toys against the newcomer in an all-out fight to discredit Buzz and remain Andy's favorite toy. Woody and Buzz would become lost later in the tale rather than near the beginning, to allow more character development. The journey portion of the plot was reduced as well, and eventually the resolution also changed. Rather than the lost toys ending up with a happy compromise, taken in by a kindergarten full of loving children, they would go from lost at a gas station to being captured by Sid, where they would learn to work together, escape, and return to their own community of toys, sharing Andy and his attention. But the screenplay continued to undergo repeated revisions. Disney also brought in the team of Joel Cohen and Alec Sokolow, who worked through multiple drafts of *Toy Story* before moving on. Next, Schneider and Katzenberg hired Joss Whedon, who had recently rewritten much of the dialogue for *Speed*. Whedon worked on dialogue but also tried to help with transition scenes, such as how Woody and Buzz could escape from the evil boy Sid's bedroom. Finally, in January 1993, Katzenberg and Disney approved the script, which paved the way for Lasseter and his team to begin building characters and sets in earnest.

Throughout preproduction, Lasseter and the Pixar writers regularly traveled from northern California to Los Angeles to discuss the rewrites and their progress toward a more unified and compelling script with Disney executives. The core team of animators also regularly updated their models and designs. Organic shapes, including the humans and Sid's dog Scud, continued to pose the biggest problems, so they avoided showing entire bodies as much as possible and covered most of the children's skin with clothing. By contrast, the central characters were based on readily manufactured toys, and they could be built from rather obvious geometric shapes. For instance, Woody's arms and legs are composed of several cylinders, not unlike tootsie rolls, and his trunk is based on an elongated sphere. Woody and the *Toy Story* characters all fit what Alice Crawford labels an algorithmic aesthetic, with "smooth, generally non-elastic and static surfaces" (116). But Woody's flexible facial features, dialogue, and nearly constant gyrations distracted audiences from seeing him as a cluster of cones, orbs, and tubes. Even the hairs on the humans were simply cones, each with several shades of color to disguise their basic shape and add the illusion of texture and variety. Lasseter also continued to watch a variety of movies for plot devices and inspiration, from Hayao Miyazaki's *Castle in the Sky* (1986) to chase scenes in *Bullitt* (dir. Peter Yates, 1968), *The French Connection* (dir. William Friedkin, 1971), and *Thelma and Louise* (dir. Ridley Scott, 1991). The animation team reportedly looked at Eadweard Muybridge's photographic motion studies as well while animating Scud the dog and his run cycles (Lemieux 120).

Lasseter also insisted on defying a long-established Disney norm by resisting the notion that his characters would break into song to explain their feelings and motives. Nondiegetic songs could comment upon the action, but Woody and Buzz would not sing like Disney princes and princesses, and *Toy Story* would not be turned into a musical comedy. Pixar wanted to retain some product differentiation from standard Disney practice. Disney finally agreed, and Lasseter hired Randy Newman to write insightful songs to reflect the concerns of the characters. Casting began as well, with Tom Hanks and Tim Allen, star of Disney's own *Home Improvement*, signed on for Woody and Buzz. When he first considered Hanks as Woody, Lasseter and his team made an initial test by animating Woody delivering the famous dialogue from *Turner and Hooch* (dir. Roger Spottiswoode, 1989), where Hanks yells at the dog not to eat the car. The animated Woody managed to mimic the accelerating frustration that Hanks had displayed in the live-action movie. This character study helped convince Katzenberg that Hanks was right for the part, and Lasseter later showed it to Hanks as an extra enticement to take the role when they all met to discuss the project (Price 129).

However, as the frequent meetings with Disney's representatives and Katzenberg accumulated, Lasseter and Catmull began to fear that the complicated contract requiring Disney approval at all stages was increasingly putting their movie at risk. As Ed Catmull recalls, all the input from a variety of sources ended up changing Woody and the action too drastically. "Gradually, over a period of months, the character of Woody—originally imagined as affable and easygoing—became darker, meaner. . . . On November 19, 1993, we went to Disney to unveil the new edgier Woody in a series of story reels. . . . Disney's completely reasonable reaction was to shut down the production until an acceptable script was written" (Catmull 57). Even Tom Hanks reportedly thought Woody was "a real jerk" by that point (Isaacson 287). Peter Schneider required that a new script be approved before Pixar could resume any animation for *Toy Story,* though Lasseter begged for a little time to prove that they could salvage the story. "We redid the whole first act of *Toy Story* within two weeks. When we showed it to Disney, they were stunned. That taught us a big lesson. From that point on, we trusted our instinct. . . . And that is when I started really giving our own people creative ownership over things" (Schlender and Tkacyzk 149). Lasseter's role as director initially involved rethinking the practical and creative chain of command in scripting and storyboarding the movie, while nonetheless incorporating some of the productive input and plot-structure suggestions from the Disney writers and producers.

Lasseter, Ranft, Docter, and Stanton had managed to convince everyone involved that *Toy Story* was indeed an engaging project with a more sympathetic Woody. He could prove self-centered and insecure at times, but he also looked out for the other toys and earnestly believed he had their best interests at heart. Even Woody's jealousy over Andy's fascination with Buzz was justified somewhat by Buzz's ridiculously clueless personality. Buzz was, after all, the only toy in the room who denied being a toy. Now, when Woody knocked Buzz out of the window, it would be more of a comical chain-reaction accident than a devious, premeditated plan. Woody grew into a complex classical Hollywood character across the course of the film, with motivations that seemed logical and consistent with his core traits, even though they were not always perfectly honorable. His character even anticipates several qualities of the Hanks character Captain Miller in *Saving Private Ryan* (dir. Steven Spielberg, 1998).

Lasseter was very active in directing Hanks, Allen, and the other actors who had to come in for multiple voice sessions as the script shifted. The voice performances in *Toy Story* established the demanding working norms for subsequent Pixar films. Central character actors are involved in the production from the earliest days of preproduction right up until final adjustments are made. As Lasseter points out, voice work for Pixar differs greatly from live-action conventions. "Tom Hanks always said that the hardest acting job he ever had was doing *Toy Story* because what actors normally do on a movie set is a page or a page and a half a day at most. But we will go through their entire performance in a four-hour period. We tried to do it in chronological order to get the emotional arcs right" (Lasseter and Anderson). Disney's Tom Schumacher praised Lasseter's work in the recording studio with the voice actors, where he was apparently quite comfortable helping perform the roles along with them: "I don't think there's anyone in animation who is better at directing actors that John Lasseter" (qtd. in Paik 87). The actors' mouths were also filmed during their read-through performances to provide additional cues for the animators.

By February 1994, the rewrite was complete, and Lasseter and Catmull were given a green light from Disney to resume full production. Steve Jobs placed himself squarely between the creative Pixar team and Disney, blaming Katzenberg openly for the delays and cost overruns, until Ed Catmull had to broker a compromise. Moreover, Jobs became a major cheerleader for *Toy Story* as it advanced. During the early stages of production, he was still open to selling Pixar, even to Microsoft, but "as the film progressed, Jobs became more excited about it" (Isaacson 288). Once he had access to sample scenes, he regularly screened them for friends. By the 1995 SIGGRAPH, just months before its release, Jobs was fully convinced of the promise of this movie, and Pixar. He told the audience that *Toy Story* would prove a "landmark" event for cinema, much like the daring *Jazz Singer,* which put Warner Bros. on the map in 1927. He also enjoyed pointing out how appropriate it was that *Toy Story* premiere in 1995, on the one hundredth anniversary of Lumière's first films (DiOrio). Jobs was positioning Pixar and *Toy Story* as equivalent to some of the major milestones in cinema history, beyond even Disney's *Snow White and the Seven Dwarfs.*

Meanwhile, Lasseter and the writing team had storyboarded most of the film, generating a revised, more comical and emotional script. They realized that the audience had to develop empathy for Buzz as well as Woody, and part of the revision included reexamining their basic character traits and narrative arcs. As the layout manager and script supervisor B. Z. Petroff explains, the writers remained committed to Robert McKee's story structures, especially consulting his methods to diagnose problems in establishing story beats and character actions (Petroff). Moreover, Lasseter, Ranft, Stanton, and Docter took into account anew the tension between a character's outward goals and inner motivations, and how their hurdles and antagonists further defined their traits. As McKee writes, "True character is revealed in the choices a human being makes under pressure—the greater the pressure, the deeper the revelation. . . . Who is this person? Is he loving or cruel?" (101). Woody's character was engineered to undergo and reveal a series of tensions, choices, and revelations.

The *Toy Story* team returned repeatedly to these existential questions for Woody and Buzz, but they also clarified the various functions and personalities of the whole community of toys, including seventy-six distinct characters, most of whom had some dialogue. Despite being toys, Pixar's characters would prove to be psychologically real and humanized, and their development benefitted from the rather predictable script construction, which fit well within classical Hollywood story norms and popular Robert McKee–type script-manual formats. The script also featured strong binary oppositions between Andy's home and Sid's house to lend formal unity to the story. Both boys have a sister, but Andy respects his toys, while Sid tortures his. Eventually, Gary Rydstrom's sound design reinforced the oppositions between the two boys and their worlds, just as the visual artists contrasted their actions and homes. The background sounds "heard outside Andy's window support his warm and playful nature. In contrast, the backgrounds accompanying Sid accentuate his sadistic and edgy qualities" (Beauchamp 72). *Toy Story*'s narrative strategies ensured that children in the audience could learn values and lessons from watching both the toy and human characters.

One of Lasseter's core storytelling devices involves emphasizing moments of personal realization by a central character. Such scenes of revelation end up forming a dominant pattern for structuring *Toy Story*. This plot strategy may have been learned from Disney cartoons such as *The Ugly Duckling*, where the newborn begins to understand why the duck family is rejecting him once he sees his own unexpected reflection in the water. Similarly, as we saw with *Tin Toy*, Lasseter's Tinny suddenly realizes he can't move without making his band noises, though he soon learns that he should use those sounds to entertain. Throughout *Toy Story*, a series of hurdles for Woody and then Buzz involves such key moments of newly gained self-awareness. Rather than simply encountering a series of predicaments from which they must escape or that they must conquer, Lasseter's characters are transformed by challenging events that reveal how but also why they need to solve a given problem. Every major decision changes our perception of Woody and Buzz in some way, but the events also reveal further some of their deepest character traits, those not always on display during routine actions. For instance, early on Woody learns that Andy's birthday party has been moved up. Parties with gifts are unsettling events for toys. They may be replaced by new, more exciting models. As Lasseter explains, "There are two days that are the most anxiety-ridden for toys: Christmas and the child's birthday. We start on Andy's birthday, and end on Christmas" (qtd. in French, "*Toy Story*," 22). That Woody attempts to mention the birthday-party problem discreetly to his trusted sidekick Slinky Dog demonstrates his concern for reducing the stress and anxiety on the other toys. He does not panic but rather decisively calls a meeting to explain and deal with the issue.

Woody's calm, commanding presence in this important scene exploits the primacy effect. The audience understands right from the start Woody's significance for the community of toys and his sense of responsibility and humor, as well as his genuine concern. For the audience, Woody is quickly established as a benevolent leader. His fellow toys are lucky to have him, and they obviously appreciate his core traits and values. Later, when Woody has to take a huge risk by calling together Sid's frightful mutant toys in a more urgent group meeting to save Buzz, a deeper level of heroism and duty will be revealed. Before they can prove successful, Buzz and Woody must "humble themselves" by asking for help from their community in what Ken Gillam and Shannon R. Wooden label the "New Man" gender models of Pixar (6). The script works hard to create intricate characters who are systematically put to a test, often in the face of looming deadlines. Similarly, the rivalry between Woody and Buzz gradually shifts from complete distrust to open complicity and cooperation by the end. These setups allow the plot to unfold in an interlaced series of functional and melodramatic scenes that emphasize the humanity and complex motives of these toys, while distracting spectators from their artificial essence as CGI pixels moving across a flat screen.

Once the storyboard and script were approved for *Toy Story*, ten "story artists" were each made responsible for specific scenes or sequences. They were handed character and key setting designs from the Art Department as well as the script and storyboards. In addition to Docter and Stanton, the story artists included Kelly Asbury, who went on to direct *Shrek 2*, and Jill Culton, who later helped write *Monsters, Inc.* According to *Computer Graphics World*, Pixar ultimately generated nearly twenty-five thousand pages of storyboards by the time Lasseter and his team had reorganized the story (Robertson). Lee Unkrich explains that as an editor at Pixar, he was also involved early on in the pipeline process that Lasseter had helped pioneer. Unkrich, as editor, gave creative input into the plot and its composition and arrangement via the storyboards before they were transferred onto the initial story reels in Avid for a better sense of pacing, shot order, and dialogue. In the process, they deliberately followed many conventions of standard and intensified continuity storytelling. As Unkrich explains, "What we decided early on in *Toy Story* was that rather than look to animation for guidance, we would instead look to live action. We really defined, I think, a whole new aesthetic for animation that is unique to Pixar, which is the fact that you are watching animation but most of the creative choices are grounded in live-action film grammar" (Spark). Much of Lasseter's control over storytelling is exerted in the storyboard and script phase, but he along with Ralph Eggleston approved and commented upon every major contribution by the various animators and technicians during the process. Creative "directing" decisions in animation are primarily forged in preproduction and production stages, including monitoring the voice work and sound effects. Throughout the process, Lasseter's input was felt across every workstation at Pixar. But it is also important to note that directing for an animated feature often involves a much longer duration than for live-action. Every element must be planned for and constructed before it can be made to "perform."

It is perhaps worth summarizing the basic pipeline process for *Toy Story,* which was adapted from the short-film and commercial procedures Pixar had set in place. Once the storyboards are approved, they are sent for lighting and color schemes to be decided by the art director, Ralph Eggleston, "working in close consultation with the director," Lasseter (French, "*Toy Story,*" 28). Next, models of the characters and figures are devised, and the layout department, managed by Craig Good, blocks out the scenes and plans out camera movements: "We assemble the scene, taking the computer models of the characters and the props, and get them in their rough positions. We're the first step into the 3-D world, and it's a big step away from the drawings" (qtd. in French, "*Toy Story,*" 28). Good's layout department next passes the shot off to animators, but it already determines the general range of allowable camera positions, to ensure scale and that it will match up to the next or preceding shot. While the general look and length of the shot are already determined, the characters remain schematics made of polygons or wire frames at this point. Animators decide on the key poses and gestures for their shot and then work with the computer program for timing and the in-betweens. The animators work from the voice track, generating the performances by their characters. But once the animation is created and programmed in, the shot still requires the surfaces, shadowing, and lighting effects from the visual-effects department. After the textures and shaders are added, the lighting technicians plan and insert the lighting effects. "We normally have a meeting with John Lasseter and Ralph Eggleston, and they tell us what their vision for the scene is" (French, "*Toy Story,*" 29). For the short films, Lasseter was intricately involved in every creative decision. With the shift to a feature, Pixar expanded and updated their established pipeline practices.

From the point when production renewed in earnest during the winter of 1994, Pixar had just over eighteen months to complete the movie. *Toy Story*'s premiere was locked in for November 1995. The final release print contained well over 1,600 shots, ensuring a rapid pace and an average shot length close to three seconds. Throughout, Pixar's staff

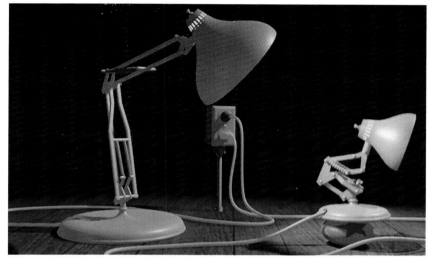

Plate 1: *Luxo Jr.* directs our gaze.

Plate 2: A confident Snowman;
Knick Knack.

Plate 3: Andy with Woody; *Toy Story.*

Plate 4: Buzz sees his TV commercial
in *Toy Story.*

Plate 5: Buzz falls; *Toy Story.*

Plate 6: Realizing that "rockets explode" in *Toy Story.*

Plate 7: Dot on the foliage
in *A Bug's Life.*

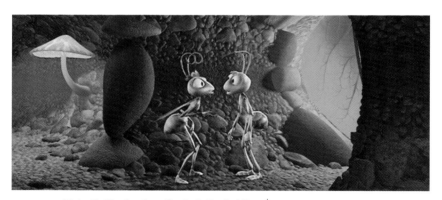

Plate 8: Staging for effect; *A Bug's Life.*

Plate 9: Hopper threatens Dot
in *A Bug's Life.*

Plate 10: Jessie explains her feelings
in *Toy Story 2.*

Plate 11: Andy, texture, and Woody;
Toy Story 2.

Plate 12: Uncanny Al versus
cartoony Woody; *Toy Story 2.*

Plate 13: Racing under virtual lights; *Cars.*

Plate 14: McQueen in Mater's
dusty lot; *Cars.*

Plate 15: McQueen and Sally's
leisurely drive; *Cars*.

Plate 16: Mater flies over London
in *Cars 2*.

included only twenty-eight full-time animators and thirty CGI technical directors, which was much smaller than a comparable Disney production crew, which could reach six to eight hundred for films like *The Lion King* (dir. Roger Allers and Rob Minkoff, 1994) or *Pocahontas* (dir. Mike Gabriel and Eric Goldberg, 1995). *Toy Story's* budget of roughly thirty million dollars was only half that of *Pocahontas* that same year. Though, as *Wired* pointed out, Pixar also had "more Ph.D.s working on this film than any other in movie history" (Snider 147–48). Adding to the film's perceived potential significance during the days leading up to its premiere, Jobs announced that he would be taking Pixar Inc. public on the stock exchange, launching what would indeed become the biggest IPO of the year. This high-stakes economic move added increased pressure on the production crew in fall of 1995, as well as placing Ed Catmull and John Lasseter even more fully into the public spotlight.

Despite the series of production difficulties, *Toy Story* proved a decisive success for Pixar and immediately secured Lasseter the "genius" label in the popular press. He was credited as the person who finally delivered Pixar's dream of a CGI feature film. For instance, when *Fortune* covered the making of *Toy Story,* it introduced readers to "Lasseter's genius as an animator," explaining how he begins each day early reviewing the night's rendered scenes, presides over meetings, and wanders around checking on the animators, offering advice and approving shots: "Today, Lasseter is studying the refraction properties of raindrops on a window. 'Each drop is a lens and should reflect everything that's going on outside,' he says. 'You should be able to see the moving van pulling up outside in miniature in each of these drops. Let's add 50 more so people won't miss the effect.'"If Lasseter gives the final okay, the scenes are spliced into the master reel" (Schlender and Tkacyzk 168). This sort of press coverage, foregrounding Lasseter as an all-involved creative mentor to the production team and a savvy entertainer, helped to condense the ownership of the feature film down to its director. It also fueled the marketing campaign by giving a sort of inside glimpse at an effect that moviegoers should want to watch for in the moving-van scene.

From its opening shots, *Toy Story* announced to the audience that a new era in animation had arrived, as Pixar transformed the Disney aesthetic for the next generation. The initial dissolve, from the blue background of the Disney logo to the blue wallpaper sky of Andy's room, quickly gives way to a complicated virtual camera dollying back and craning down, then panning left, revealing a child's cardboard-box western-town setting. Suddenly, Andy's humanoid arm thrusts a Mr. Potato Head with a large water pistol taped to his hand toward the camera. Andy, in voice off, warns the township toys, "Don't anyone move." At first, of course, this comment seems childish, since the toys obviously cannot move without his hand shaking them. Andy, as a sort of playful stand-in for the animators, speaks for each toy as he sets up a quick scenario in which Woody saves the day, ordering the Potato Head bandit, One-Eyed Bart, to "Reach for the skies." Within one minute, most of the central characters, from Andy and the slinky dog to Bo Beep and Rex the dinosaur, have been rapidly and comically introduced. Even Andy's drooling little sister Molly, an older version of the *Tin Toy* baby with yellow, carpet-like hair, enters the scene before Woody's string is pulled for a second time and he mechanically tells Andy that he is his favorite deputy. Randy's Newman's "You've Got a Friend in Me" cues the title sequence over a montage of Andy playing cowboy with Woody in tow (plate 3).

During this opening sequence, nearly every Pixar visual trait is put on display, including realistically reflective floor surfaces, self-shadowing, attention to plausible details in the background, and motion blur. *Computer Graphics World* was duly impressed: "Andy's room looks like a kid's room, not a drawing of a kids's room" (Robertson). For all its seeming realism, however, this CGI setting involves distortion: "We caricatured the sets. The doorknobs are oversized and the doors are a little taller and thinner than they would be in reality," according to Ralph Eggleston (qtd. in Street 83). The action during the song becomes increasingly frenetic as Andy hyperactively makes a playful tour of his favorite places in the house with Woody. Importantly, this sequence also begins providing a glimpse into what will become one of the film's dominant narrative strategies, as multiple shots from Woody's subjective point of view begin to focalize our attention. He is rapidly established as the central figure of *Toy Story*'s narrative space. By the end of this title sequence, Woody's vision reveals the mother putting the finishing touches on preparations for a birthday party for Andy, which will soon jump-start the story's initial action.

Lasseter also builds *Toy Story* with the camera close to the ground, foregrounding the world as experienced by the toys. The audience even manages to share the army men's vision, looking through their opaque plastic binoculars onto the actions of Andy and his friends. From the beginning, *Toy Story* guides the audience to see but also hear from the toys' perspective. Gary Rydstrom and a crew of foley artists and sound editors continued the Pixar tactics of reinforcing weight, texture, and volume cues with sounds. For instance, when the disgruntled Potato Head sticks his nose back in, there is a plastic blurp sound that seems to fit the echo one might hear within his orb of a head, and the army men's cheap plastic clomping down the hall further anchors the brown pixels beneath their feet as a wooden floor. Attention to visual and audio detail, as when an offscreen toy horn toots softly to accompany punch lines, helps combine the images and sounds into an efficient storytelling mode, lending increased presence to the character animation.

This opening accomplishes a great deal more than introducing a nostalgic space and set of toys, however. As Jay Telotte explains, the opening scenes of *Toy Story* overtly address digital animation's potential. Telotte labels this strategy "surface play," as it displays the 2D clouds on a flat blue wall and Andy's "artlessly constructed" boxes, before revealing the much more convincing sky, clouds, and buildings outside Andy's window, all generated in stunning 3D CGI. "This surface play directly addresses the work of animation and especially the perceived power of the new digital regime to offer a different level of realistic reproduction, a major leap beyond traditional 2D animation" (Telotte, *Animating Space,* 203). By unfolding steadily an increasingly complex, textured, and multiplane visual world in this opening sequence, Pixar clears the way for their own brand of highly stylized animation to supplant the conventions of Disney and the past (205). That the toys all come fully "to life" the minute Andy leaves the room further announces what Pixar has been proving steadily for the past few years: inanimate objects can make convincing 3D characters. A prime example of this sort of hybrid cinematic-meets-animated world can be seen in the several shots where Woody, standing in front of a western-themed background from the bedspread, tries quietly to tell his trusty friend the Slinky dog that there is bad news. The other toys in the room screech to a halt, which further underlines how quickly the audience has already accepted the CGI toy models as independently moving, thinking, embodied characters. Once everyone is aware of some impending problem, Woody calls the meeting. *Toy Story*'s collection of playthings is conceived as more than an extended family; it is a workplace for toys, a functioning community with its own hierarchy and even history. The toys interact as if they have known each other for years. Their teasing proves that they understand each other's natures and vulnerabilities. In other words, they display functional, plausible, small-group dynamics.

The opening scenes thus demonstrate clearly the narrative strengths of the Pixar aesthetic, as well as Lasseter's brand of storytelling. Pixar is concerned that the audience learn the rules of their fantasy worlds right from the start. The toys have apparently agreed on a sort of contract to move and speak only when there are no humans within earshot. As Ed Hooks reminds animation writers, "Your audience will go anywhere with you just as long as you tell them the rules of the game up front" (Hooks, *Acting for Animators,* 65). Further, the *Toy Story* figures may magically come to life, but they do not have superhero strength. This is no science-fiction fantasy film. The army men do not turn into "real" men or shoot bullets, the dinosaur cannot breathe fire, and no one can magically fly around the room on their own power. These are not super-natural figures but only "realistically" limited living toys made of plastic, cloth, and fake fur, though with distinct personalities. One of Lasseter's keen abilities involves bridging creatively the worlds of classical story-telling and computer animation. From the beginning, with Wally B, he understood that motivation is central to characterization. Lasseter was also vitally interested in the materiality of his toys and how that would be seen to affect plausibly their mobility and character traits.

Importantly, *Toy Story*'s cast of characters, and their voice actors, were not simply dropped into random wire-frame toy models and bodies. Lasseter asked the team to figure out "each toy's physical and conceptual essence" by considering its basic character traits, materials, purpose, and physical flaws. "Cheap-plastic Rex doesn't thunder around like a living tyrannosaur from *Jurassic Park*; he's stiff and tentative and unsure of himself because his construction makes him limited in what he can do." Similarly, Mr. Potato Head is naturally cranky because his facial features keep falling off, and they decided that Bo Peep, while "a delicate flirt," must act slowly and with caution, since she is made of porcelain. The slinky dog is happiest following Woody's lead, since it cannot move well on its own power; it prefers to be pulled along by another (Lasseter and Daly 16). Thus, the story artists and animators connected the material shapes to the toys' behavior and narrative functions before casting the voice actors, while they also used the rigid computer models to their advantage whenever possible. Even a character with no audio voice, however, could "speak" and project a sense of humor and personality. For instance, the Etch-a-Sketch "draws" a gun when jokingly challenged to a duel by Woody. Lasseter created this character by following the rule of basing the animated version on the toy's materials, leaving it without facial features or a voice: "Toys like Etch-a-Sketch walk around, and there's no question they're alive, but . . . they don't have a face that disappears when there is no one around" (qtd. in French, "*Toy Story,*" 21). A plausible consistency results, even in this fanciful world of embodied toys with minds of their own.

Further, Lasseter wanted to ensure that each toy has its own physical gestures and locomotion traits, and even that a given toy would move differently at various times depending on its mood or dramatic situation. "Each of the toys behaves consistently, yet displays a custom vocabulary of movement and gesture" (Laybourne 241). Their speed and gait should help cue whether they are hesitant or confident. Even the remote-controlled car does not always roll at a set speed. Yet, no other toy ends up displaying as wide a range of emotions and moods as Woody. William Schaffer credits Lasseter for recognizing "the poetic affinity between the plastic and the digital" that results in thinking characters like Woody and Buzz Lightyear, who have one foot in reality and one foot in the virtual CGI world (85). As a result, Lasseter sees this bedroom community "as a little urban microcosm. It is a melting pot that isn't so melted. It's got toys of different plastics and colors and sizes and recommended age groups all doing their jobs together" (Lasseter and Daly 16). Add to this group a self-assured newcomer, Buzz Lightyear, who sees himself as saving whole worlds in outer space, and the necessary array of toys was complete, save for the unfortunate mutants in Sid's bedroom across the way. Woody and his crew would worry first about being replaced or ignored by nice Andy, and second about being captured and blown apart by bad-boy Sid. Their world is full of potential drama.

Woody's initial goal is to organize and calm all the other toys as they watch for new competing gifts at Andy's birthday party. Just when the presents all seem harmless and Woody reassures his fellow toys that there is nothing to worry about, a new big gift is announced by the spying army men on their walkie-talkie. However, interference prevents the toys from hearing what the gift is, and the editing cuts upstairs to their frantic chaos. At fifteen minutes into the movie, Buzz is delivered to Woody's treasured spot on the bed, though it takes the toys a few minutes to discover "what the heck is up there" sitting in Woody's spot. This turning point begins act 2, the story's complicating action, which features increasing tension in the toy room as Woody, feeling his dominance threatened, begins by mocking Buzz, but then gradually realizes unhappily that the foolish spaceman is indeed winning over the other toys. The mise-en-scène helps demonstrate the ultimate point when the bedspread is suddenly switched from the cowboy theme to Buzz Lightyear and outer space. Woody also acts less and less like their level-headed, trusty leader—as Mr. Potato Head observes, Woody has developed "laser envy."

A flustered and increasingly desperate Woody accidentally knocks Buzz out the window, losing the trust of the other toys and initiating the prolonged search-and-rescue portion of the plot. After a series of back-and-forth exchanges between the two competing central toys, a major character development occurs precisely at the film's midpoint, thirty-three minutes into *Toy Story,* at the gas station. Woody and Buzz physically fight, falling beneath the van, until Andy and the family drive off without them. The perceptive Woody realizes that his battle with Buzz has gotten them both lost and abandoned. He must now work with Buzz if he ever wants to see Andy again. This scene marks the beginning of act 3, the development of the plot, after the first two acts, which are roughly fifteen minutes each. The sight of the Pizza Planet delivery truck then provides Woody with new hope and two distinct goals: he must trick and manipulate the naive Buzz to return to Andy, but he must also be sure they both return home safely together, so the other toys realize that Woody is indeed heroically and selflessly helping Buzz.

From the plot's midpoint on, Woody struggles to regain the respect of his fellow toys by fighting to return Buzz to Andy, even if he cannot be sure of remaining Andy's favorite toy anymore. Woody's new task presents a complex agenda and displays a rich set of personal traits. This deeper perspective on Woody is revealed by his newfound predicament and helps generate increased empathy from the audience. As Torben Grodal has argued, humans have "a hardwired disposition to tenderness" toward youngsters and helpless figures (148). While Woody and Buzz are embodied as grown-up toys and voiced by adults, their status as children's playthings who are technically younger and physically much smaller than their child owners allows them a more heightened vulnerability than would be the case for live-action adult characters. Like children, they are still learning to negotiate and survive within this human world. The narrative also follows an intensified variation of a sentimental "separation-reunion" journey plot built around children who temporarily lose his family and protective home (Tan and Frijda 56). That Woody and Buzz are indeed lost in a gigantic, dangerous world accentuates the spectator's fears for their safety.

But just when Woody and Buzz are nearly reunited with Andy in the pizza restaurant, Buzz foolishly enters the rocket-ship claw machine. Delayed again in his heroic scheme, Woody opts to join Buzz in the crowded claw game rather than leap to safety alone into Andy's basket. Oblivious to the risks, Buzz allows evil Sid to select and remove him from the claw machine, and Woody, sticking to his vow to save Buzz, clutches on until they both wind up in Sid's dreaded backpack. That Sid takes pleasure in dismembering toys and recombining their parts into grotesque new hybrids further aligns the audience with Woody's warnings, reinforcing his status as a wise and valuable leader: Woody could have avoided being captured with the clueless Buzz, but he remained true to his long-term goal of returning together. Earlier in the film, he had ordered all the other toys to select a moving buddy to ensure that no one is left behind. Buzz is now Woody's moving buddy and Woody's responsibility.

Toy Story's separation-reunion portion of the plot incorporates roughly fifty pages of the ninety-page script and just over one half of the screen time, from the moment Woody and Buzz tumble out of the van fighting at the gas station until they drop back through the van's sunroof triumphantly near the end. As the *Film Comment* review pointed out, "If *Toy Story*'s journey from the Pizza Palace back to Andy isn't epic, I don't know what is" (Jones, "Beyond," 24). This third act also features two of the film's most emotional, melodramatic scenes. First, while trying to escape and evade Sid's creepy dog Scud, Buzz witnesses the television commercial for Buzz Lightyear toys and hears all the tag lines about his proud features, including his same voice simulator. He also he sees the "not a flying toy" disclaimer. As the French philosopher Ollivier Pourriol points out, the shocked Buzz experiences a sort of trauma of misrecognition: "Curiously, what he sees on the television is simultaneously him and not him" (111). Buzz realizes that Woody was right all along (plate 4).

But if Buzz is a mass-produced item, it means that he has no individual identity, and his whole existence has been an illusion, which he is clearly not ready to accept. Moments later, he engages in a final existential test as he climbs to the top of the stairs to try flying out the window and beyond. Randy Newman's "Sailing No More" accompanies Buzz's sad grappling with his identity, which alternates indecisively competing refrains that suggest "yes I can, no I can't" themes. Buzz also recalls Woody's angry "no, you can't fly" taunt, before scaling the railing and then falling brutally to the hall floor below, disconnecting his arm. This personal realization and test, with Buzz's thoughts translated and amplified by Newman's song, generates strong witness emotions in the spectator, as well as an intensified affective congruence between the music and Buzz's mental state. Images of his contorted face in close-up and his determined climbing gestures combine with the evocative music to create strong, sentiment-provoking stimuli, cueing intense identification from viewers. Newman was aware of the music's functions here as well: "The songs became the one place Woody and Buzz really manifest their feelings explicitly. It's where they voice stuff they don't otherwise admit to people, or even to each other" (qtd. in Lasseter and Daly 94). Once Buzz drops to the floor, he is a broken toy, mentally and physically (plate 5). To add insult to injury for Buzz, Sid's little sister Hannah picks him up and makes him part of her toy tea party, where Woody witnesses his drunk and despondent behavior. The confident space ranger has hit bottom and lost all sense of himself and any purpose, which may have delighted Woody earlier, but only poses a new challenge for him now.

Soon, too depressed to run, Buzz is grabbed by Sid, who tapes him to a rocket. Ironically, of course, Buzz's goal all along has been to be relaunched into space. He may finally get his chance, though he now knows it spells his doom. The rainy evening delays the launch, while Andy falls asleep next door, missing his favorite toys and oblivious to their fate. Meanwhile, a pleading Woody convinces Buzz that being a toy for Andy is the highest calling and that Buzz is the best toy possible. As Woody reassures Buzz, he also realizes for the first time that being an old-fashioned cowboy with a string to pull makes him the most expendable of toys. It is logical that Andy should prefer Buzz. A close-up reveals Buzz screwing up his face, gaining a new determination, while sad Woody looks away, feeling sorry for his low-tech self, caught in his milk-crate jail. However, the newly energized Buzz takes the initiative to free Woody and notices the moving van arrive next door, adding a deadline to their escape, which is reinforced by Sid's alarm clock. These turning-point scenes of self-discovery slow the story action to deepen Woody and Buzz as thinking, feeling characters. These scenes also further strengthen the audience's sympathies for the toys' plight and garner respect for their ultimately mature decisions.

Once Buzz and Woody have finally adopted a new cooperative attitude and confided in one another, Buzz recognizes his real mission as a toy. But Sid wakes up and runs off to launch Buzz. After the thirty-minute-long act 3, the film's fourth act, its fifteen-minute climax, begins in earnest. Stuck in Sid's room alone, Woody quickly decides to appeal to the mutant toys who had helped repair Buzz's arm the night before. He even accepts all the guilt, confessing that Buzz is about to be blown to bits, all because of Woody's past mistakes. In the background is a shot-up poster of a man's outline from target practice, reinforcing Sid's violent potential and keeping Buzz's doomed fate visually present. He is a sitting target. As the other toys rally round him, Woody devises the final plan to frighten Sid in the yard, involving the toys working together and coming to life in front of Sid, breaking the rules to warn him never to be cruel to his toys again or they will take their revenge. This sort of scene, which includes a collective action by previously oppressed or weak characters, fits Judith Halberstam's notion of "Pixarvolt," in which "communitarian revolt" repeatedly overcomes the dominant order (29). As a result of Woody and the toys' antics, the emasculated Sid runs off, further scared at the sight of Hannah and her doll arriving.

The immediate crisis for Buzz is averted, but Andy's car is leaving, adding a new, more pressing deadline. Woody could jump on just in time, but he is forced yet again to delay saving himself, turning back instead to make sure that Buzz is not left behind, in a Pixar nod to *The Defiant Ones*. A frantic series of chases, beginning with Scud the dog and then involving the remote-controlled car, allows Woody to display all his leadership skills, though the toys in the moving van still distrust him. Thanks to teamwork, Buzz and Woody overcome their toy car's loss of battery power, exploiting the previously dreaded rocket to blast off, return the toy car to the moving truck, and fall with style back into the family van, satisfying every narrative trajectory in a rousing climactic scene. Their success depends upon the new understanding and even sympathy between Woody and Buzz, who contribute equally to their shared mission. Finally, the epilogue reveals that the community is happy again in a new house, until Woody and Buzz learn that Andy has gotten a new puppy for Christmas, and now they will both have more competition for Andy's attention.

Ultimately, the *Toy Story* script and its story beats are easy to diagram, with the screenplay moving elegantly through the sort of contemporary four-act structure described by Kristin Thompson, including the setup, complicating actions, development, and climax (Thompson, *Storytelling*, 27–36). Ultimately, the short, clever, classical Hollywood epilogue anchors the narrative with a secure termination effect of simultaneous narrative resolution and stylistic closure. Buzz and Woody have struggled against daunting hurdles before returning together to Andy. Moreover, Woody has regained the trust and respect of the community of toys, including romantic attention from Bo Peep, and Buzz is happy with his place among this extended earthbound family. The resolution functions as doubly satisfying for the audience, since it accomplishes both cognitive and affective concerns.

As the story unfolds, spectators become invested in the plot, anticipating and retrospectively revising assumptions as they evaluate causal cues. As Ed Tan points out, such cognitive investment in perceiving and comprehending story information is directly related to our pleasure and affective engagement. Spectators actively posit their preferred final situation as the story progresses. Here, the toys' safe return home is every spectator's narrative goal. This mental process generates a parallel affective investment that is eventually rewarded, since the ending is in accordance with the sympathies and value systems of the protagonists as well as the viewers (98). That an embodied character such as Woody has a set of goals and acts upon them is not in and of itself adequate to create highly emotional responses or strong affective concern from the audience. Spectators require clear markers of the character's emotional arc. We do not only follow a movie's story line to get to the ending; we watch movies for the engagement with the various cognitive and emotional structures that get us there. The characters' choices are key to this double process. *Toy Story* features a number of highly pertinent cardinal story points, where Woody has to make an important decision, and the results further develop his character traits while allowing the audience to construct likely scenarios for the film's eventual outcome that then are rewarded logically and emotionally by the end.

One tactic that allowed Pixar to distract audiences from the mechanics of their constructed world was Lasseter's training in character animation and his knack for timing, as well as careful observance of conventional Hollywood editing, sound, and mise-en-scène norms. Building on facial-action systems and the human ability to judge character intentions immediately from subtle eye movements and facial gestures, Lasseter creates characters who seem to be constantly thinking and surveying their options: "To convey the idea that the thoughts of a character are driving its actions . . . always lead with the eyes or the head. If the character has eyes, the eyes should move first, locking the focus of its action a few frames before the head. The head should move next, followed a few frames later by the body" (Lasseter, "Tricks," 45–46). Moreover, when two characters converse, the alternation between looking away and shared gazes helps organize the narrative space. For instance, when Woody and Buzz suddenly lose all battery power during the final chase sequence, their toy car slows to a crawl and actually hunches down slightly as it wheezes and stops, sounding like the deflating ball from *Luxo Jr.* Meanwhile, the escaping moving van continues on, diminishing in perfect mathematical proportions as the duo sits dejectedly in the middle of the road, and Buzz drops the useless remote control. However, in a close-up, Buzz shifts from sad to excited as he looks offscreen toward Woody and reminds him of the rocket. A newly energized Woody spins around in close-up to announce "the match!" The next cut reveals his arm grabbing the match from its holster, followed by a reestablishing shot of Woody leaping out of the driver's seat. A match-on-action covers the lighting of the match, and then a reaction shot of Buzz reveals his apprehension just before another shot suddenly includes a blurred car passing by in the foreground, blowing out the match.

The chase is saved, however, when Woody drops to his knees in frustration over the extinguished match. The virtual camera reframes, tilting down, to make sure his head does not touch the bottom of the frame and ensuring that the audience can witness his change of attention and mood as Woody notices the hot spot and magnifying effect from Buzz's helmet. He realizes that they can use Buzz's helmet as a magnifying glass to light the fuse. Moreover, both toys stare offscreen right first in confidence, then panic—"Rockets explode!"—before blasting down the street in a trail of smoke that mirrors the strict monocular perspective of the street setting (plate 6). Even within the moving truck, amid the frantic gestures of the agitated toys watching Woody and Buzz try to catch up, Mr. Potato Head's intense eyes, centered consistently in the frame, help anchor the audience's vision, fixing our gaze upon him as the most important viewer. Then, of course, he is slammed by the incoming car, blasting parts of his face all around the truck and screen.

The characters' eyes have guided the audience's attention through these twenty-nine shots and brisk 2.3-second-average shot lengths. An eye-tracking experiment on this scene reveals just how concentrated the audience's attention is here, despite the great amount of visual detail in the background and edges of the frame. Most of the essential action, and certainly all facial gestures, take place within the middle third of the frame, the essential area. This scene is not only about the daring way the toys solve their problem; it also delivers their shifting emotions, made clear with eye movements, facial expressions, body gestures, and a carefully motivated mise-en-scène and editing rhythm.

The critical reception upon the release of *Toy Story* was almost universally positive, with many of the initial reviews building on Pixar's marketing department's talking points. There was a constant attempt to address both the stunning accomplishment of the first truly computer-generated feature film and its inventive storytelling. For instance, *Newsweek*'s pre-release story labeled Lasseter a genius and a big kid whose office "looks like Toys-R-Us after an earthquake" (Kaplan 54). They also explained that rendering took eight hundred thousand computer hours, while "each second has to be programmed manually." To provide Woody just the right gestures as he speaks, there are 712 avars to control on his body, with 212 for his face alone (56). As Eben Ostby explained, they had to provide the animators with enough controls to provide a wide range of facial cues in "believable" performances: "Woody had to act in over seventy minutes of the movie" (Street 84).

The technological achievements were readily foregrounded as part of the ballyhoo. Many reviews mentioned that animators actually have to perform like actors, as they informed their readers that Pixar animators are not mere technicians manipulating computer programs. There was a concerted effort by Pixar's marketing and publicity wings to align the work of making a CGI feature with the more traditional creative roles identified with animation and live-action filmmaking. Most reviews followed this pattern of acknowledging the groundbreaking CGI process before evaluating the resulting story's qualities. For instance, David Ansen observed that "Lasseter and his team have resisted the temptation to merely show off the computer's limitless spatial freedom. *Toy Story* is a marvel because it harnesses its flashy technology to a very human wit, rich characters and a perception no computer could think of: that toys, indeed, are us," complete with paranoia and anxiety over their job security and personal future (89). Further, the Italian historian Gabriele Lucci points out that much of *Toy Story*'s success came from its synthesis of ultramodern visuals with hyperclassical storytelling that emphasizes such identification with the characters and their plight (130). *Toy Story* was celebrated both as the first CGI feature and as a well-told, even gripping tale. It was all new and yet provided mainstream, high-quality entertainment.

Roger Ebert in particular compliments Lasseter on getting such great performances from the groundbreaking CGI process, then adds the ultimate praise: "Watching the film, I felt I was in at the dawn of a new era of movie animation, which draws on the best of cartoons and reality, creating a world somewhere in between" (Ebert, Rev. of *Toy Story*). The tech-savvy *San Francisco Chronicle* reviewer credits Lasseter for the directing and cowriting: *Toy Story* "is a gem of fast action, sophisticated wit and inspired comedy. After a minute to get used to the novel plastic-rubbery 3-D look, it clicks as a delightful romp" (Stack, "Computers 'Toy'"). Typically, reviews mention that the CGI effects are spectacular, before stating that *Toy Story*'s real accomplishment is the surprisingly engaging story that Pixar and Lasseter deliver. Character and computer wizardry are both celebrated in the reviews, echoing Lasseter's stock quote that art inspires the technology, and the technology challenges the art. The *New York Times* included statements from Lasseter explaining the process of locating animators for this brave new project and the need to teach them how to make characters perform. It also included his references to the new artistic and technical practice of texture mapping, pointing to the synthesis of conventional animation with newfangled technology (Sragow 28). The *Village Voice* continued the praise for Lasseter's balance of groundbreaking CGI and storytelling: "As with the best animation, the combination of tech elements serves to draw us into the drama" (Klady 48).

Toy Story went on to earn $191 million at the domestic box office and another $170 million internationally. According to *Variety,* "*Toy Story* took the foreign box office by storm." In Mexico it had the second highest opening weekend (*The Lion King* remained number one), with the fourth best opening of all time in the United Kingdom, while it "rocketed to the top spot in Japan" ("Story Tells" 15). However, one German booker complained to *Variety* that the movie was not drawing as many adults as children and that the characters lacked the usual Disney "warmth," "due partly to the 'hard lines and cool quality' of John Lasseter's pic" ("*Toy Story*" 10). Strangely, the reference opposes the generic Disney look with that of Lasseter, rather than identifying it as CGI or Pixar's style. By the next year, *Toy Story* had sold a record-breaking twenty-one million videocassettes in the United States alone. While its script was the first animated feature nominated for best original screenplay at the Academy Awards, John Lasseter was awarded a special-achievement Oscar for his "inspired leadership." It also won eight Annie Awards that year, including for directing and best feature. Further, it is only the second animated feature to make it onto the American Film Institute list of top one hundred American movies, along with *Snow White and the Seven Dwarfs.* In 2005 it was voted into the National Film Registry.

The prestigious French journal *Cahiers du Cinéma,* which is often cautious with its praise for highly commercial American products, gave Lasseter and his movie a glowing review: "The best proof that *Toy Story* is a complete success is that there is absolutely no need to know that this is a total revolution in digital imagery while watching it" (Malandrin

79). The reviewer Stéphane Malandrin concluded that *Toy Story*'s contributions were narrative as well as technical, since for him the film is a very adult existential drama. The central theme is "What are we doing here?" Buzz's personal journey is in fact philosophical, since he must realize and then accept that he has no metaphysical mission or professional purpose: "Buzz learns there is no heaven or outer space up there for him and he is just a toy like thousands of others made in a far-off factory. And, there are no women here, except the shepherdess. They all just stand before the absurdity of the world." Finally, however, *Cahiers* concludes that, this being Hollywood, the movie must end by reinforcing American morality, and obviously the one male figure with both feet firmly planted on the ground, the cowboy, has to be the most loved of toys. "Ideology, did we say ideology?" (Malandrin 79).

Within the world of animation history and criticism, *Toy Story* holds a special place. Though many cultural theorists express more reservations than *Cahiers* about the movie's ultimate social functions, the historical significance of *Toy Story* is unanimously agreed upon. For Stephen Prince, Pixar's feature fits well within the trajectory of digital special effects and filmmaking since such films aim for "an immersive illusion," in which spectators recognize the characters as living in a convincing fictional world. "A viewer watching *Toy Story* is responding to Woody and Buzz and their cohorts, who are designed not to be effects but characters" (Prince, *Digital Visual,* 190). Moreover, Andrew Darley argues that *Toy Story* exceeded the old standards of Disney realism, especially thanks to its cues for texture, weight, and movement, achieving new levels of visual sophistication: "Nowhere is this more apparent than in the degree of surface accuracy and the greatly enhanced illusion of three-dimensional space and solidity" (84). Pixar had revolutionized animation, blending traditional storytelling and character animation with the potential of new digital forms. As Paul Wells observes, with *Toy Story,* Lasseter "has explored the interaction between cartoonal aesthetics and the new potentialities of the computer-generated interface in a way that fully exploits the material nature of the objects which serve as characters in the films and the geometric space and synthetic gloss of the graphic environment" (Wells, *Animation,* 151).

Ultimately, *Toy Story* presents a reassuring fictional world within a completely unprecedented new medium that straddles a line between cartoonal and live-action realism for a result that was closer to puppet animation than traditional hand-drawn paper or cels: "It is an *other* world neither more nor less real than the actual, physical world outside. It is wholly different at the same time that it is familiar" (Sarafian 216). Some label the resulting aesthetic outcome as the Pixar "feel" or "touch," and these summaries regularly include a sense of awe, part of which is encouraged and shaped by the Pixar marketing team. For instance, Loren Carpenter explained how he merged images of gravel and sand to make a random pattern for the asphalt, but then concluded "it's semi-magic" (qtd. in Robertson). The CGI process was part of the film's attraction, and it managed to retain a sense of respect and even mystery within the discourse surrounding the movie and its reception. *Toy Story* became the most important animated feature since *Snow White and the Seven Dwarfs* for a number of reasons, and Pixar's technical triumph made for a great story in its own right.

That *Toy Story* could be described as familiar, even nostalgic, while simultaneously introducing an entirely new mode of production for feature-length animated features only proves further Lasseter's powerful synthesis of classical and innovative techniques. Jennifer Barker believes that much of *Toy Story*'s significance owes to its illusion of concrete physical objects and shapes. The film's "nostalgic charm and kid-appeal are inseparable from its tactile allure. . . . American audiences of a certain age will remember the feel of those little plastic green soldiers. This film entices us to run our fingertips over it, and its tactility invites a childish kind of tactile enjoyment in its viewers, both young and old. . . . *Toy Story* recalls sensual memories of a particularly urban, consumer culture" (Barker 45). The surfaces are almost too perfect, as they evoke a nearly forgotten era for adults, merging "emotion, memory, and history" into in a highly sentimental viewing experience (46). By populating its fiction with recognizable figures from childhood, *Toy Story* manages to distract audiences from the digital technology behind the illusions. William Schaffer agrees that Pixar had changed the playing field: "Before *Toy Story,* digital images may have recalled the artificial, depthless textures of plastic in the 'bad' sense. After *Toy Story,* digital images recall the intimate, animated, resonant plastic of childhood toys. Digitality is thus never cold or distancing in *Toy Story,* as parents raised on warm, soft, analogue features like *Bambi* might fear. Digitality here becomes warm, nostalgic, and loyal, like the toys whose life it reveals" (Schaffer 88–89). Lasseter's story thus successfully reassures children about the fate of Woody and Buzz while simultaneously winning over wary adults worried about how emerging media may betray the hand-drawn animation experience and artistry.

Yet how can a film based on stylized plastic figures and a completely new technological mode generate "nostalgia"? The ideological functions of *Toy Story* have attracted as much discussion as its technical and narrative accomplishments. However, any nostalgia seems to be created in the audience rather than among the fictional characters. This story of a single mother raising two children and suddenly deciding to move for no apparent reason is not based on any overt story point that signals a loss of security, much less a father or husband as a factor in their lives. Unlike the clearly nostalgic Disney princess stories with their long line of dead or absent fathers and mothers, or even Hayao Miyazaki's compelling family melodramas, *Toy Story* makes no mention of an earlier, more whole, idyllic family. There are no references to whether Andy and his sister ever had a father and no photos of past birthday parties on the mantel with a smiling conventional nuclear family. Fans and poststructuralist theorists alike have offered hypotheses on the absent father, positing death and/or divorce. For instance, Alan Ackerman argues that the films in the *Toy Story* series "seem a fulfillment of the Oedipal dream in which Andy gets to live alone with this always available, non-professional mother, treating his infant sister with his own brand of benevolent paternalism" (903). There is no textual effort to offer a psychological profile of Andy as a suffering boy transferring his lack of a father onto two male-authority-figure toys, though some critics try to impose such psychological analyses via extratextual moves. As Dennis Tyler productively observes, "Though heavily invested in representing 'safe' family values, Pixar nonetheless has managed to respond to the current cultural landscape and the changing nature of family and family relationships. . . . From *Toy Story* forward, the 'family' does not just refer to the heteronormative nuclear family, but to a wide ranging affective network" (269). *Toy Story* is clearly directed at a time before VCRs, cell phones, and the internet—a rather mythical consumerist era. It encourages adults and growing children to think back to caring deeply for certain toys and making up stories around them. However, *Toy Story*'s sort of nostalgia does not simply evoke a conventional patriarchal past that is now somehow lost forever.

Nonetheless, the ideological structures of *Toy Story* leave many cultural critics justifiably unsettled. The leftist critic Jyotsna Kapur complains that the central characters are "cynical and jaded postmodern toys" who "accept matter-of-factly that being a toy is no more than a job" (241). Further, as mentioned, Lasseter referred to this insulated community of toys as a melting pot that never quite melted. However, his toy world is strikingly homogeneous. For Lasseter, the materiality of the toys may represent a sort of diversity, yet the dialogue is all voiced by famous white actors. Woody's name may be a tribute to Mr. Strode, but his voice is by Tom Hanks, not Denzel Washington. As Thomas Dumm points out, "*Toy Story* is relentlessly white, relentlessly straight, and relentlessly male." For him, *Toy Story* cynically reveals a world order based on inequality in which toys, Buzz included, must learn to submit to the established order to find peace and "commodious living" (Dumm 92). In other words, some see Pixar's leading male characters as a rejection of generic "alpha male" roles. Rather, characters such as Woody and Buzz are dramatically emasculated as they "learn, reform, and emerge again with a different, and arguably more feminine, self-concept" (Gillam and Wooden 5). *Toy Story* thus participates in a transitional era in American masculinity for symptomatic cultural critics. Woody and Buzz have also been interpreted by Wells as "icons for an America caught between innocence and experience; expectation and fulfillment; instability and reassurance" (Wells, *Animation,* 155).

That Pixar's film featured brand-name mass-produced toys such as Slinky, Barrel of Monkeys, and Mr. Potato Head also reinforced many fears about commercialism and the highly capitalized requirements of computer animation: "It was no accident that the first full CGI feature to debut in cinema was exclusively focused upon the myriad of manufactured object forms yielded by the children's toy market" (Gurevitch 133). The convergence of advertising campaigns to sell the movie, Pixar as a new IPO stock option, and Woody and Buzz toys and products seemed either the height of cynical capitalism or postmodern self-consciousness, depending on the observer. Consumers could buy Buzz Lightyear toys, but also Buzz Lightyear sheets, much like those in Andy's room. Leon Gurevitch argues that Pixar's features "mainline the viewer into the process of industrial fabrication and consumption simply through the act of spectatorship" (136–37). *Toy Story* clearly fits contemporary Hollywood norms for high-concept productions. Yet, despite the suspicions some held for these highly capitalized Disney-Pixar figures, they also helped market and valorize CGI itself as a successful new medium for generating embodied characters. Ollivier Pourriol goes so far as to claim that after *Toy Story,* "nothing will ever again be as individuated and alive as the plastic figurines of Woody or Buzz Lightyear" (114). The *Toy Story* characters have since become canonical members of motion-picture history, making them truly "post-human reconstructions" for our age, according to Paul Wells (*Animation* 160).

Toy Story's resounding success at the box office and later in home-video sales, combined with the launching of Pixar as a public company, secured the financial security of the studio and catapulted Catmull and Lasseter to the top level of American animation. The new status for Pixar also meant that Lasseter's duties would continue to move him toward functioning more as a producer, beyond animator, writer, and director. Yet he also managed to continue directing a few personal projects, including the short in-house documentary *Who Is Bud Luckey?* (2005). The Pixar style, so carefully constructed and synthesized over the years by Lasseter and his colleagues, was now firmly in place, and he would begin cautiously guiding those principles forward while mentoring others to continue the Pixar look. Moreover, in addition to the box-office profits and ancillary toy sales, *Toy Story* left Pixar with an inventory of incredibly valuable material. As *Fortune* pointed out to its readers, CGI technology "makes possible for the first time the stockpiling of digital characters, sets, props, and even scenes. Stored in the computer, they can be reproduced and adapted economically and infinitely, in film and video sequels and spinoff products like toys, TV shows, and games" (Schlender and Tkacyzk 156). Once Woody, Buzz, and their fellow toys and environments had been created, their completed digital files provided an incentive for Disney and Pixar to exploit them well into the future. Thus, the temptation to generate a number of subsequent sequels makes even more economic sense for a CGI property like *Toy Story* than it does for a live-action franchise.

While Pixar's next production lacked some of the immediate pressures and insecurities felt during *Toy Story,* the studio also had to maintain its momentum and retain and pay as many of its employees as possible during the long process of generating another feature-length film. From the beginning, Smith and Catmull had been dedicated to protecting their talent, both technical and artistic, seeing them as their biggest assets. Now, Catmull had a much larger pool of people to keep engaged. Financially, the ideal model for keeping the studio working at a sustainable level would be to release one feature each year. Given the three to four years required to complete an animated feature, having several titles in various stages of production at any given time would allow steady work for everyone from preproduction through publicity. This production-schedule model would allow the sort of stability enjoyed by classical Hollywood studios, just on a smaller scale.

Pixar had developed its own version of an animation pipeline, but covering costs before the prospective box-office returns from *Toy Story* arrived had been a major challenge. Further, Catmull and Lasseter were well aware that a demanding slate of future feature films would require more writer-directors beyond Lasseter. Thus, from the beginning, they were assessing everyone for their future potential. Joe Ranft, Andrew Stanton, and Pete Docter were Lasseter's closest animators and among his favorite storytellers, so they were entrusted to take on more responsible roles and independence. As Steve Jobs observed, "John realized very early on that he was really running the John Lasseter School of Animation Direction. Sure, he wants to direct his own movies forever, but he also tries to surround himself with, and nurture, the best and brightest people" (qtd. in Kurtti 14).

During the summer of 1994, while *Toy Story* still had nearly a year to go before its completion and release, Lasseter, Catmull, and his colleagues were already concerned about Pixar's all-important second feature. Given that their contract with Disney required approval of each script, and in light of the delays and difficulties of forging a final screenplay for *Toy Story,* they had to look into new story ideas even before knowing how well *Toy Story* would be received. In one now-legendary discussion about future stories, the central cohort of Lasseter, Ranft, Docter, and Stanton met for lunch at the Hidden City Café in Point Richmond, California, to compare ideas they had each been considering. This lunch meeting, which was actually part of a long string of conversations among many Pixar employees, has now become a major story point in Pixar's own history. As Andrew Stanton states, in the "teaser" trailer for *Wall-E*, "In the summer of 1994 there was a lunch . . . so we knocked around a bunch of ideas that eventually became *A Bug's Life, Monsters, Inc., Finding Nemo*, and the last we talked about that day, was the story of a robot. . . ." Pixar was indeed searching for new story lines as well as new directors or codirectors to work with Lasseter on the subsequent projects. It was apparently Ranft and Stanton who began discussing the potential merits and challenges of adapting Aesop's "The Ant and the Grasshopper" fable. During their discussion they began pitching the more dramatic notion that the hungry grasshopper might just come steal the food raised by the ants. The ant colony, however, would ultimately fight back. As this idea developed, the writers would also look to Akira Kurosawa's *The Seven Samurai* (1954) and the western *The Magnificent Seven* (dir. John Sturges, 1960) for inspiration and parodic material, since those tales too involved oppressed communities hiring some unlikely helpers in their desperate attempt to protect themselves from returning bandits.

A Bug's Life was at least doubly motivated as the next Pixar project. First, Lasseter was attracted by a story involving insects because their segments were easy to build in a computer. They could be designed from various geometric shapes, much like toys, but Lasseter also isolates other advantages: "In thinking of subject matter that lends itself to this medium, one that came up very quickly was insects—because of their physical attributes: exoskeletons, color, iridescence, translucence. All of these properties translate to our medium beautifully" (qtd. in Sarafian 213). Second, *A Bug's Life* was timely because the computer division was perfecting a crowd-technology program to animate hundreds of figures moving seemingly independent of one another. While certain sorts of intricate and mobile organic figures were still too difficult to render convincingly, an ant colony could exploit large numbers of nearly identical insects moving autonomously. Ants may move in rhythmic unison, but they need not always appear in perfect sync with one another. Alice Crawford's concept of the algorithmic aesthetic within contemporary CGI, including its digital replication of objects, settings, and even camera optics, could be said to be hard at work in justifying and creating this animated movie about insects (Crawford 116–17).

In addition to advances in the modeling program, Bill Reeves and Michael Fong developed software to allow large clusters of figures to move in some general ways to cue shared emotional states, expressing collective joy, fear, curiosity, and so on. But the program also allowed for individual movements and even permitted small sections of the group to turn and look in specific directions. The self-guided crowd animation could help synthesize story and style in an efficient, functional manner, especially since Flik's quirky, individualized gestures would need to be distinguished readily from the obedient worker ants around him, who typically move in relative unison. For instance, the mass of ants will collectively shift their angry glance toward Flik on occasion, but at varying speeds and angles. Further, though they all may run in panic at the same time, their gestures and routes are not mechanical or obviously cycled or programmed (figure 17).

The gender theorist Judith Halberstam even argues that CGI and its technological ability to render convincingly swarms of figures has created a demand for stories such as *A Bug's Life*: "You need narratives about crowds, you need to animate the story line of the many and downplay the story of the exception" (176). *A Bug's Life* ended up including 430 shots involving crowds, with seven hundred ants in the largest instance. Moreover, the computer-graphics team had just developed new subdivision-surface processes for more flexible bodies (Porter and Susman 25). The ants could be built around initially simple geometric

Figure 17: Multiple figures and eye movements in *A Bug's Life*.

shapes. For instance, young Dot has a particularly rigid, spherical bottom, and the rubbery caterpillar Heimlich is composed of a fixed series of segments. Yet their body parts could shift subtly as the characters change their speed or move over the uneven terrain, suggesting that their concrete surfaces or shells are indeed organic and malleable. When the ants throw a party, every minor figure from the foreground or snaking into the background dances in one of a wide variety of styles, though they all move in synch to the same rhythm.

Given Lasseter's ongoing responsibilities directing *Toy Story* and his frequent duties as a chief spokesperson representing Pixar to the press, Andrew Stanton was put in charge of drafting the initial script. By July 1995, the treatment was ready enough to be pitched to Disney. In the initial story, the normally passive ants decide to stand up to the grasshoppers, who will soon return to collect their food for winter. The Queen sends for warrior insects to protect them. The ringleader of a circus group, Red the fire-ant, convinces his troupe to go along with the naive ant scouts and pretend they will defend the colony, when in fact they would just stay long enough to devour as much food as possible before sneaking away in advance of the grasshoppers' arrival. Eventually, however, the circus bugs would be won over by the ants and grow to accept their mission. The newly responsible Red would lead them all to fight and win against the grasshoppers.

While Disney approved this initial outline, Stanton eventually decided that the script included a wildly unrealistic change of heart for Red and the circus bugs, and that the story fell into the same pattern as the earliest versions of *Toy Story*: the main character, a self-centered liar throughout much of the screen time, risked becoming too unpleasant and ultimately unlikable. Stanton, following the lead of the *Toy Story* screenwriting teams, decided to rethink the central character, his motivations, and the overall functions of the communities of minor characters around him. He shifted the protagonist from the ringleader circus ant Red to the ant colony's desperate scout, Flik. Now it would be a tale about how one clumsy, outcast ant unleashes the collective power of the multitude of tiny ants while simultaneously proving the value of this incompetent circus troupe. As Halberstam explains, "*A Bug's Life* is not just about bravery in the face of tyranny; it showcases the ability to think in multiples, to move as a crowd, to identify as many" (184). In a Stanton and Lasseter Pixar world, the best actions are those proven to benefit the community as a whole.

Only after Stanton tested his revised treatment on two trusted colleagues, story artist Ash Brannon and editor Lee Unkrich, did he pitch it to Lasseter, who apparently readily agreed that Flik would be a more compelling main character in this stronger and more satisfying plot. Thomas Schumacher, president of Disney Feature Animation, agreed that the new version was better as well. "It got down to the fundamental issue that, in life—and the movies—you want that key character to be empathetic, because you want people to cut you the same break you're gonna cut that guy" (qtd. in Kurtti 31, 33). And, having learned from the challenges in constructing those multiple drafts of *Toy Story,* Lasseter and the story team worked to be sure Flik would never become too confident or mocking, even though down deep he believes that the entire colony needs to change its fundamental attitudes and behavior. All the insects ultimately learn a valuable lesson and find a new respect for each other as well as a reassuring confidence in themselves. As Lasseter explains, "Flik grows quite a bit, but more importantly, everyone around him, because of his influence, also grows a tremendous amount. . . . It's a really apt emotional core to the film that fits everyone's everyday lives" (Lyons). Over and over, Lasseter's explanations of Pixar characters return to their own emotional essence and the effects their personality and life choices will have on those around them. There is a real belief at Pixar in the unifying potential of plot points driven by character motivation and progressive social change.

The final script and storyboard for *A Bug's Life* were the products of a core group and designed to satisfy a number of internal creative and managerial requirements, all while appealing to a wide commercial audience of children and adults. Lasseter became increasingly involved in this second feature as the final stages of *Toy Story* wrapped up. For Stanton, the story artists, and the concept artists, model builders, and animators, Lasseter was their most important audience. The story team regularly sought his input and opinion, and he was essential for greenlighting every aspect of the production, from story points to the visual style. As a result, Stanton generously shares authorship: "it is Lasseter's sensibility that pervades both *Toy Story* and *A Bug's Life.* . . . He has both the kid's perspective and the filmmaker's perspective" (qtd. in Booth

100). But for the popular press, Lasseter was always the central directing force behind *A Bug's Life*. In 1997, a full year before its release, *Wired* was already building anticipation for the film, reporting that *A Bug's Life* would undoubtedly "adhere to Lasseter's Law: Flashy f/x may get people into the theater, but the essentials—plot and character development—are what keep them in their seats" (Daly, "Hollywood 2.0," 212). Lasseter was marketed as the gatekeeper for every aspect of visual storytelling at Pixar.

For *A Bug's Life*, Lasseter again encouraged the artists, designers, and technicians to do their research on every object, investigating the core traits and functions that would lend realism and purpose to props and characters alike. Further, while the insects were primarily composed of primitive polygonal shapes—cylinders, hemispheres, cones—Lasseter called for the inclusion of as many organically shaped objects within the environment as possible. Leaves, for instance, were important for the story line because their varying colors signaled the passage of time and seasons. But they could serve as aesthetically pleasing backgrounds as well and were designed to show off their naturally complex networks of veins and how they could distort and enhance the lighting, often by tinting nearby objects. He also recommended early on researching what a natural setting might look and feel like from an insect's perspective. Lasseter's interest in how lamps and toys experience the world inspired a curiosity in how a bug's miniaturized perspective could defamiliarize mundane, everyday items in nature, including seeds, flower petals, and rain drops, making them surprisingly new and even dramatic.

The visual artists studied plants and insects under microscopes as well as in the real world for inspiration. Lasseter consistently reminded the crew to stay close to the insect world's scale and explore that creative vantage point. This sort of concern for investigating the environment from a fresh perspective motivated the "bug cam," devised by the engineer Neftali Alvarez. The camera, wheeled through the fields at one-half inch from the ground, inspired extremely low camera positions but also revealed an impressive variety of lighting effects and colors. As Lasseter explains, "The one thing you noticed down at that level was how translucent everything was . . . to see these huge clover leaves like giant stained-glass windows—it was stunning" (qtd. in Kurtti 124). Among the most striking environmental effects resulting from these experiments were the silhouettes of ants seen through leaves as well as the intricate shifts in colored light as it filters through layers of vegetation (plate 7). The visual concepts behind *A Bug's Life* built upon lessons learned within *Toy Story* but also warranted some drastically new options as well. The supervising layout artist Ewan Johnson explains that they were not designing concise, enclosed spaces as in *Toy Story* but rather a "completely organic world where nothing is going straight up or down and nothing is perfectly level" (qtd. in Kurtti 67). And, given the complex exteriors and large number of characters interacting in many shots, Pixar's Ralph Eggleston suggested creating *A Bug's Life* in a widescreen format of 2.35:1, which would offer a larger playing space with expansive horizontal zones of action complementing the occasional deep-space planes of action. Widescreen opened up the narrative space and reinforced the mock-epic quality that pervades the movie, including its visual and musical references to Hollywood westerns and adventure films. Randy Newman's expansive, lyrical soundtrack even won a Grammy Award. As Price points out, "Lasseter had come to envision the film as an epic in the tradition of David Lean's *Lawrence of Arabia*" (162).

Pixar's division of labor famously allows story input from a wide range of talent. Beyond the initial story and script, with Joe Ranft as story supervisor, there was a story manager, Susan E. Levin, the storyboarders, and the story artists, as well as B. Z. Petroff as a production supervisor. For both *Toy Story* and *A Bug's Life,* part of Petroff's job was to serve as a liaison between the story artists and the editorial and technical departments. For instance, story artists were asked to create a variety of comical circus acts for the insects in *A Bug's Life.* She points out that they were also instructed not to worry initially about whether any scene or action was "possible" in CGI. Catmull and Lasseter were devoted to their slogan that the story comes first, and the technology merely serves the narrative. These proposed scenes were then considered by the larger team, but Lasseter and Stanton finally decided which worked best and helped advance the plotlines. Hence, a number of humorous individual scenes were never used because they did not adequately affect the charted path of the central characters, though several, like the bug, voiced by Lasseter, flying into a bug zapper—"I can't help it. It's so beautiful"—were retained. For the scenes that were chosen, it was Petroff's task to break those sequences down and assess their practical or narrative challenges, meeting with the animators and technicians to discuss ways to accomplish the action or make workable compromises (Petroff).

In the end, *A Bug's Life* involved a great number of distinct characters with conflicting or overlapping goals. As Petroff explains, "You had the circus bugs, you had Flik and the ant colony, and then you had the grasshoppers. And all of those characters need to have great character arcs. . . . It's hard to tell that many stories in that short a period of time" (qtd. in Price 162). Storytelling responsibilities were shared across a range of personnel and departments. In a practical sense, key aspects of authorship for *A Bug's Life* were dispersed throughout Pixar. Moreover, everyone involved was well aware of certain themes and graphic tendencies that were now part of the successful Pixar style, which the studio often continued to promote and market effectively as John Lasseter's personal style.

The overall plot structure as well as the evocative visual and audio style are built around the consistent development of the entire range of characters, from Flik and Atta to the circus bugs and little Dot. Much like *Toy Story*, this narrative is composed in four clear acts of relatively comparable length. The introductory setup act runs for twenty-five minutes, establishing the colony's transitional matriarchy, Flik's bumbling experiments, Dot's faith in him, Hopper's annual raid, and his new threat to return for twice as much food when the last leaf falls. The second act, or complicating action, begins with Flik setting out for town to redeem himself, meeting the circus troupe, and bringing them back to Ant Island. Atta, still suspicious of Flik's actions, throws a party welcoming the warriors, who then discover the misunderstanding and decide to abandon the ant colony. However, just as the troupe is secretly leaving, they team up with Flik to rescue young Dot from a pesky bird. Flush with their accomplishment and cheered by the appreciative ants, the circus insects decide to stay and help, at the film's precise midpoint, forty-five minutes in.

The development, or third act, involves the alignment of all ant and circus-troupe goals, as everyone works happily together to build the fake bird to frighten away Hopper, even though the ant colony is not yet aware that the insects are inept circus performers instead of fierce fighters. However, once Atta and the colony learn that their warriors are circus clowns, and Atta shames Flik for lying to everyone, a new turning point arises. The scene recalls the moment when the toys turn on Woody after he knocks Buzz out the window. Even little Dot is held back from comforting the banished Flik. However, the circus troupe, appreciative of Flik's help in making them feel confident, decides that they are willing to stay and fight. But it takes little Dot, repeating the same encouragement that she had received from Flik earlier, to convince Flik that he should stick to his original battle plans and redeem himself. Flik's resolve to fight back follows the pattern established with Woody and Buzz. After feeling helpless and even ridiculous, these Pixar protagonists rally thanks to the most supportive members of their community.

Act 4 of *A Bug's Life* thus includes the harrowing, climactic return of the grasshoppers, plus the circus bugs responding bravely by presenting their best performance ever. They distract Hopper and his gang while Flik and the young blueberry ants launch the fake bird, turning the tables against the grasshoppers. Most importantly, when the bird catches fire and Hopper is about to regain control, seeing through their hoax, the masses of ants band together in solidarity to fight against the remaining gang of grasshoppers. However, even as they win and Hopper is about to be jettisoned in a cannon, a rain storm disrupts the ants' triumph. Hopper abducts Flik, flying off into the night during an intricate chase scene in which all the circus performers aid in the pursuit, and even the bumbling Tuck and Roll manage to break off part of Hopper's antenna, keeping it as a sort of castration trophy. Hopper is thus comically emasculated even more thoroughly than Sid had been in *Toy Story*. Thanks to her incredible flying abilities, Atta finally rescues Flik, who leads Hopper to his death in the bird nest. A brief epilogue reveals springtime, when the proud circus troupe leaves amid thunderous applause, Flik is thanked, and Atta is crowned queen. A new prosperity for the colony is also suggested by the fact that many ants are now joyously harvesting with the same technology that Flik was testing unsuccessfully at the beginning of the story. The old feudal system has been conquered, leaving an enlightened monarchy. The network of story points are all resolved happily, and the termination effect is reinforced by the camera pulling back in a shot that reverses the opening, bracketing the telling of this tale and reinforcing the film's carefully unified narrative space.

It came as a shock, however, when Pixar learned in 1996, while *A Bug's Life* was still in production, that there was another CGI feature film about ants in the works. One of the consequences of the success of *Toy Story,* and of Pixar's willingness to share information with their other colleagues at SIGGRAPH and beyond, was that they had indeed helped jump-start the entire niche of computer-animated feature films. Moreover, over the years, Lasseter, Catmull, Smith, and Jobs had all engaged in long discussions with Disney executives about the potential of CGI for their own future. They had worked to convince Jeffery Katzenberg among others of of computer animation's value, and Katzenberg had often proven a keen ally for Pixar. Lasseter in particular forged a good working relationship with him. Even after Katzenberg's very public, very bitter exit from Disney in 1994 and his cofounding of DreamWorks SKG, he and Lasseter remained on friendly terms. Lasseter reportedly met with Katzenberg in 1995 and described Pixar's new ant project. A year later, however, as a sort of revenge plot against Disney and Michael Eisner in particular, Katzenberg announced that his first animated feature at DreamWorks, in cooperation with Pacific Data Images (PDI), would be *Antz,* not the previously announced *The Prince of Egypt.* Moreover, DreamWorks would release *Antz* in October 1998, weeks ahead of Pixar's scheduled premiere of *A Bug's Life.* Katzenberg was using a story of an ant colony, initially proposed by Nina Jacobson, as leverage to retaliate against Eisner and Disney for their apparent attempt to steal the thunder from the release of the first DreamWorks animated feature by the timing of *A Bug's Life*'s opening. It remains unclear whether the announcement of the *Antz* project was initially just a threat, or whether Katzenberg really intended to go through with the insect movie to counter Disney's distribution plans.

Even before the announcement of the *Antz* project, there had been competitive tension between some at Pixar and Katzenberg's animation wing at DreamWorks. In one interview, the normally generous Ed Catmull turned quite sarcastic: "I keep reading all the announcements about what Jeffrey is going to do, and they call their company DreamWorks. Well we're actually doing it, so we're thinking of changing our name to RealityWorks" (qtd. in French, *"Toy Story,"* 19). Steve Jobs deeply resented Katzenberg's *Antz* stratagem as well, but later he claimed that he felt worse for Lasseter: "People started saying how everyone in Hollywood was doing insect movies. [Katzenberg] took the brilliant originality away from John, and that can never be replaced" (qtd. in Isaacson 428).

It is worth mentioning, however, that insects were already a standard feature of early CGI prior to *A Bug's Life*, including within the curriculum of introductory computer-animation classes. An early MFA project from the new computer-animation program at the University of Georgia, *The Birds and the Bees* (dir. Scott Stevens, 1996), was begun in 1995. Bugs offered practical subjects for early 3D modeling. Regardless, the Jobs quote also reinforces the tendency by many people associated with Pixar to keep Lasseter's face and name front and center. Jobs did not mention feeling sorry for Andrew Stanton, Joe Ranft, or even Ed Catmull because of the *Antz* affair. Rhetoric surrounding Pixar often tends toward personifying the studio as an extension of John Lasseter, their creative core and avatar. When Lasseter suffers, the studio suffers, and vice versa.

John Lasseter therefore had to move rapidly to confront and deflect this betrayal from someone he had considered a friend in the business. According to David Price, Jobs and Lasseter rallied the Pixar staff to carry on and endeavor to make the better film. However, they were also secretly approached by Katzenberg. He was willing to delay or even shelve *Antz* if Jobs and Lasseter could get Disney to shift their release date away from the projected premiere of his *Prince of Egypt*. Pixar refused (Price 171–72). Lasseter took the entire *Antz* saga quite personally and claims never to have seen the DreamWorks movie, refusing to speak to Katzenberg for years.

The two features are clearly made in opposition to one another and have subsequently been compared and contrasted relentlessly by reviewers, critics, and film students. Even the opening shot of *A Bug's Life*, with a leaf landing on a water surface that initially looks like a shot of the bright sky, could be read as a response, reversing the DreamWorks logo with its reflection of the night sky disrupted by the fishing lure. Despite all the creative cast and crew involved in both films, over time the press has regularly assigned authorship of *Antz*, with its snappy, more mature dialogue, to Katzenberg as much as, or more than, to the directors Eric Darnell and Tim Johnson, while *A Bug's Life* was often referred to as the competing Lasseter film. Katzenberg and Lasseter were seen as sources of their animation studios' styles, which reviewers clearly opposed in tone and temperament. One tiny detail reveals some of those perceived differences: In *Antz*, the worker ants drink beer from the anus of live aphids. In *A Bug's Life*, the Queen keeps an aphid as her cute little lap dog. The DreamWorks and Pixar stories and sensibilities clearly diverged despite the parallels in their plots.

Thus, while the story lines of *Antz* and *A Bug's Life* are similar, each being organized around a rather weak, bumbling, individualist male ant who has to strike out on his own in order ultimately to strengthen the colony, the characterization and visual styles in the two films are far from identical. *Antz* opens right away with a voiceover from its main character, the self-centered and depressed Z (Woody Allen), explaining his recurring discomfort and dissatisfaction with his life, blaming much of it on a lack of attention from his mother, who had five million other children as well. Z even complains about his feelings of inadequacy to an analyst who quickly assures him that he is indeed insignificant and therefore not deluded. This introduction situates Z as a direct descendant of Allen's Alvy Singer in *Annie Hall* (1977). Z is consistently cynical and mocking, though he tries half-heartedly to be a team player and "be the ball" in one of his first scenes. His emotional style stands in direct opposition to the more optimistic, big-hearted Flik, who understands the benefit of the colony and just wants to help everyone improve things for the future well-being of all.

Visually too their worlds are opposed. The underground world of *Antz* is a dim, brown place with dirt walls from a seemingly simple texture-map program. The characters are composed of an array of flatter surfaces that seem to be stretched across rigid skeleton rigs, so that in some close-ups, as they speak, their materials shift in ways that suggest that these are costumed figures, almost as if Woody Allen or Sharon Stone were wearing rubber ant suits. When these figures move, they rarely show any convincing signs of shifting muscles or weight. They remain cartoonal caricatures with few subtle gestures. As Rita Kempley's review laments, the story also violates the first commandment of fairy-tale movies: "The protagonist must learn a moral lesson in the end." Z does not really grow up.

By contrast, the Pixar characters not only learn and mature, they are also more mobile, moving with perceived physical weight and purpose through their more textured and colorful environments, with lush lighting cues and deep-space staging that often exploits motion blur and rack focus to mimic live-action motion-picture film optics. Flik and Atta are more engagingly embodied animated characters than the comical performers Z and Bala, who fit closer to figurative animation as defined by Don Crafton. Figurative performances are typically more extroverted, with characters seeming overtly constructed. They employ reflexive styles to signal emotion, appearing to play a role rather than truly embody the character (Crafton 23–24). *Antz* is also dialogue-centered, with its characters striking performative stances and poses as they explain themselves. As Paul Wells points out, *Antz*, with its star-voicing, quotations of live-action films, and historical connection to earlier insect movies such as *The Cameraman's Revenge* (dir. Wladyslaw Starewich, 1911), has been interpreted as more obviously allegorical and self-conscious than *A Bug's Life* (Wells, *Animation*, 157–58).

While *Antz* may have been rushed by Katzenberg's accelerated production schedule and lacked many of Pixar's proprietary software programs, it managed to compensate for some of its technical shortcomings with scenes that exploit some of those limitations. For instance, when Princess Bala sneaks out of the palace to visit the bar and dance with Z, the rows of background ants all move heavily in unison, with few of the variations seen in a dance scene from *A Bug's Life*. DreamWorks and PDI may have lacked crowd controls as sophisticated as those at Pixar, but in the bar sequence the dull repetitive movement of the scores of ants helps serve as a monotonous backdrop that allows the spontaneously dancing Z to distinguish himself as he tries to impress Bala. Z and his freewheeling attitude lead into a joyously chaotic ruckus as a fight breaks out. Most of the fight scene is filmed in short takes, soft focus, and rather grim low-contrast lighting, which all helps disguise the fact that the clusters of ants are moving in cycles and set rhythms. Nonetheless, as the *San Francisco Chronicle* review complains, "It's a bit tedious (all those earth tones, the sameness of millions of insects, etc.)" (Stack, "Bugs"). Clearly, the interiors in *Antz*, with tiny blue lights affixed to the walls, generating a purple and reddish effect from the reflective brown dirt walls and bodies, do not feature the sort of exotic, motivated lighting of the glowing phosphorescent mushrooms of *A Bug's Life* or its visually appealing array of subtle colors. Even in the battle scenes, the armies in

Antz walk in strictly computed rows that foreground the repetition so easily accomplished in CGI, though the rapid, clever dialogue tries to distract from the rather limited range of movement for these animated characters.

However, *Antz* is not always less visually rewarding than *A Bug's Life*. Once Z and Bala leave the colony and undertake their adventure to Insectopia, the intense colors and expansive natural sets generate a bright, inventive spectacle. On their journey, the bickering Z and Bala become trapped in a drop of water and soon after try to eat picnic food protected by plastic wrap (figure 18). Their faces are distorted in both sequences, recalling *Tin Toy's* glance at the baby from inside his toy box. Z and Bala's further ordeal, stuck on a gigantic human's tennis shoes, with moving cameras and an ant's perspective, make the sequence a parody of generic action films. The alternation in *Antz* between their liberating adventure outside the ant hill and the developing plot of betrayal inside the dark colony structure this story in a more contained, claustrophobic narrative space than the personal journeys that organize *A Bug's Life*. If *A Bug's Life* is inspired by Aesop and Kurosawa, *Antz* is more a reworking of *Annie Hall*, with some serious allegorical plot points distilled from *Metropolis* (dir. Fritz Lang, 1927), among others.

Visually, *A Bug's Life* continues Lasseter and Pixar's philosophy of presenting a world that is stylized yet anchored in realism and plausibility.

Figure 18: Stuck in a water droplet; *Antz.*

Beyond the bug cam's influences and convincing crowd movements, complete with waves of shifting eye directions, the mise-en-scène reinforces the finely textured environment and the precise gestures of these hectic, purposeful insects. Even the opening, with the virtual camera flying in to Ant Island and entering the tall grasses, foregrounds the contrast between the grand epic widescreen expanse of landscape and the minuscule creatures who inhabit this world. After the shot isolates one tiny ant hard at work scaling a stalk to harvest a seed, a digital rack focus immediately reveals a number of identical ants hard at work on neighboring stalks. The film's art direction will build throughout on this strategy of making seemingly mundane little actions, like dropping a seed or walking in an organized ant line, seem surprisingly important. Philippe Lemieux points out that one of the greatest innovations in *A Bug's Life* "is surely the wind. Invisible to the naked eye and absent from the virtual world, wind is one of the natural phenomena that computer animation cannot replicate easily. . . . However, Pixar's technicians solved the problem and the gigantic grasses and plants move together depending on the force and direction of the wind" (121–22). He even connects his amazement with the wind effects to the early critics who wrote with astonishment at seeing the moving leaves in Louis Lumière's *A Baby's Breakfast* (1895). When Flik later rides off into the distance on a dandelion flower or wind surfs down on a leaf, the sense of wonder and palpable diegetic space prove just as compelling and spectacular as the adventurous events themselves.

As for its narrative space, *A Bug's Life* follows fairly classical shot composition with a very functional pacing and some intensified continuity editing. Thanks to the careful storyboarding, Lasseter's style encourages readable individual shots organized into a seamless plot structure for easy narrative comprehension and strong cues for time and location in the design layout and lighting scheme. In general, the camera movement is determined by character action, with the lighting motivated by mood and diegetic sources, whether sunlight as a key source, with fill light reflected off nearby rock surfaces, or those mushroom lamps emitting pastel lighting within the colony underground. The fanciful mushrooms, which also function as glowing performance stages in some scenes, seem influenced by *Fantasia*, Miyazaki, and those Parrish paintings from the *André and Wally B* days.

One good example of an efficient two-shot that combines all these elements is the moment when Atta pulls Flik aside within the tunnels to confide that she did not initially trust his warrior bugs. It is an honest, personal moment for her, though Flik obviously feels guilty during her confession, since he still has not revealed that her hunch was actually correct and the supposed warriors are mere circus performers. He has to decide quickly whether he too should confess the truth, stay and play along, or run out of the room. A mushroom in the far left zone casts an aqua light, while the leaf-curtain doorway on the far right glows from the lights outside. The staging resembles a John Ford setup, since the two are poised between going privately deeper into the tunnels together, or returning back out in public, where she has to act more like a princess (plate 8).

Comical scenes, unfolding out in the expansive exteriors with many players, also fit conventional staging norms, with rapid continuity editing guiding our attention and helping personify the CGI minor characters via their eyeline matches. In the opening scene, when the long line of bugs bringing their harvest to the offering pile is suddenly disrupted by a falling leaf, the line stops in panic, and Mr. Soil (Roddy McDowall) carefully guides them around the obstacle. The sequence takes only fifty seconds to unfold but is presented in eighteen distinct shots. This small scene alone incorporates shot/reverse shots, eyeline matches, matches on action, high-angle shots, and mobile camerawork. It also displays Lee Unkrich's flair for quick, clean shot-to-shot ordering, with the spectator's eyes fixed upon specific portions of the frame during the transitions. David Bordwell points out that Pixar's editorial teams "sometimes use laser pointers to track the main areas of interest within shots and across cuts, especially when characters' eyelines are involved" (Thompson and Bordwell). The overall shot length for the film as a whole huddles right around the same pacing as this scene and *Toy Story*, with a rate of just over three seconds per shot. Further, the early moment when Flik is testing out his new harvesting machine, which churns out sawdust that flies by in randomly generated patterns that recall the snowflakes in *Knick Knack*'s snow globe, are typical of the ways *A Bug's Life* includes multiple elements moving in the frame simultaneously to lend depth and spectacle to the already brief shots. This constant motion, combined with the editing strategies, establishes a convincing scenographic space that is reinforced by the enhanced realism of the diegetic sound cues.

Moreover, *A Bug's Life* fits previously established Pixar story norms, with central characters forced to face their own failures and disappointments before rallying and working with their supportive communities. Flik initially believes that he can help everyone until he is forced to agree with Atta that he has misled and disappointed the colony and he should just go away. But, just as Woody and Buzz help each other when they each lose all hope, Dot, Flik, Atta, and the circus troupe rally and reinforce one another in what turns into a can-do tale of self-discovery and cooperation. Every eccentric character gets to use some unique quirky ability to contribute to the group's success. Lasseter and Stanton concentrated on creating emotionally engaging characters so that even the minor figures are cleverly developed and any character can spout an important or comical line as needed. As a result, the array of figures in *A Bug's Life* could be said to project even more distinct personalities than the secondary line of toys in *Toy Story.* Woody and Buzz dominate their movie, while the range of developed, embodied figures in *A Bug's Life* is much more extensive. One helpful way to think of the cast of characters in *A Bug's Life* is as an array of well-defined persons with their own often complicated emotional histories and trajectories. These Pixar characters are also given many more significant traits than are seen in the caricatured figures in DreamWorks films like *Antz* or *Shrek.* Lasseter's emphasis on character animation helps create animated characters with active, functional personalities.

Each of the named characters in *A Bug's Life*—and there are fifteen core players, from Flik to Princess Atta and her family to the circus bugs and Hopper and his sidekick Molt—displays complex human traits with an emotional style all their own. In their book *The Emotional Life of Your Brain*, Richard J. Davidson and Sharon Begley argue that individuals have specific emotional styles that are partially determined by their brain patterns. Coping skills and emotional reactions thus vary and can change across time, but everyone has their own unique emotional profile (Davidson and Begley 2). This concept of an emotional style proves particularly useful in narrative, both in the fictional creation of logical, embodied characters, but also from the vantage point of spectators. We all have our own emotional style and are also very accomplished at recognizing and assessing emotional style cues in others. It follows that the most emotionally engaging characters, whether live-action or animated, will be those who provide the most diverse cues to their personalities, allowing spectators to comprehend why they act as they do and also how they will react in given situations.

Davidson has isolated six different dimensions of emotional style, each of which has a distinct neural signature in specific regions within our brain. Among those six dimensions comprising emotional style are the degree of *resilience* (how quickly one recovers from adversity), whether one has a positive or negative *outlook*, the extent of *social intuition* and whether one recognizes easily the feelings of others, *self-awareness* (one's awareness of one's own emotional state), *sensitivity to context* and social rules, and finally *attention*, or how focused one is during regular activities (Davidson and Begley 5–6). The character-animation traditions that impressed Lasseter so much in classical Disney also rely on basic human emotions and how clearly those thoughts and feelings are represented in the animated figures. Further, humor often results from characters who are particularly inept at recognizing social context and the emotional style of others around them.

In addition to setting up the story's context, characters, setting, and action, the opening scenes in *A Bug's Life* begin to establish the emotional styles for the central figures. For instance, in the first few moments of the film, Princess Atta proves to be nervous and in a panic, though at least she recognizes that she is overly stressed and anxious. Down deep she is most worried about someday having to replace her mother, the much more focused and calm Queen. Atta is not adequately resilient, displays a nervous, negative outlook, is aware of her neuroses and social context, yet remains unfocused. When the alarm is blown announcing the approach of the grasshoppers, it is the Queen who gets everyone to escape into the colony in an orderly fashion. Thus Atta is established as an inadequate replacement for the Queen, and one of her biggest problems is that she knows she is not yet competent.

By contrast, Flik remains resilient, with a positive outlook that borders on the ridiculous. The audience readily recognizes that he should not be so confident. For instance, even when he has accidentally flattened Atta twice with his new stalk-cutting contraption, he continues to try to impress her with his invention. His intuition and sensitivity to context are flawed, and he is often clueless, focusing on the wrong things as if wearing blinders. Thus he remains relatively oblivious to the critical attitudes of those around him and the problems he poses for others. Yet it is this unique cluster of traits that makes it plausible that Flik will be the only ant to leap rashly out of the group to protest when Hopper threatens little Dot in front of the whole colony, though he quickly comes to his senses and retreats back in place (plate 9). He has not yet learned when to stand firm. Clearly, Atta and Flik need to learn from one another, synthesizing or balancing their opposed emotional styles. In scene after scene, Atta and Flik gain increased insight into themselves and others as the audience witnesses their ongoing maturing. Their emotional style progresses throughout the narrative, while Hopper's remains fixed and inflexible.

Flik's faulty emotional style angers Hopper and shifts the plot dramatically. After Hopper and his gang leave the first time, Princess Atta decisively pulls together a sort of trial, but Flik's shame changes when he misunderstands their plea for him not to help anymore, and he rashly hatches the scheme of leaving the island in search of stronger bugs to protect them. The other ants, however, understand that his leaving the island will either get him killed or bog him down in a long, fruitless journey far away where he cannot ruin anything new for them. They readily accept his plan and pretend to send him forth with their best wishes. Flik is overly resilient, full of faith in his mission. He even mistakes everyone's cheer of relief when he leaves as a tribute to his heroism. Yet his particular brand of emotional style and naive optimism ironically allow him to accomplish his task of rounding up a bug brigade to return and eventually help successfully turn the tide against the grasshoppers. The emotional style of each of the circus bugs, from the feisty male ladybug to the overly kind black-widow spider, also reinforces the Pixar theme of everyone having a keen significance for the community. These various insects, in the tradition of *Toy Story*, display personalities that are determined by their own physical limitations and abilities. The conventional thematics, including having the weak but ambitious "little guy" save the day and win the hand of the princess, however, includes pointing out the value in trusting in outsiders who are different from the fixed society's usual norms. In the end, *A Bug's Life* celebrates diversity, modernity, and progress over a mindless adherence to traditions and routine (Lucci 256). Admittedly, however, the sense of inclusion is still relative, since the voice cast is again almost exclusively white.

The emotional range of the characters and themes was also reinforced by the highly talented sound team, featuring Gary Rydstrom's effects and Randy Newman's music and songs. For *A Bug's Life*, Rydstrom remained in charge of sound design, working with his team from Pixar, Skywalker Sound, and beyond, including the regulars Gary Summers, Tim Holland, and Michael Silvers, among many others. Rydstrom exploits heightened realism throughout the film, often drawing the viewer's attention to minor insect figures in a frame with a suddenly loud buzzing of wings or the noise of their tiny feet paddling along the ground. Even with hundreds of ants on screen at once, there are times when a single sound cue will foreground one figure from all the others. Rydstrom's soundtracks are not only evocative, adding directional and spatial audio cues, they also repeatedly expand on the movie's sense of humor. And they can be ironic.

A Bug's Life opens with the idyllic chirping of birds and crickets, yet the story will reveal that the world pits bugs against birds and is rarely peaceful or harmonious. Birds and large insects are the ants' constant enemies. On a more practical level, Rystrom's mix punctuates the action with loud prompts but also occasional abrupt cuts to silence that further emphasize the sound's creative role. For instance, during the hectic scene when the angry grasshoppers, finding no food above ground, punch holes in the colony's ceiling and descend to terrorize the ants, there are a series of marked blasts as the earth is bashed in. But when Hopper suddenly drops down in front of Flik the soundtrack goes nearly silent. Hopper bends down, creaking as the sound effects call attention to his leathery exterior plates rubbing against one another and his noisily flicking eyes, with no other diegetic or nondiegetic noise heard. Next, the sound of an initially speechless Hopper stomping among the recoiling, stunned ants is all that is needed to heighten the tension and denote Hopper's pent-up anger as well as the wordless fear of Atta, the Queen, and all their subjects. It is a creative solution to the initial showdown of the offended Hopper and the humble, frightened ants, slowing down the action to allow the audience to contemplate the thoughts of all the major players as it generates increasing suspense.

The expressive soundtrack underlines the rhythm and tone of every scene and adds greatly to the overall emotional impact, helping make each situation more compelling. Rydstrom and his team place a great deal of importance on multiple functions of the sound effects but also on forging surprising sound-to-image relations by combining often unlikely source sounds with concrete image cues. As he explains, "Usually you can come up with a better idea sound-wise for a given moment in a film if you just step back and think about it non-traditionally" (LoBrutto 237). Rydstrom also warns that relying too much on overly faithful, realistic sound effects can limit the emotional and psychological impact in a scene. Even with characters like personified bugs, Rydstrom likes to allow the sounds to communicate in ways that replace or at least modify what language might be able to accomplish. He gives a "voice" to actions, objects, and gestures: "I always like sounds that have a vocal characteristic. I love real-life sounds that have the same emotional envelope a voice does. There are some sounds in real life—squeals, squeaks, and air hisses—that remind me of a voice. I like sweetening non-voice events with voice-type sounds to give them intelligence, a resonance" (LoBrutto 241). Sometimes even manipulated string instruments can replace dialogue. For instance, when Flik arrives in the big city searching for fighting bugs, the city pulsates with Hollywood musical themes that recall Gene Kelly as a bumpkin in a *Singin' in the Rain* (dir. Stanley Donen and Gene Kelly, 1952) routine. When he accidentally backs into a pathetic beggar bug scratching his legs together, we only hear grating violin strings. It is not clear whether the sounds are to be understood as diegetic or extradiegetic effects, and this uncertainty helps communicate Flik's disorientation among all the hustle and bustle. The music and sound effects consistently corroborate the specific scene's tone and bolster the narrative rhythm throughout the film, reinforcing Lasseter's storytelling tactics.

Certainly, one of the most raucous examples for sound design in *A Bug's Life* is the climactic rainstorm-and-chase scene. The rain sequence begins with Flik noticing a rapid flow of water already heading down the gully toward the ants. He even leans in during an extreme close-up to look and listen, further concentrating the audience's attention on his facial reactions and the accompanying sounds just before the explosive splats of rain fall like artillery shells, battering the ground and tossing the ants about. It should be no surprise that Rydstrom worked on *Saving*

Private Ryan that same year. "The raindrops are sweetened with the sound of jet engines and missiles to represent the magnitude of rain from a bug's perspective," as the sound designer Robin Beauchamp explains (21). As Hopper's escape and the abduction of Flik gets increasingly hectic, however, the sound effects come and go in highly functional and even abstract ways. Despite the constant visual downpour, the sounds of thunder and rain nearly disappear during the bursts of dialogue, as when Francis the ladybug temporarily loses Slim the stick bug in the tree branches. As soon as Slim delivers his line, "I'm the only stick with eyeballs," the soundtrack suddenly shifts from low background noises back to loud sound effects and rising music to return us to the chase. But once Atta flies in to save the day, jolting Flik out of Hopper's grasp, the music loudly signals a change in the mood, delivering triumphant, even pleasantly clichéd strains of strings and horns announcing that the tables have been turned.

As Atta carries Flik close to the surface of the water, the rain drops look and sound their most abstract yet, until the pair land on a leaf and flop onto the ground, bursting their water bubble in a scene mirroring Z and Bala's splashing fall in *Antz*. Finally, Hopper steps into Flik's trap as the bird is lured from its nest to grab Hopper for its hungry chicks. Screeching music and screaming characters reinforce the violence of his disappearance into the black abyss of a chick's mouth, in a shot that resembles a radical graphic transition from an Ub Iwerks scene back in the earliest days of Disney cartoons. But the sound of a horn accompanies the camera pulling back out of the darkness from the mouth of a shell as an ant blows the horn to announce a work stoppage, signaling the departure of the circus bugs. The sounds and music have been functionally embedded in Lasseter's storytelling. Rydstrom bolsters the emotional style of each of the characters, anchoring them within their fictional worlds. Similarly, Randy Newman's poignant musical compositions round out the rising and falling dramatic stages of the action, contributing affective cues for individual as well as group sensations and attitudes. Rather than resorting to known songs with calculated recognition and response cues—as is the case in DreamWorks' *Antz*, with Z singing "Almost Like Being in Love," for instance, and especially their later *Shrek* series—Newman's original music builds its own connotations specific to this movie and its singular context.

Initially, some reviewers seemed hesitant about *A Bug's Life* and its potential to top *Antz,* much less *Toy Story,* at the box office. *Variety's* Todd McCarthy, for instance, considered *Antz* "more sophisticated," adding, "John Lasseter's second film won't reach the exalted B.O. levels of this 1995 *Toy Story,*" though he had faith in it reaching a wide family audience. Yet Lasseter's second feature ended up with a very strong release and extremely positive reviews. One of the more enthusiastic reviewers was the *San Francisco Chronicle's* Peter Stack, who wrote, "Give it six thumbs up and a crawling ovation! *A Bug's Life* is one of the great movies—a triumph of storytelling and character development, and a whole new ballgame for computer animation. Pixar Animation Studios has raised the genre to an astonishing new level" (Stack, "Bugs"). Where *Antz,* which cost around $105 million to produce, earned ninety million dollars in the United States and fairly lackluster sixty-one million dollars internationally, *A Bug's Life,* with its $120 million production budget, set records for a Thanksgiving release and eventually captured $163 million at the domestic box office and another $200 million internationally for a total of $363 million, which was roughly equivalent to *Toy Story's* total first run. It earned a very strong $8.2 million in Japan during its first two weeks, and by late March 1999 *A Bug's Life* was the top-grossing American movie abroad. In France, where it sold 3.4 million tickets, surpassing *Toy Story, Le Monde* newspaper pointed out Lasseter's excellent use of widescreen to compose a very fine "Fordian epic." *A Bug's Life* tied or outperformed *Toy Story* in a number of foreign markets, where it was acknowledged as standing up technically and aesthetically to the *Antz* challenge.

With the reassuring box office and growing critical success of *A Bug's Life,* Pixar received a new wave of attention. *Business Week* profiled Steve Jobs, the "Movie Mogul," but Jobs's biographer Alan Deutschman claims that everyone at Pixar was focused on executing Lasseter's vision. Lasseter was the nurturing and positive manager who ensured Pixar's continuing growth. "While Steve's photo appeared on the magazine covers, John Lasseter was the overwhelming creative force at Pixar. . . . John signed off on every commercial, every THX trailer, even the details of the attraction at Disney's theme park in Florida, where the characters Flik and Hopper sing 'It's Tough to Be a Bug'" (Deutschman 274). Moreover, while *A Bug's Life* was still in production, Joe Roth at Walt

Disney Studios initially pitched the idea to Michael Eisner of purchasing Pixar. Disney's recent films had been losing money, while spending what many saw as an exorbitant amount on those productions. According to Leonard Maltin, the Disney management team of the late 1990s openly questioned whether some of their recent animated films initiated under Jeffrey Katzenberg, including *Pocahontas* and *The Hunchback of Notre Dame* (dir. Gary Trousdale and Kirk Wise, 1996) may have weakened the Disney brand and reputation. However, their *Hercules* (dir. Ron Clements and John Musker, 1997) "wasn't the megahit Disney had hoped for," though it earned a healthy $250,000,000 worldwide, with nearly $100 million in the United States and selling over four million tickets in France alone, beating out *A Bug's Life* (Maltin, *Disney,* 332). With the animation portion of their budgets running quite high, and even *Hercules* apparently losing money when overhead was taken into account, Roth argued that digital was the future of animation and could eventually save them money. Further, "Jobs is a darling of Wall Street and you'd get John Lasseter, the greatest creative mind that's come out of Disney" (qtd. in Stewart 288, 290). Eisner was not interested in owning Pixar, however. But Pixar's chief assets by this point were clearly perceived, as John Lasseter and the creative management style he and Catmull had proven time and again.

With the completion of *A Bug's Life,* Pixar had completely defined its place in American animation. Lasseter's second feature had helped firmly plot out a viable and reliable production model for the studio. As Lasseter repeatedly argues, Pixar's success depended in large part on the fact that it is managed by creative filmmakers and not by business executives. But there was also a new confidence and sense of responsibility among Pixar's core creative-production managers. However, though the studio had managed to achieve solid income and assets, their cycle of new, overlapping projects placed renewed pressure on their teams of technicians, animators, and editorial staff. In order to retain their large stable of employees and generate profits for stock holders, a demanding production schedule was established.

Two years before *A Bug's Life* hit the movie theaters, Disney had announced plans to create a direct-to-video sequel to *Toy Story,* along the lines of their *Return of Jafar* (dir. Toby Shelton, Tad Stones, and Alan Zaslove, 1994), which was a shorter, cheaper follow-up to *Aladdin* (dir. Ron Clements and John Musker, 1992). Pete Docter was already assigned to the early planning and development stages of *Monsters, Inc.*, so Lasseter named the relatively new Ash Brannon to direct the *Toy Story* video sequel. Soon, however, Disney executives complained that the Pixar sequel was already proving more expensive than expected. Rather than cut production costs, an optimistic Catmull proposed a more radical solution, turning the video project into a full-scale theatrical-release version of *Toy Story 2* to help justify the costs and maintain a high level of quality and help protect the Pixar brand. As he explains, "Suddenly we were making two ambitious films at once. . . . This was a little scary, but it also felt like an affirmation of our core values" (Catmull 68). The budget and staff increased, and as soon as *A Bug's Life* was completed, Lasseter and Lee Unkrich would take over as codirectors on the expanded version of *Toy Story 2*.

By the time of the late-1998 premiere of *A Bug's Life*, however, Catmull and Lasseter were growing concerned with the progress and general condition of *Toy Story 2*. "The story was hollow, predictable, without tension; the humor fell flat" (Catmull 69). Lasseter decided to call together his central collaborators Stanton, Docter, Ranft, and Unkrich for a weekend retreat to rethink the script. Their initial version had Woody suffering a torn arm and then being left behind at the last moment as Andy goes away without him to cowboy camp. Woody would be abducted at a garage sale by Al, a greedy toy collector who wants to reunite him with the other members of his original toy set, a horse named Bullseye, an old prospector, never out of his box, and Jessie the cowgirl sidekick. Al also has to refurbish Woody, who has now lost his arm in a scene that recalls Buzz's loss of an arm in the initial *Toy Story*. The ultimate buyer is to be a toy museum in Tokyo that insists upon the complete set of toys. Woody would have to decide whether to live a pampered but idle life, preserved forever in a glass case in front of adoring fans, or return to Andy, who might soon outgrow him.

However, some of the basic character motivation and ensuing tension was underdeveloped. Lasseter and his team added a new penguin character who explains to Woody how tough it is to be a broken, neglected toy, but they also increased the role of Jessie, who even sings about how devastating it was to be abandoned by a child who outgrew her. Lasseter included stronger female characters for *Toy Story 2*, in part apparently thanks to encouragement from Nancy Lasseter. Jessie's cautionary tale and loneliness would directly affect Woody's perspective on his limited options as a toy and deepen the emotional impact of the story and his being torn between two potential families and two very different fates. Even with improved characterization and new story events, the most pressing practical problem was that the release date for the feature was fixed for November 1999, giving the Pixar team less than a year to rework the movie. Lasseter insisted on storyboarding the entire film anew, a process that began in earnest that January, plunging Pixar into a frantic and daunting production schedule for the rest of the year.

Throughout the preproduction and production processes, the Pixar team continued to follow its usual, if intensified, collaborative work model and pipeline. However, given the previous problems and accelerated schedule, Lasseter imposed the final say on key designs as well as story elements. Of central concern were the emotional hooks for Woody, Buzz, and Jessie, as well as their competing communities, and the resulting empathy from the audience. The overall plot falls comfortably into a clear four-act structure. The initial setup of a damaged Woody being left behind by Andy and then abducted by Al changes over to act 2, the complicating action, twenty-two minutes into the story. At that point Woody discovers his past as the popular TV host and star of *Woody's Roundup,* followed quickly by Buzz and his decision to lead a rescue party bound for Al's Toy Barn. In the massive store, another Buzz Lightyear takes the "original" Buzz's place, complicating further the gang's task of locating and retrieving Woody. Act 3, the development, begins at the midpoint of *Toy Story 2,* fifty-two minutes into the screen time. Woody learns from Jessie's sad song that she was abandoned by her owner Emily. He decides that he cannot break her heart yet again by leaving to return to Andy, especially since she is correct that Andy, like all growing children, will inevitably abandon Woody in the near future. Thus, Woody vows to remain with Stinky Pete, Bullseye, and Jessie.

Toy Story 2's major turning point, however, arrives just after the end of the development, when Woody has explained to Buzz and the rescue party that he will not be returning home with them. As soon as Buzz and the old gang leave, Woody hears his own character's voice singing "You've Got a Friend in Me" on the old TV show, which reminds him of his long history with Andy, and he quickly discovers that the Prospector has been deceptive and selfish. Thus, Woody changes his mind, deciding to return to Andy, but he offers to take Jessie and his horse Bullseye along so they too can avoid being locked up in a museum. The climactic fourth act, beginning at sixty-six minutes, involves a series of chases and challenges, including the interference of Buzz's nemesis Zurg and the impending flight to Tokyo. Once Jessie is rescued from the cargo hold of the airplane, the short epilogue reveals everyone safely back home at Andy's house. The resolution is also built around the promise of a cluster of romantic couples, including Buzz and Jessie, Woody and Bo Peep, and the reunited Potato Heads. Moreover, buddies Buzz and Woody seem content to grow old and face the future together, while it is also suggested that Andy's little sister will undoubtedly extend the ultimate playing lives for Jessie, Woody, and Bullseye, guaranteeing a doubly happy and secure narrative termination point for all. The solid closure and epilogue also leave plenty of options for sequels into the future.

The revamped script was a group project credited to Stanton, Rita Hsiao, who had worked on *Mulan*, Doug Chamberlin, and Chris Webb. Their final version developed further the emotional states of a number of characters, especially the timid Rex the dinosaur, who learns to confront and overpower his enemy Zurg, and Buzz, who exhibits a new sense of social intuition as he temporarily takes on Woody's role as leader of the toys, motivating and guiding their rescue operation. In fact, *Toy Story 2* opens with a particularly evocative scene that provides a nod to its commercial and constructed natures, as the initial battle between Zurg and Buzz turns out to be a computer game, played by Rex with Buzz looking on, lending encouragement: "You're a better Buzz than I am." . Thus, the film begins with a mise-en-abyme as a toy plays a computer game, posing the question of whether these toys are indeed just images on a screen or actually exist as objects (Tesson 41).

But it will again be Woody whose emotional journey structures the plot and ethical themes of *Toy Story 2*. His sensitivity to context and self-awareness initially cause him to decide to stay with Jessie and her cohort, before he has a revelation that echoes Buzz and his "falling with style" moment in the first *Toy Story*. Woody realizes that yes, someday Andy will outgrow and abandon him, but everything in this world has an expiration date. He accepts that everyone must shape their own destiny, remaining true to themselves and others along the way. Whether he goes to the museum or returns home, Woody's decision involves some measure of a personal sacrifice, but his resilience, outlook, and self-awareness guide his decision to go back to Andy and take his new TV-show friends along. His emotional style thus reveals a new level of maturity and growth, and the Pixar team's script highlights and celebrates his character's decisions and values over all the others as he decides to return to his "true" family of Andy and the toys and insert Jessie and Bullseye into his rewarding world.

The emotional turning points for Woody, Buzz, and especially Jessie are consistently cued by character gesture and facial expressions and eye movements. One pivotal example is the sequence in which Woody, happy with his repaired arm, is about to follow Buzz down the air shaft and back to Andy. However, Jessie surprises Woody with her anger and goes off to sulk by the window, while the wily Prospector points out to Woody that Jessie has suffered greatly from the rejection by her owner, Emily. Further, Bullseye directs his sad, oversized eyes at Woody, giving him a guilty glance that delays Woody's escape. In fact, Bullseye's pathetic look is reminiscent of the collective glances of the toys hiding under the couch in *Tin Toy* as they turn their attention to Tinny, challenging him to act. Bullseye's silent reproach motivates Woody to go appease Jessie before leaving.

Once Woody confronts Jessie, he is stunned to learn that her feelings for Emily match perfectly his relations with Andy (plate 10). As Jessie, voiced by Joan Cusack, looks out the window at a blue and pink sky that recalls the original *Toy Story* wallpaper in Andy's room, a melancholy sort of music video, with the song "When She Loved Me" by Sarah McLachlan, unfolds, telling Jessie's story in condensed fashion. Jessie's song provides a bittersweet reply to the fast-paced and energetic "You've Got a Friend in Me" montage of Andy playing with Woody that opens *Toy Story.* During Jessie's montage, there are slow pans and dissolves to reinforce her loss and nostalgia. The entire mental subjective scene includes distorted colors and a dreamlike animation style. At one point, young Emily can be seen running across a field with Jessie in tow, but the girl's feet do not even to touch the ground, as if she were on a separate cel above a conventional painted background. The spatial cues are quite different from the rest of the movie and may be motivated as much by the rushed production schedule as by the music-video flashback aesthetic. Her run cycle recalls that of André racing away from Wally B, his body floating just above the forest floor.

During this flashback scene's two most sentimental moments, Jessie's eyes register the devastating realization that she is being outgrown and abandoned. First, when she has fallen under the bed, Jessie peers out to witness Emily and another girl preferring nail polish to her. Unlike Woody, Jessie does not seem to have any friends. She is the only toy we see come alive in Emily's room. Moreover, by the end of the song, she is dropped off at a bleak donation and recycling site and stares dumbfounded as an insensitive Emily heads off without her. This is nearly the same setting where Emily earlier ran happily with Jessie. Now, only Jessie's eyes and fingers are visible in the cardboard box's handle hole, as if she were locked in a prison cell (figure 19). By the end of the song, after Woody looks down the long, empty heating-duct exit, Woody resolves to stay behind, as the Prospector again lays out his options: the future can mean impending abandonment by Andy, or eternal pampering and security in front of generations of devoted, appreciative fans. Clearly, the latter is deeply needed and seemingly deserved by the roundup gang, and Woody's emotional style justifies his temporary decision to abandon his own goal of returning to Andy.

Beyond the engaging story progression, created under severe time constraints, there had been many important technical advances at Pixar

Figure 19: Jessie abandoned in *Toy Story 2.*

since the first *Toy Story*. Textures were rendered with much more detail on everything from clothing, floors, and plastic surfaces to the background setting and environment. Moreover, beyond the increased ability to control the individual toy characters' gestures, there are more realistic skin and hair cues for the humans, who also earn more screen time than in the first installment. Andy receives a number of close-ups, though his facial shape and features retain a fairly geometric, even toy-like quality. He and his mother still move rather stiffly, sometimes appearing less lifelike than the more flexible toys (plate 11). By contrast, the toy merchant Al is particularly striking and even quite naturalistic-looking in some scenes. Much like his parallel antagonist Sid from the first *Toy Story*, Al must be made to look menacing. His heightened photorealism underlines his difference from Andy and his family. It is as if the Pixar team wants Al to hover uncomfortably on the edge of the uncanny valley effect. In one shot, as Woody sneaks up on the sleeping Al to retrieve his own severed arm from Al's shirt pocket, there is a slightly unsettling tension between the glossy, cartoony Woody and the convincing fabric of Al's corduroy shirt, hyperrealistic eyeglasses, and faithfully rendered skin and hair. This is one moment where the CGI toys risk appearing to be composited into a live-action scene (plate 12). By the end, the visual style for representing human figures presents a spectrum from the familiar, more stylized Andy and his mother to the increasingly human gestures and surface details present in *Toy Story 2*'s devious Al, voiced with gusto by Wayne Knight.

As Ed Catmull proudly writes, "In the end, we would meet our deadline—and release our third hit film. Critics raved that *Toy Story 2* was one of the only sequels ever to outshine the original, and the total box office would eventually top $500 million" (Catmull 73–74). A number of key reviews were indeed exceptionally positive. Roger Ebert noted how well Pixar overcame the challenge of shifting from a made-for-video product to a full-fledged theatrical-release version. He applauded the smart screenplay: "It isn't just a series of adventures (although there are plenty of those) but a kind of inside job, in which we discover that all toys think the way every kid knows his toys think" (Ebert, Rev. of *Toy Story 2*). The *San Francisco Chronicle*'s Peter Stack again spoke for many other critics as he praised the sequel and the creative team: "The Pixar wizards with their amazing computer animation have outdone themselves with this generous and dramatically rich . . . story that takes real chances as a sequel and hits pay dirt with heartfelt dramatic nuances. . . . Unlike most sequels, this one expands the lives of its characters (from Mr. Potato Head to Slinky Dog and Hamm), putting them into new situations with substance" (Stack, "Toy-ing"). And the BBC underlined that the sequel is at least as good as the original: "Watched back-to-back you can see how it surpasses *Toy Story* in technical excellence (leaves, dogs, and humans are all more lifelike)" (Hilditch). Pixar had in fact reworked many basic modeling controls, and the render farm for *Toy Story 2* alone included 1,400 Sun Microprocessors, seven times more than *Toy Story* (Price 201). Beyond the technology, the *New York Times* review concentrated on the film's emotional resonance: "Lasseter's avowed fondness for Frank Capra's films can be seen in the nostalgic world summoned here, and in the fundamental goodness of the toy characters themselves. Without undue sentimentality, this film lets its playthings pull together in ways that would be sweet and funny in any format" (Maslin, "*Toy Story 2*"). Most reviews echoed these central traits of *Toy Story 2*, as surprised and impressed critics had expected a potentially disappointing or at least less inspired sequel.

One of the most insightful reviews of *Toy Story 2* came from the French critic Charles Tesson. In *Cahiers du Cinéma*, he praised the movie's ability to establish the perceptual and affective perspective of these toys so convincingly: "In *Toy Story 2*, the tiny toys look upon humans with a nervous eye" (40). Tesson also points out that the film acknowledges and pays homage to film history, from D. W. Griffith and Alfred Hitchcock to *Lady from Shanghai* (dir. Orson Welles, 1947), Federico Fellini's *8½*, *Star Wars*, and *The Terminator* (dir. James Cameron, 1984). Even the title of Tesson's article, "Toys Also Die," refers to *Statues Also Die* (dir. Ghislain Cloquet, Chris Marker, and Alain Resnais, 1953). Moreover, Tesson sees Woody's biggest decision as a significant cinephilic moment: "He must make the choice between a Fordian world (rejoining his community, that of the western, while retaining the memory of his identity) and a Hawksian world, with his community of alliances, the toys of Andy's room who belong to many different categories and types" (40). Either way, Woody realizes that he is selecting one mode of death over the other, and his days of freedom and happiness are finite. Many of the melancholy aspects that recur in

Pixar's subsequent feature films, including *Finding Nemo, Wall-E,* and *Up* (dir. Pete Docter and Bob Peterson, 2009), are already major components of *Toy Story 2.* Tesson even ponders whether these toys have a soul, but he concludes that what they benefit from the most is Lasseter's direction: "In John Lasseter's film, the classical style of the mise-en-scène guarantees the character's humanity . . . and helps familiarize the audience with the represented universe, which is naturalized despite its openly unrealistic dimensions" (42). By the end, very real, human, and ethical issues of personal loss, fate, and sacrifice are addressed by this most artificial, generic, and commercial of media, American CGI animation. Woody had become a successful existential character indeed, as *Toy Story 2* sold an impressive 4.5 million tickets in France, nearly two million more than *Toy Story.*

Thus, precisely one year after the acclaim over *A Bug's Life,* Lasseter was seen as driving his Pixar team to yet another triumphant premiere, this time under the toughest of production schedules. Beyond the positive reviews and earning $245 million in its American first run alone and another $239 million abroad, on a $90 million budget, *Toy Story 2* swept the Annie Awards, grabbed the best comedy or musical award from the Golden Globes, and won Randy Newman a Grammy for "When She Loved Me." Moreover, in six select locations, *Toy Story 2* was projected as a digital format, proving that "a film could be entirely made, released, circulated and exhibited without the actual use of acetate" (Venkatasawmy 28). But as Lasseter continued to emphasize that the technology only serves the storytelling, it had become clear by the end of this third feature that "story" to Lasseter means building a plot around engaging, embodied characters set within complicated personal situations that determine their preferences and final actions. In both *Toy Story* tales, Woody and Buzz and their cohort grapple with fundamental life choices that are in part determined by their own traits and emotional styles. Lemieux sums up this fundamental stage of Pixar's output: "Despite all the technological innovations within computer animation, the secret to success still rests with emotion and the animators' ability to translate the heart of the scripts into images that are both moving and engaging. In brief, the spirit of Walt Disney walks the hallways of Pixar" (126).

After the exhausting experience of *Toy Story 2,* during which up to one-third of the animators and technicians encountered symptoms of overworking, including serious repetitive stress injuries, Lasseter and Catmull vowed to ensure a healthier working environment in the future, built around more realistic production timelines. At the final-wrap party in the San Francisco's Castro Theatre, Lasseter apologized to the employees: Pixar would never again force the staff to work this hard to meet a schedule. But there were other changes under way for Lasseter personally as well. By the summer of 2000 he had made the transition to executive producer, allowing others from his "brain trust" cadre to take over directing. Lasseter and his family took a road-trip vacation while Pete Docter, Lee Unkrich, and David Silverman prepared *Monsters, Inc.* Next, Andrew Stanton would begin work on *Finding Nemo,* before Lee Unkrich joined him as codirector. Lasseter continued to consult with the animation teams on key decisions, especially with story structure, and he participated in the reviews of footage and reels. He forged an engaged executive style and remained the most recognizable face of the studio. Thus, Pixar entered the new century with a stable and incredibly profitable business and production model, still under the firm control of Ed Catmull and John Lasseter. Their unique management style had proven that an upstart studio could remake animated cinema. They had also launched the most respected brand name in animation and perhaps in contemporary cinema as a whole. Pixar reliably drew enthusiastic critical praise and audience loyalty, as well as attracting a steady stream of job applications from the best young computer animators in the world.

Cars and Beyond: Executive Producer and Animation Auteur

John Lasseter accepted ever-increasing responsibilities at Pixar and put his imprint on the stories and styles of every Pixar feature, including *Monsters, Inc., Finding Nemo,* and *The Incredibles.* The central characters of Pixar shorts and features, including *Ratatouille* (dir. Brad Bird and Jan Pinkava, 2007), *Wall-E, Up,* and *Monsters University* (dir. Dan Scanlon, 2013), would all owe a debt to Lasseter and accumulating studio influences and for their design, their emotional styles, and their ethical dilemmas. With the merger with Disney, Lasseter also became an executive producer for their features, beginning with *Meet the Robinsons* (dir. Stephen Anderson, 2007). However, he refused to give up on directing.

For his own next feature, *Cars*, Lasseter was able to combine his interests in animation and automobiles. For the prepublicity, he stressed his very personal connections to this story, and in interviews and later on the DVD supplement track he hints at a strong connection between the central character and himself. Both are incredibly successful but then learn to slow down and appreciate life, in large part thanks to the influence of an intelligent and caring female role model. He not only found inspiration from road trips, both with his family and the animation team, but he also referred back to a classical Disney cartoon, *Susie the Little Blue Coupe* (dir. Clyde Geronimi, 1952), animated by Ollie Johnston. Susie begins as a "latest model" in a showroom, flashing her smile (her grinning grill) and flirting with potential owners. The entire windshield is taken up by her large eyes, and it is a cartoon in which every car in the parking lot expresses its status and mood via gestures rather than dialogue. Eventually the anthropomorphic Susie ages and fades, until finally being refurbished into a peppy hot rod by a teenage boy. While the production team retained a few traits from *Susie,* including a sort of rebirth motif, *Cars* would shift the lead role to a cocky, male race car who must learn to look beyond his own success, maturing and learning from an unlikely community of vehicles that resemble the ensemble cast of characters in *Toy Story* who surround and influence Woody. Lasseter retained a blue female car, Sally Carrera, as the influential love interest in *Cars.*

Cars surprised many at Pixar when it did not receive the stunning level of critical praise lavished on the preceding Lasseter features, or *Finding Nemo* and *The Incredibles.* For instance, Roger Ebert, normally one of Pixar's biggest fans, wrote, "The movie is great to look at and a lot of fun, but somehow lacks the extra push of the other Pixar films. Maybe that's because there's less at stake here, and no child-surrogate to identify with" (Ebert, Rev. of *Cars*). The *Village Voice* critic Robert Wilonsky complained that *Cars* was like a commercial product rolling off an assembly line: "Yet it's also director John Lasseter's most elegiac offering, an ode to the bygone days of dusty roads winding through small towns in which nothing ever happens except the crawling of time. That probably explains the turgid pace, with all the traction of a boxcar going uphill in molasses." And the BBC proclaimed sadly, "It had to end sometime. After a run of standard-setting CGI movies, Pixar has finally delivered a dud. . . . [The car] learns valuable lessons about (yawn) the importance of community and teamwork. It's Capra with hubcaps" (Arendt). The *Guardian*'s review was titled "Pixar's *Cars* Stalls with Reviewers," and even Mick LaSalle's review in the loyal *San Francisco Chronicle* admitted that *Cars* "runs out of gas." Several reviewers pointed out that Lasseter's plot seemed like an uninspired retread of the movie *Doc Hollywood* (dir. Michael Caton-Jones, 1991), played out with less than compelling cars. However, the French critic Gilles Ciment championed *Cars* in *Positif*, celebrating Lasseter's proven mastery of lending personality to mechanical objects. Ciment also points out that the director's nostalgia for retro office lamps and discarded toys is transferred here onto automobiles to comment on an America that is fast disappearing. With *Cars*, Lasseter joins the ranks of filmmakers such as Wim Wenders who pay homage to a remote western spirit often ignored now, and far off the interstate. For Ciment, "Lasseter shines on," thanks to his sensitive, humanistic portrayal of misfits and freaks who are all valued by the movie's end (15).

Despite the cautious and even occasionally mocking critical reception, *Cars* earned $244 million in its American first run, second only to *Pirates of the Caribbean: Dead Man's Chest* (dir. Gore Verbinski, 2006) for that year. Eventually it took in nearly five hundred million dollars globally at the box office and won a number of prizes. Randy Newman's "Our Town" won the Grammy Award for best song, and *Cars* was awarded the Golden Globe for best animated feature, as well as five Annie Awards, including best feature, animation effects, and character animation. Pixar's movie also defeated *Happy Feet* (dir. George Miller, Warren Coleman, and Judy Morris, 2006) at the box office, despite the latter's winning the Academy Award for best animated feature. Thus, as David A. Price points out, any disappointment in the critical reception for *Cars* was purely relative (256). In most circles it was deemed a success, and its ancillary products added a whole new line of characters for Pixar and Disney to market.

Even some of the weaker reviews complimented the film's striking graphic style. There is an intense visual energy unleashed right from the opening title sequence, with its Sheryl Crow music-video montage for "Real Gone." Subsequent racing scenes, on and off the tracks, display a constant barrage of virtual camera movements and intensified continuity editing. Further, Pixar had once again delivered ever more impressive and expressive cues for texture and lighting, with water splashes, glints of sunlight, and McQueen's trademark "ka-chow" greeting, all sparkling brightly thanks in part to advances in ray-tracing technology. (For Pixar's explanation of the process, see http://renderman.pixar.com/view/raytracing-fundamentals.) As Kristin Thompson writes, Pixar's filmmakers regularly engage with some new technical challenge: "Every film pushes the limits of computer animation in one major area, so that the studio has been perpetually on the cutting edge. In *Cars,* that area is light and reflections . . . the filmmakers forced themselves to devise ways of showing light realistically bouncing off their painted surfaces. This happens in virtually every scene, but the moment when the refurbished town of Radiator Springs turns on its array of neon lights in the evening is a real *tour de force*" (Thompson, "Reflections").

Research into paint and light proved crucial for the final look of *Cars.* According to the shading supervisor Thomas Jordan, "At the local body shop, we watched them paint a car, and we saw the way they mixed the paint and applied the various coats. . . . We figured out that we needed a base paint, which is where the color comes from, and the clear coat, which provides the reflection. We were then able to add in things like metallic flake to give it a glittery sparkle, a pearlescent quality that might change color depending on the angle" (qtd. in "Look of *Cars*"). The realistic effects for dynamic reflections on shiny metallic car surfaces as well as intricately complex shadowing allowed greater control over depth and texture cues in complicated environments full of rapidly moving objects, extreme motion blur, and sudden reframings. As the production crew explains, the story warranted improved resolution, shadows, and lighting effects. They argued that *Cars* "has scenes that are much more complex than past Pixar movies; for example, wide desert landscapes with many sagebrush and thorn-covered cacti, and a racing oval with 75,000 cars as spectators," all of which demanded more efficient lighting algorithms (Christensen et al.).

Conventional sorts of shadow maps were no longer adequate for scenes in which the production team had to manage as many as one thousand separate light sources, including the waves of flash bulbs firing from the race stands. Plus, the new ray-tracing software's calculated effects challenged the potential to render surfaces and textures in greater detail, from elegantly curved chrome bumpers to rusty and crusty metallic fenders, with appropriate reflections on each (plate 13). Smoke and exhaust appeared more layered and palpable as well. Jay Telotte points out that *Cars* foregrounded breakthroughs in RenderMan software to create more naturalistic illusions to imitate how we typically perceive objects in motion. During race scenes, some elements blur, "whereas larger images such as car numbers and the 'facial' details that have been created for the personified autos—visual elements that we need to see clearly for narrative reasons—remain distinct. The result, even in mobile shots, is an intense spectatorial sense, as if we were witnessing real movement through real space" (Telotte, *Animating*, 217–18). Some of Pixar's most hyperrealistic environments to date resulted from the new processes, including the desert settings, the "Life Is a Highway" truck montage, and even Tow Mater's junk-filled shop and dusty impound lot (plate 14). The results are particularly evident during the pivotal scene when Sally Carrera (Bonnie Hunt) convinces the narrow-minded race car Lightning McQueen (Owen Wilson) to take a drive through the stunning countryside. Their shiny bodies careen through a wide range of impressively generated settings, shadows, and lighting setups. Moreover, the environment retains the sorts of complementary colors within the shadows that Lasseter insisted on way back during the *André and Wally B* days, though the pine trees and rocks in *Cars* clearly belong to a whole new century of CGI software and hardware (plate 15).

Beyond the new visual tools for the design and animation teams, the increased options for character expression and the film's extended 116-minute run-time allowed Lasseter and his team to lend emotional style and subtle traits to the wide variety of vehicles, helping transform these normally inanimate objects into thinking, feeling characters. *Cars* is also heavy on mental subjective scenes, including daydreams and memories. Nonetheless, since the automobiles retain their essential materiality, weight, and volume, they have to express their thoughts and motivations in somewhat cruder ways than could the fine-grained faces of Woody or Flik, much less the large and flexible heads and faces of *Monsters, Inc.* and *Finding Nemo. Cars,* much like *The Incredibles,* exploits an uneasy synthesis of cartoonal expressions and realistic mise-en-scène cues. These sorts of stylized gestures by the car characters tend to deliver clearly marked cues for expressing their thoughts, moods, and even intentions. Ironically, as Stephen Prince explains, less photorealistic animation may actually deliver more effective information: "Caricature conveys emotion in concentrated form" (122). McQueen, Sally, and the brooding Doc Hudson (Paul Newman) may lack some of the precisely detailed movements and subtle gestures of Woody's facial features, but they nonetheless generate very immediate emotional cues.

With *Cars*, Lasseter also continued the narrative device of matching his lead with an antithetical sidekick, here the tow truck Mater, and opposing him to an evil male nemesis, this time the ruthless race car Chick Hicks of the Hostile Takeover Bank team. However, this lead character has more to learn than Woody or Flik. The competitive and brash Lightning McQueen has to become lost and even arrested in Radiator Springs before he can learn humility, life skills, and racing tips from everyone in this hick town, especially Tow Mater, Sally Carrera, and the veteran Doc Hudson. Early on, the overly confident McQueen ignores advice and assistance from the aging Dinoco King and his own pit crew, and he dismisses his Rust-eze sponsors and fans as embarrassing losers. In a plot twist that recalls *The Wizard of Oz* (dir. Victor Fleming, 1939), many of these earlier characters have a sort of alternative double in Radiator Springs. Now, the forced period of community service and ensuing leisure activities far from the fast-paced racing world allow McQueen to develop, slowly, a completely new outlook and emotional style, aligning him more with the Pixar ethics of a Woody, in contrast to the mean, self-centered motives of his rival Chick Hicks.

During the heart of the story, at the plot's midpoint, an accumulating series of scenes reveal McQueen gradually becoming genuinely intrigued by the folks of Radiator Springs. First, he is surprised to enjoy the simple pleasure of tipping tractors with Mater, then he discovers that Doc Hudson was once famous, winning three prestigious Piston Cup races, and most importantly, McQueen takes the scenic drive with Sally as she teaches him to slow down and appreciate the world around him. He nearly forgets his central goal and race deadline for a day. Gradual changes in camera position, editing rhythm, and music increasingly signal McQueen's shift in perspective, while shots of his startled, responsive eyes gazing around with wonder prove that the conceited race car is seeing the world anew. By the end of their drive, his self-realization process is nearly complete.

While writing and storyboarding the plot, Lasseter and his team revisited some of the problems initially caused by an overly harsh Woody in the first *Toy Story*. They built McQueen from the beginning as a talented, self-centered, immature character, but he is never as obnoxious as Chick Hicks, so he remains potentially worthy of our allegiance. Owen Wilson's endearing voice work also helped temper McQueen's cocky traits. Later, before leaving Radiator Springs, McQueen acquires a fresh view on life that brings with it a best friend, a girlfriend, and a new adoptive family. At the final race, the distracted, unfocused McQueen benefits from Doc as crew chief and his comically supportive pit team. He also earns the respect of the crowd when he gives up winning the Piston Cup, sacrificing his lead to help the damaged Dinoco King finish the race. Surprisingly, however, the tiny three-wheeled Guido may give the best performance of the race, changing McQueen's tires in record time, proving once again that everyone, no matter how small, has an important part to play in a Lasseter film.

With *Cars,* just as in *Toy Story* and *A Bug's Life,* the central character is not the only one to learn from others. In this highly structural and ethical universe, McQueen makes a huge impact on the sleepy town of eccentric vehicles, and his presence forces Doc Hudson to face his past and move on (figure 20). After McQueen's sacrifice of the race title to help the battered Dinoco King cross the finish line, *Cars* ends with an extended epilogue, especially lengthy by Pixar standards. In the final sequence, Radiator Springs is rediscovered by tourists, Sally and McQueen are reunited for good, and Doc teaches McQueen another a trick or two on the dirt track. By the resolution, McQueen's taming echoes some of the trajectory of Woody and Buzz. According to Ken Gillam and Shannon Wooden, *Toy Story* and *Cars* culminate in offering a New Man model and signal a new era in animated masculinity: though Woody, Buzz, and McQueen "strive for alpha-male identity, they face emasculating failures." Eventually they all participate in a sort of homosocial development, and "finally they achieve (and teach) a kinder, gentler understanding of what it means to be a man" (Gillam and Wooden 3). There is a sense of loss but also resignation in the films. Moreover, during the end titles, Pixar offers a touching tribute to Joe Ranft, Lasseter's close friend and collaborator, who had died during the summer of 2005, ironically, in a tragic automobile accident. *Cars* was

Figure 20: Mater and Doc Hudson; *Cars.*

dedicated to Ranft, and he is listed as codirector alongside John Lasseter. Despite the film's many jokes—"He did what in his cup?!"—and clever references to previous Pixar films, a palpable sense of nostalgia permeates *Cars*. That theme of loss is reinforced with the dedication to Joe Ranft. The repeated refrain, "There's a lot more to racing than winning," proves central to *Cars* on many levels.

Admittedly, in contrast to the *Toy Story* franchise, and the expressive insects of *A Bug's Life*, the vehicles of *Cars* remain more like computer-game avatars than engaging, embodied characters. Shot/reverse shot conversations between vehicles tend not to be as lively as those between toys or insects, where close-up facial features deliver much of the emotional impact. In some ways, *Cars*'s story resembled an extended episode of a public television show for kids, with characters talking through their predicaments and learning to trust others along the way. When the cars speak, the pace is slowed. But if *Cars* is weighed down somewhat by its heavy reliance on musical sequences and moralizing, which left some critics bemoaning its tangents and sluggish rhythm, its sequel, *Cars 2* (2011), codirected by Lasseter and Brad Lewis, offers a much more fast-paced, even childish romp. In this second installment, Lasseter shifts much of the narrative attention to Mater and the theme of friendship.

Set in a wide array of locations, *Cars 2* employs a rather convoluted plot in which a billionaire invents a revolutionary alternative, nonfossil fuel and hosts a series of races in Tokyo, Italy, and London to showcase its value. However, he and a bunch of disgruntled "lemon" cars, including Pacers and Gremlins, secretly conspire to sabotage their own fuel because they have discovered a new untapped oil field in the ocean. British spy cars, voiced by Emily Mortimer and Michael Caine, get involved, and everyone on both sides mistakes the rusty old Mater as an undercover spy with a clever cover as an idiot rusty truck. Mortimer's Holley Shiftwell replaces Sally as the lone active female character. McQueen's biggest challenges are his racing duels with Italian Francesco Bernouili (John Turturro) and learning not to be embarrassed by Mater. As the *Guardian* review observes, however, "Mater finds himself at the centre of this new movie, out of his depth and emotionally vulnerable. He is the star, but doesn't have really anything funny or interesting to say or do." They found the tale disappointing and not at all up to expectations of a Pixar story (Bradshaw).

The plot unfolds as an alternating series of scenes, with fast-paced chase and action sequences and then long conversations to help explain rapidly changing events and character motivations. Thematically, it also includes many mistaken-identity moments, disguises, and all sorts of surveillance, though its position on renewable fuel gets lost with each new plot reversal. Plus, the spy cars have a number of *Mission: Impossible* and James Bond sorts of special abilities and features, though it is unclear whether they sometimes forget that they can fly like jets or turn into submarines. Even Mater gets a pair of secret machine guns, jet engines, and a parachute that allows him to tow McQueen across the London skyline (plate 16). By the ending, the accidental hero Mater is knighted by the Rolls Royce Queen before returning happily to Radiator Springs with McQueen and his proud community of cars, in a script that lacks the usual poignant Pixar characterization. The characters have little time to develop a specific emotional style in this sequel, much less make any personal discoveries that allow growth or new understandings of the world around them.

The *Cars 2* visual style is also much more overtly cartoonal in its mise-en-scène, with the cars often appearing more rubbery than metallic, fitting an overall concept that is clearly aimed at a younger audience than *Cars*. These changes appealed to the *San Francisco Chronicle*'s Mick LaSalle: "This time out the cars no longer seem so earthbound, so locked into being heavy hunks of metal that can barely touch. The cars, as physical entities, have been reconceived as more pliable and interactive" ("*Cars 2*"). The background locations are less realistic and concrete as well. The international settings are 3D postcard versions of famous cities and their landmarks, "with buildings, windows, and archways redrawn to suggest grilles, bumpers, and headlights" (Osmond 57). City squares feature automotive fountains, and the ancient buildings are even equipped with automobile-shaped gargoyles. Where *Toy Story, A Bug's Life,* and even *Cars* offered compelling new perspectives on intricate three-dimensional spaces, *Cars 2* provides comic book-inspired compositions and frenetic mobile framing.

By moving the story beyond the American Southwest, with races and varied escapades taking place in Japan and across Europe, Pixar managed to generate increased interest globally with its sequel as well. *Cars 2* earned three times as much in Japan as the original. *Variety*'s Justin Chang observed that "[t]his time, Lasseter abandons Route 66 nostalgia to deliver a giddily escapist action-thriller that moves too swiftly and assuredly for the viewer to do anything but sit back and enjoy the ride . . . not a frame goes by where you can't hear Lasseter's inner child squealing with pleasure." Roger Ebert also found pleasure in *Cars 2,* which rekindled childhood memories of playing with toy cars on his bedroom floor. That Proustian recollection was "inspired by the spirit of John Lasseter's movie. I believe in some sense, the great animator was sitting Indian-style on the floor of his Pixar playroom and hurtling his cars through time and space with sublime reckless delight. We learned from *Cars* that Lasseter loves automobiles, and here we learn that they can serve him as avatars in an international racing-and-spying thriller as wacky as a Bond picture crossed with Daffy Duck" (Ebert, Rev. of *Cars 2*). *Cars 2* evokes a childish world, recalling playful Matchbox-car adventures and giddy fantasies of exotic voyages and dangerous encounters in some audiences.

Others were less impressed with *Cars 2* and its frenetic generic mashup, especially in light of the huge hit of *Toy Story 3* (dir. Lee Unkrich, 2010), which proved much more emotionally engaging. The *Village Voice* found *Cars 2* to be "stuck in neutral" (Schager), while the normally supportive *Cahiers du Cinéma* announced that the film confirmed the fears of many that Pixar may be slipping into a disappointing Disneyfication of their stories (Malausa 56). *Cars 2* felt closer to a DreamWorks product than a Pixar film to such critics. Interestingly, the *Wall Street Journal*'s Joe Morgenstern proved most cynical about the commercialism and weaker plot of *Cars 2*:

> In the five years since *Cars* was released, the movie has sold something in the neighborhood of $10 billion in merchandise—cute little cars, trucks and other vehicles that keep rolling off the toymakers' assembly lines in epic numbers. To sustain such financial numbers—and to pave the way for next summer's opening of a 12-acre Cars Land at Disney's California Adventure Park—Pixar and Disney . . . needed a hard-sell crowd-pleaser . . . *Cars 2*. This is something new for Pixar, a movie in which characterization and deep feelings take a back seat to breakneck pace, and something new for Pixar lovers, including me, who may find themselves wondering if Disney's master merchandisers are starting to call the tune for Pixar's master storytellers.

Such critical complaints about the rambling story and overt commercial motivations were routinely blamed on the corporate level, with some reviewers openly asking how John Lasseter could allow himself to be drawn in to such a venture. *Sight and Sound* even complained that it was Pixar's "least feature to date" and "inferior to any of the other big computer cartoons released in the past few months (*Tangled, Rango, Rio, Kung Fu Panda 2*)" (Osmond 57). Despite its British locations, *The Guardian*'s reviewer Philip French agreed, "This 3D animated movie does not show the formidable Pixar team at its best. . . . It is flat-footed stuff" (French, "*Cars 2*").

While not a huge hit, *Cars 2* earned nearly two hundred million dollars in its American first-run and raised an impressive $368 million at the foreign box office, though this seemed a bit disappointing to some, given that *Toy Story 3* had earned well over one billion dollars and nothing but rave reviews the previous year. Nonetheless, the *Cars* franchise remains a very personal project to Lasseter, and he plans to write and direct *Cars 3*, as well as *Toy Story 4*. The demanding Pixar production schedule, with overlapping feature-film products and franchise properties, continues in a highly successful series that is now synchronized with Disney's output and slate of films as well. Sequels obviously function to expand the economic and narrative lives of their presold stories, reinvigorating the value of the characters for Disney parks, games, and other ancillary products. For Pixar, they also help provide a strategy to maintain full employment during all the various stages of production for these presold product lines.

Though Pixar and Lasseter continually emphasize the big-happy-family aspects of their vast corporation, some of the central themes in the Pixar story are problematic. Lasseter repeatedly mentions having faith in everyone's input and allowing the creative minds at Pixar to follow their instincts, yet often key writing and directing personnel have been removed or forced to share their duties. Brenda Chapman, who initially wrote the story for *Brave* (2012), was replaced as director by Mark Andrews; Steve Purcell was codirector. That the woman who initiated the story project was removed and a male director put in her place generated a good deal of public attention. Ironically, or fittingly, *Brave* won the Academy Award for best animated feature, making Chapman the first woman ever to receive that Oscar. Unfortunately for Pixar, by that point she had left to return to DreamWorks. Ultimately, she complained about the hierarchy and culture of Pixar and argued that DreamWorks offers more creative freedom. As she told the *New York Times,* "At Pixar, it's all John's show" (qtd. in Barnes). Amid Amidi cautioned that if Lasseter's micromanagement was motivating Chapman and a few others to migrate from Pixar and Disney "to DreamWorks for its liberal creative environment . . . the times they are a-changin" (Amidi, "Brenda Chapman"). Moreover, from 2010 on, the U.S. Justice Department has been investigating illegal strategies by Pixar, Disney, DreamWorks, and others to repress wages and discourage poaching of employees at one another's studios. The press, however, does not seem comfortable investigating Ed Catmull and John Lasseter the same way they might target other seemingly ruthless producers. Pixar continues to benefit from a great deal of good faith within popular culture.

Another embarrassing concern for Pixar was the series of production delays for *The Good Dinosaur* project. Originally scheduled for 2014, *The Good Dinosaur* saw a change in director similar to that of *Toy Story 2.* Bob Peterson was completely replaced by his codirector Peter Sohn. The change involved revisiting the script and disrupted the planned 2014 release. The lack of a fall 2014 Pixar feature led to the layoff of fifty employees, though *The Good Dinosaur* was placed on the calendar for a late 2015 premiere, making that year rare with two features released. *Inside Out* (dir. Pete Docter and Ronaldo Del Carmen, 2015) was their summer film event. Both these instances, however, reveal the high stakes involved in each new feature project and remind us that the mythologies built around Pixar's business strategies and Lasseter are in large part the product of their publicity machines. For instance, when the *Huffington Post,* like many news sources, reported that Peterson had been removed from *The Good Dinosaur* for creative reasons, they calmed fears and reassured their readers: "No replacement has been named for Peterson, but that's almost academic: Pixar will use its brain trust to work on the film, a group of studio elders, like Pixar CEO John Lasseter, who are familiar with the ins and outs of production at the animation powerhouse" ("Bob Peterson"). Pixar and Disney, like all major brands, are quick to respond to any sort of story that might tarnish their reputations or sow doubts about their purported core values. Moreover, Lasseter's name is still the mark of quality in the popular press, and his stature metonymically covers over both vast corporations.

Separating John Lasseter as director out from John Lasseter as animator, writer, and producer has become as pointless as it is impossible by this point in his career. Lasseter has been at the core of character animation and storytelling and marketing of Pixar films and the Pixar brand since the beginning, and his influence continues to permeate every project they undertake. Lasseter's guidance and input as executive producer have also shaped Disney's feature-length animation, from *Meet the Robinsons* and *Bolt* (dir. Byron Howard and Chris Williams, 2008), right up to *Frozen* (dir. Chris Buck and Jennifer Lee, 2014). While this book has concentrated on Lasseter's contributions to the rise and establishment of Pixar's storytelling and style, subsequent studies should investigate his role as mentor and chief creative officer throughout Pixar and Disney's many short and feature productions. Clearly, Lasseter's input and status continue to grow at an impressive pace.

Already, by 2004, Steve Jobs and John Lasseter were listed as Hollywood's most powerful deal makers by *Premiere* magazine. With Walt Disney Company's $7.4 billion purchase of Pixar in 2006, Lasseter's significance for American film production only accelerated. He became the most influential person in international animation. In 2011, John

Lasseter was honored by *Variety* with their Creative Leadership Award and labeled "the World's Greatest Boss" (Blair; DeBruges). More than ever, Lasseter stands as the representative figure for Pixar and even computer animation in America. However, Pixar should not be reduced to just one person, or even the central cadre of Catmull, Lasseter, Docter, Stanton, and Unkrich. Pixar is a complex corporation with hundreds of active participants. As Alvy Ray Smith explains, "Lasseter is an astonishing talent." But, he adds, "[i]t is a mistake to isolate Lasseter away from the technically creative people he depends on" ("Re: Questions").

Nonetheless, no other single person at Pixar, or perhaps in American film production at large, has managed consistently to earn the sort of praise and box-office revenue that John Lasseter has achieved over the past thirty years. In 2006, *Entertainment Weekly*'s story on Lasseter and Pixar was titled "The Man Who Could Save Animation," as if animation were about to topple over the brink into extinction without him (Daly). Lasseter has also become one of the most vocal and visible advocates for computer animation as a genre and medium. In 2010, when there were concerns over the fragile economy's effect on Hollywood and the box office, Lasseter reassured *Newsweek* that movies remained an inexpensive form of family entertainment and that "animation is the one type of movie that really does play for the entire audience. Our challenge is to make stories that connect for kids and adults" (qtd. in Yabroff).

With the merger, Lasseter also brought a sense of reassurance to Disney, its employees, and its investors, promising continuity as well as an adherence to both studios' histories and visions: "Ed and I both say, the test is to make both studios a big success—to make movies that are really, really fun and entertaining. And emotional. And of course you want them to do well at the box office. You wanna make sure they are profitable so you can carry on doing what you want to do and make sure everyone is creatively inspired and fairly compensated" (Day). John Lasseter may well be the most important animator-writer-director-producer in history, though he repeatedly tries to play the humble role of just an average guy hard at work to bring us all entertaining stories. With his deferential, playful persona, he presents himself as a family man as much as a company man. And he is a good-natured joker for the Pixar publicity machine. "When he first appeared on a power list many years ago, ranked 35, he said then that must make his wife, Nancy, No. 34" (Athorne).

Throughout his career, Lasseter has acknowledged his desire to balance his corporate and creative responsibilities with his private life. In the press, he openly forges personal connections to each title, making parallels and analogies with his own life and especially with being a parent. When *A Bug's Life* was about to open in theaters, he declared, "I always equate it to having a child and then raising it. At a certain point, your son or daughter graduates from high school and goes to college. You give them to the world and hope that you did okay. That's very much like these movies. When we get to the release date, we realize that the movie doesn't belong to us anymore. It belongs to the world and you just hope that you did okay" (qtd. in Lyons). Not only is this a great marketing strategy, entrusting the audience to help keep watch over the progress of Pixar's nearly personified features, but this sort of quote also reveals his self-promotion as a compassionate, familial fellow entrusting his characters to us. He often sounds as if he actually lived in a *Toy Story* world. Yet surprisingly, especially for someone who is such a family man, Lasseter has included relatively few references to traditional parents and families in his feature films. The toys, insects, and cars all form new cooperative communities to replace the nuclear family; they are not temporary sanctuaries or inadequate substitutes. Perhaps the most pertinent models for Lasseter's fictional worlds are the sorts of cohorts of animators he found in film school and his fellow creative friends and colleagues at Pixar. Lasseter's films valorize a collaborative culture for their residents and the resulting close-knit respectful community that allows everyone to thrive.

Among Lasseter's most impressive legacies are the sorts of character animation and storytelling that came to distinguish Pixar. From the beginning, when he developed André as a clownish figure rather than a conventional robotic spaceman, Lasseter melded the world of CGI with classical Disney animation principles. The best of CGI characters owe to this synthesis. Eric Herhuth points out that computer animation contributes to posthuman culture because "the illusion of life relies on external, visible markers to denote the invisible, ephemeral qualities of personality and vitality. . . . Pixar films can be considered a primary means for audiences to acclimate to the technologies of today and the future" (63). Catmull, Smith, Lasseter, and their initial Pixar team helped bridge computer graphics, commercial storytelling, and character animation in ways that inserted their work within a larger tendency in culture formation. Paul Wells insightfully notes that John Lasseter in particular "recognized that if an intrinsically American art-form was to speak to its own history, its own progress and its own place in contemporary Hollywood, it would once more have to speak to the dilemmas at the heart of American culture" (Wells, *Animation,* 149). By integrating the worlds of Disney character animation with computer graphics and commercial tales embedded with a popular nostalgia, Lasseter and Pixar have helped create an immensely dynamic and engaging medium. Pixar's characters are as familiar as they are original, and thus highly compelling. As Andrew Darley observes, Pixar's figures become significant thanks to the combination of codes of live-action narrative cinema with the codes of animated cartoons, as well as "a naturalism based on illusionism, and the result is a new sort of ambiguity in its figures. Are they more like puppets, cartoons, or live action?" (Darley 84). They are indeed a new form of embodied cartoonal figures that mix caricature, realism, and technology.

John Lasseter successfully negotiated daunting administrative hurdles as he combined his talents to become an animator, director, and producer, struggling all along to help maintain the aesthetic and economic survival of Pixar. While all directors have the huge task of getting their current films profitably completed so as to continue their ongoing auteurist careers, Lasseter bears the rare responsibility of writing and/or directing his own films while simultaneously watching over the continued economic and aesthetic vitality of Pixar and Disney Studios Animation. In many ways, he actually exceeds the role played by Walt Disney, since Disney did not write and direct feature films. Like Disney, John Lasseter has now become a brand name, but he also protects, along with Ed Catmull, two larger corporate brand names. Thus, he far exceeds the conventional role of the commercial director, even more that of the individual cinema auteur. For better or worse, Lasseter is personally identified with the engaging themes, characters, and styles churned out by Pixar Studios, regardless of who finally wrote, directed, or animated the films. He has been granted a rare sort of auteurist function and reputation by Pixar and Disney, as well as the general public. Even though Ed Catmull, Alvy Ray Smith, and their original team of graphics technicians did most of the initial heavy lifting to launch Pixar and put it on the map, John Lasseter stands alongside Luxo Jr. as a representative icon for what is a complex, highly capitalized, and deeply loved string of motion pictures that changed the landscape of animation forever and ever.

Interview with John Lasseter |

This interview by Denis Rossano° was originally published in French at the time of the release of *The Incredibles* and reveals many of the recurring motifs, anecdotes, and insights pertinent to Pixar and John Lasseter. Further, it provides a condensed and revealing glimpse into some of Lasseter's perspectives on his career and computer animation by 2004. Translated by Richard Neupert.

* * *

He was named the most powerful person in Hollywood by *Premiere* magazine, ahead of Steven Spielberg, Tom Cruise, and all the others. At age forty-seven, the soul of Pixar and father of *Toy Story, Monsters, Inc., Finding Nemo,* and most recently *The Incredibles,* all films he directed

° Denis Rossano, "Chez Pixar, nous sommes tous des enfants" (At Pixar, we are all kids), *L'Express* 2785 (November 22, 2004): 70–73. (Copyright obligatoire © Denis Rossano / lexpress.fr / 22.11.2004)

or produced, transforms everything he touches into gold and dollar bills. After an underwhelming time at Disney, John Lasseter landed at Lucasfilm in the early 1980s, where he understood that the future of animation would be given over to digital imagery. He was in the minority but held tight to his vision. In 1986, when Steve Jobs, the founder of Apple, bought the newly baptized Pixar division, Lasseter followed him. Ten years later, when *Toy Story* became a worldwide triumph, his ambitions were realized. If the jovial, talkative Lasseter admits to being obsessed by his art, he is just as obsessed by his work ethic.

DENIS ROSSANO: It is no exaggeration to say that Pixar, just born in 1986, has revolutionized animated cinema. How did this adventure get started?

JOHN LASSETER: The evolution of animation has unfolded in a number of stages. When Walt Disney began working in the 1930s, a single idea guided him: produce and direct films that he himself wanted to see. They were stories aimed at adults as well as children. But he was not alone. Over at Warner Bros., Chuck Jones [the creator of Bugs Bunny and Daffy Duck cartoons], one of my mentors, considered his career as addressing almost exclusively an adult audience. Everything changed with the rapid expansion of television during the 1960s. Initially, animation was also aimed at adults and therefore presented during the evenings, with *The Jetsons* and *The Flintstones*. But rapidly cartoons were programmed increasingly for children late in the afternoons and Saturday mornings. Animation was now only directed at a young audience. The result, not unexpectedly, was a rapid decline in the genre. When I began to work at Disney in the late 1970s, we were far away from the golden age.

DR: But, little by little, the genre regained its value.

JL: For me, the second turning point arrived in 1977, thanks to George Lucas and *Star Wars*. It made me realize that no other film had ever managed to entertain such a wide audience. With this movie, Lucas managed to rebuild a connection between the generations. This was a revelation for me, and I immediately wanted to do the same thing within animated cinema. I was not the only one to feel this change, since after the doldrums of the 1960s and 1970s, *Who Framed Roger Rabbit, The Little Mermaid, Beauty and the Beast*, and *The Lion King* all appeared.

The genre had been relaunched. At Pixar, we openly played the same card with *Toy Story* in 1994, offering animation that did not exclude any portion of the audience.

DR: Yet, from *Toy Story* to *Finding Nemo,* childhood pretty much remains the principal theme of your work.

JL: True. This work lets me remain the child I was. As an adolescent, I had a secret: I continued to love to play with my old toys. Plus, as soon as I got home from high school in the afternoon I rushed to the television to watch cartoons. At that time, I never admitted it to anyone for fear of looking ridiculous, but once I started to study at CalArts I was happy to discover that I had not been alone in my passion. At Pixar and elsewhere, we are all a bunch of kids who never really grew up. My office is filled with toys from floor to ceiling.

DR: Let's discuss your work in detail. How do you go about constructing this trademark universe of yours?

JL: The story is always at the heart of each of our projects. It determines everything, including the characters. But to really set it off—and this may be what makes us different—we create a world where every element can develop. The universe for *The Incredibles,* for instance, can be summed up with a single word: "cool." That setting allows us to propel the story in the right direction. We work up what we call a "color script," which then helps us create the emotional palette for the story and establishes a parallel between the overall aesthetics and the psychology of the characters. We never set out to make the universe of our films realistic, but we do want it to be credible. Nothing should bother the spectators or remind them that what they are looking at went through computers.

DR: But technological progress surely will not stop. . . .

JL: Undoubtedly. One does not hear engineers declaring, "That's it. It is over. There will never be a computer chip faster than this one." Of course not. Nonetheless, we never begin a film by saying "Okay, what new technology will we be able to invent?" The story, which is our point of departure, often contains some elements that we do not yet know how to show on the screen. At that point, we consider ways to get there. Thus, the story is always the driving engine, but the technology stimulates us. The art challenges the technology, and for its part, technology inspires the art. It is a marvelous balancing act.

DR: Pixar has earned a reputation as an animation studio that is in a class of its own. What accounts for this difference?

JL: It is very simple. Pixar is the only studio managed by creative people. Everywhere else it is administrative types who choose the projects, decide on the director, and decide how the film will be made. With us, this is not the case. Our success has allowed us to gain our autonomy, and as a result no bureaucrat gets in the way. This process is also one of our founding principles. All our colleagues are passionate about animation and do not want to do anything else. Here, the directors are surrounded by teams that want to help them, support them, and criticize them when necessary. At Pixar, I want to work with artists who carry a story and a universe inside. It is up to me to give them the means to succeed.

Obviously, an ongoing dialogue is necessary. As vice president of creative development, I am there to protect them, but also to speak with them if something is not going right. There are no egos with us! In fact, Pixar resembles the group of passionate young animators that were taught at CalArts, where I also went to school. Nothing mattered besides animation.

DR: Seen from the outside, Pixar looks like a refuge for unconventional talent who possess a personal vision of their art.

JL: You can see it that way. In my mind, Brad Bird, the author of *The Incredibles* [and director of *The Iron Giant*], is very representative of this sort of personal vision. We had met at CalArts in 1975, in our first year of study, in a course titled "Character Animation," which has now become essential for anyone studying animation. All the important animators today have taken it. Brad's passion for his art always impressed me. He does not accept any compromises. The only thing that matters for him is the quality of the work. Hollywood does not always function by those standards. When he and I were working at Disney, this was the era of *The Fox and the Hound* [1981], I could tell Brad was very frustrated. I left to work at Lucasfilm, and then Pixar was created. I always wanted Brad to join us. I knew he would feel at home there. Now, it is a done deal. He does not have any manager looking over his shoulder. He had never before experienced these conditions.

DR: What motivates you today to keep moving still further ahead?

JL: One of the philosophies at Pixar is to give our employees the opportunity to work on projects they can be proud of. Just recently in Sonoma, where I live, I met a family who spoke with a great deal of emotion about their grandmother, who had been one of the colorists on *Snow White and the Seven Dwarfs*. This really touched me. I hope the same thing will happen for us at Pixar.

Another trait that is specific to Pixar is that we are the only studio that does not hire its animators on short-term contracts. I want to surround myself with people who want to work with us rather than those that must work with us. Our animators could probably earn more money elsewhere and have more time off, but they would surely not have as much creative freedom. One aspect of my job is to verify that what we do reaches the highest standard of quality possible. This is why we systematically search out that which has never before been accomplished. This goal may require greater investments, but it is also infinitely more satisfying.

DR: Do you think that animation is a reflection of its era in the same way as any other movie?

JL: Whether we are artists or filmmakers, we all live in the same world today, we all know what is going on, and that certainly has an influence on the ways we treat any given subject. I do not think any of our films are overtly political, but there is always a certain degree of reality in our stories. In *The Incredibles,* for instance, we touch on some problems specific to American society, like the proliferation of legal trials, which really can lead to abuses. Thus our super hero is prosecuted for saving a guy who did not want to be rescued. The other theme, which runs through the film from end to end, was inspired by Nelson Mandela's inaugural address when he was elected president of South Africa. He declared that one should not be jealous of those who have a particular talent or hinder their advances; rather, we should instead encourage them so they might teach us. That said, we want to create films that can touch all generations and are timeless. Therefore, we avoid jokes that are tied specifically to our era, to politics, or a precise social situation. Instead, we strive to develop humor that is born from our characters, their interactions with others, or the emotions they experience. That is what makes stories endure. I like to imagine that our grandchildren will enjoy these films with just as much pleasure as today's audiences.

DR: Now that we understand more about how you work, what, for you, are the qualities for a good animation artist?

JL: A good artist is above all a good observer. This is one of the essential things instilled in us by the veterans at Disney when we were still apprentices. Everywhere they went they carried drawing pads, and their eyes stopped every second on some special detail. Much of what you see on the screen—motions, character behavior, various events—come from what was seen in daily life. This brings us back to what I said at the beginning: these powers of observation are linked to a child's sense of wonder. And, in particular, this allows us to show the spectators something that seems familiar but that they never saw done in this manner. In *Toy Story,* this involved re-creating for adults the toys they themselves had played with as children, by telling the inner lives of those objects. For *The Incredibles,* Brad seized upon an overexploited genre in Hollywood, the super-hero film, but he completely reexamined and renewed it by inventing a very ordinary family, including a father with a boring job and a housewife raising their squabbling son and daughter. Any family can identify. The core idea, which refers back to the Mandela speech, consists of imagining children with extraordinary abilities, though they have never been able to put them to use. From there, Brad created an unreal universe and made it real by inserting part of his own childhood and, undoubtedly, that of the audience, including a passion for all these films of the 1960s with secret agents, spies, or gangsters who live in fantastic and supercool places. The island where our super hero's enemy lives is a good example. There is a detail here that is typical of Brad's sense of humor and precision. The island is called Nomanisan, for "no man is an island." This is typical of Brad; he loves these sorts of playful ideas.

DR: Another distinctive feature of Pixar is that its headquarters are located outside San Francisco, and your work space has become famous for its open atrium in the center, where one can see employees getting around on roller skates, and the offices are decorated in rather fantastic ways. To what extent is this architecture representative of your work philosophy?

JL: We are based near San Francisco because Pixar was born at Lucasfilm, George Lucas's studio, whose headquarters is based in that area. That said, I am sure that one of the factors in our success is our relative distance from Hollywood. The daily life of the people working here does not revolve around cinema. None of my friends outside work belongs to the film industry. This allows us to stay in touch with reality, and as a result, with our real public.

As for our building, I call it "the Steve Jobs movie," because he was the one who designed it, and its construction took as long as the making of one of our feature films. Initially, we were housed in separate buildings, and each one seemed to have its own culture. There was little communication. When we bought the land at Emeryville, we first considered creating a studio based on the old model, with a number of bungalows. But that would give the impression of a number of various companies. Then Steve decided to reunite the group in a single building, and since all of them worked individually on their own computer, which amounted to their only work partner, he conceived of this central hall that one must systematically cross to get a coffee, check the mail, go to a meeting, or head to a screening. Suddenly, everyone's paths crossed. I am convinced that this way of life has a beneficial impact on our work.

DR: Your work is constantly praised. But do you have the impression that you have been adequately recognized as artists?

JL: Not as much as I would have hoped. One of the first things that you are supposed to learn in animation classes is that the individual drawing has no value; it is only a means of inspiration. For *The Incredibles* we made some twenty-five thousand rough drawings before constructing the story and arriving at a satisfying final result. Well, that does not prevent these drawings from being magnificent! For Pixar's twentieth birthday, I hope to launch an exhibit that will demonstrate his aspect of our work to the general public. Animation should be truly creative and magical, but it continues to be undervalued. When *Toy Story* became the number-one film of 1995, people said to me, "That's good, now you can direct a real movie with real actors." We still have not gained the respect we deserve.

Directed by John Lasseter

Short Films

Lady and the Lamp (1979)
Production: California Institute of the Arts
Direction, Story, and Animation: John Lasseter
Music: Norman Sholin
Voices: Jack Hannah, Nancy Bieman
4 min.; black and white

Nitemare (1980)
Production: California Institute of the Arts
Direction, Story, and Animation: John Lasseter
5 min.; black and white

André and Wally B (1984)
Production: Lucasfilm
Direction and Concept: Alvy Ray Smith
Animation: John Lasseter, Tom Duff, Eben Ostby
Sound: Ben Burtt
Visual Effects: Loren Carpenter, Ed Catmull, Don Conway, Rob Cook, Tom Duff, Sam Leffler, Tom Noggle, Thomas Porter, William Reeves, David Salesin, Alvy Ray Smith
2 min.; color, digital

Luxo Jr. (1986)
Production: Pixar Animation Studios
Producers: John Lasseter and William Reeves
Direction and Story: John Lasseter

Sound Design: Gary Rydstrom
Visual Effects: Don Conway, Paul Heckbert, John Lasseter, Sam Leffler, Eben
 Ostby, William Reeves
2 min.; color, digital

Red's Dream (1987)
Production: Pixar Animation Studios
Direction and Story: John Lasseter
Sound Design: Gary Rydstrom
Music: David Slusser
Visual Effects: Don Conway, Eben Ostby, William Reeves
4 min.; color, digital

Tin Toy (1988)
Production: Pixar Animation Studios
Producer: William Reeves
Direction and Story: John Lasseter
Sound Design: Gary Rydstrom
Animation Department: Craig Good, John Lasseter, Eben Ostby, William Reeves
5 min.; color, digital

Knick Knack (1989)
Production: Pixar Animation Studios
Direction and Story: John Lasseter
Music: Bobby McFerrin
Sound Design: Gary Rydstrom
Animation Department: Eben Ostby, William Reeves, Ralph Guggenheim,
 Craig Good, Don Conway, Flip Phillips, Yael Miló, Tony Apodaca, Deirdre
 Warin
4 min.; color, digital

Tokyo Mater (2008)
Production: Pixar Animation Studios
Producer: Kori Rae
Direction: John Lasseter, Rob Gibbs, Victor Navone
Story: Scott Morse
Music: BT
Film Editing: Torbin Xan Bullock
Production Design: Anthony Christov
Voice Cast: Larry the Cable Guy (Mater), Keith Ferguson (Lightning
 McQueen), Michael Wallis (Sheriff), Mach Tony Kobayashi (Kabuto),
 Robert Ito (Ito-San)
7 min.; color, digital

Feature Films

Toy Story (1995)
Production: Pixar Animation Studios
Producers: Bonnie Arnold, Ed Catmull, Ralph Guggenheim, Steve Jobs
Direction: John Lasseter
Original Story: John Lasseter, Pete Docter, Andrew Stanton, Joe Ranft
Screenplay: Joss Whedon, Andrew Stanton, Joel Cohen, Alec Sokolow
Music: Randy Newman
Sound Design: Gary Rydstrom
Editing: Robert Gordon and Lee Unkrich
Art Direction: Ralph Eggleston
Voice Cast: Tom Hanks (Woody), Tim Allen (Buzz Lightyear), Don Rickles
(Mr. Potato Head), Jim Varney (Slinky Dog), Wallace Shawn (Rex), John
Ratzenberger (Hamm), Annie Potts (Bo Peep), John Morris (Andy), Erik von
Detten (Sid), Laurie Metcalf (Mrs. Davis), R. Lee Ermey (Sergeant), Sarah
Freeman (Hannah), Penn Jillette (TV Announcer)
81 min.; color, digital

A Bug's Life (1998)
Production: Pixar Animation Studios
Producers: Darla K. Anderson, Kevin Reher
Direction: John Lasseter, Andrew Stanton
Original Story: John Lasseter, Andrew Stanton, Joe Ranft
Screenplay: Andrew Stanton, Don McEnery, Bob Shaw
Music: Randy Newman
Sound Design: Gary Rydstrom
Cinematography: Sharon Calahan
Editing: Lee Unkrich
Production Design: William Cone
Art Direction: Tia W. Kratter, Bob Pauley
Voice Cast: Dave Foley (Flik), Kevin Spacey (Hopper), Julia Louis-Dreyfus
(Atta), Hayden Panettiere (Dot), Phyllis Diller (Queen), Richard Kind (Molt),
David Hyde Pierce (Slim), Joe Ranft (Heimlich), Denis Leary (Francis), Jona-
than Harris (Manny), Madeline Kahn (Gypsy Moth), Bonnie Hunt (Rosie),
Michael McShane (Tuck/Roll), John Ratzenberger (P. T. Flea), Brad Gar-
ret (Dim), Roddy McDowall (Soil), Edie McClurg (Dr. Flora), Alex Rocco
(Thorny), David Ossman (Cornelius), John Lasseter (Bug Zapper Bug No. 1),
Andrew Stanton (Bug Zapper Bug No. 2)
95 min.; color, digital

Toy Story 2 (1999)
Production: Pixar Animation Studios

Producers: Sarah McArthur (Executive Producer), Karen Robert Jackson, Helene Plotkin
Direction: John Lasseter, Ash Brannon, Lee Unkrich
Original Story: John Lasseter, Pete Docter, Ash Bannon, Andrew Stanton
Screenplay: Andrew Stanton, Rita Hsiao, Doug Chamberlin, Chris Webb
Music: Randy Newman
Sound Design: Tom Myers
Cinematography: Sharon Calahan
Editing: Edie Bleiman Ichioka, David Ian Salter, Lee Unkrich
Production Design: William Cone, Jim Pearson
Voice Cast: Tom Hanks (Woody), Tim Allen (Buzz Lightyear), Joan Cusack (Jessie), Kelsey Grammar (Stinky Pete), Don Rickles (Mr. Potato Head), Jim Varney (Slinky Dog), Wallace Shawn (Rex), John Ratzenberger (Hamm), Annie Potts (Bo Peep), Wayne Knight (Al the Toy Collector), John Morris (Andy), Laurie Metcalf (Andy's Mom), Estelle Harris (Mrs. Potato Head), R. Lee Ermey (Army Sergeant), Jodi Benson (Barbie), Jonathan Harris (Geri the Cleaner), Joe Ranft (Wheezy the Penguin), Andrew Stanton (Evil Emperor Zurg)
92 min.; color, digital

Cars (2006)
Production: Pixar Animation Studios
Producers: Darla K. Anderson, Thomas Porter
Direction: John Lasseter, Joe Ranft
Original Story: John Lasseter, Joe Ranft, Jorgen Klubien
Screenplay: Dan Fogelman, John Lasseter, Joe Ranft, Kiel Murray, Phil Lorin, Jorgen Klubien
Music: Randy Newman
Cinematography: Jeremy Lasky
Film Editing: Ken Schretzmann
Production Design: William Cone, Bob Pauley
Voice Cast: Owen Wilson (Lightning McQueen), Paul Newman (Doc Hudson), Bonnie Hunt (Sally Carrera), Larry the Cable Guy (Mater), Cheech Marin (Ramone), Tony Shalhoub (Luigi), Guido Quaroni (Guido), Jenifer Lewis (Flo), Paul Dooley (Sarge), Michael Wallis (Sheriff), George Carlin (Filmore), Katherine Helmond (Lizzie), John Ratzenberger (Mack/Hamm Truck/Abominable Snow Plow), Joe Ranft (Red/Jerry Recycled Batteries/Peterbilt), Michael Keaton (Chick Hicks), Richard Petty (The King), Tom Magliozzi (Rusty Rust-eze), Ray Magliozzi (Dusty Rust-eze), Dale Earnhardt Jr. (Junior)
117 min.; color, digital

Abraham, Adam. *When Magoo Flew: The Rise and Fall of Animation Studio UPA.* Middletown, Conn.: Wesleyan University Press, 2012.

Ackerman, Alan. "The Spirit of Toys: Resurrection and Redemption in *Toy Story* and *Toy Story 2.*" *University of Toronto Quarterly* 74.4 (Fall 2005): 895–912.

Amidi, Amid. *The Art of Pixar Short Films.* San Francisco: Chronicle Books, 2009.

———. "Brenda Chapman Acccuses John Lasseter of Micromanagement." July 16, 2013; accessed May 25, 2015. http://www.cartoonbrew.com/pixar/brenda-chapman-acccuses-john-Lasseter-of-microman agement-85910.html.

———. *Cartoon Modern: Style and Design in Fifties Animation.* San Francisco: Chronicle Books, 2006.

Ansen, David. "Disney's Digital Delight." *Newsweek,* November 26, 1995; accessed June 22, 2014. http://www.newsweek.com/Disneys-digital-delight -181300

Arendt, Paul. Rev. of *Cars. BBC.* July 28, 2006; accessed December 22, 2014. http://www.bbc.co.uk/films/2006/07/12/cars_2006_review.shtml.

Artz, Lee. "Monarchy, Monsters, and Multiculturalism: Disney's Menu for Global Hierarchy." In *Rethinking Disney: Private Control, Public Dimensions.* Ed. Mike Budd and Max H. Kirsch. Middletown, Conn.: Wesleyan University Press, 2005. 75–98.

Athorne, Scott. "Me and My Big Mouse." *Sunday Times,* September 23, 2007.

Aubron, Hervé. *Génie de Pixar.* Nantes: Capricci, 2011.

Barker, Jennifer. *The Tactile Eye: Touch and the Cinematic Experience.* Berkeley: University of California Press, 2009.

Barnes, Brooks. "The Quiet Force behind DreamWorks." *New York Times,* July 15, 2013; accessed July 30, 2015. http://www.nytimes.com/2013/07/16/business/media/the-quiet-force-behind-dreamworks.html.

Barrier, Michael. *Hollywood Cartoons.* New York: Oxford University Press, 1999.

Beauchamp, Robin S. *Designing Sound for Animation.* New York: Focal Press, 2013.

Bernstein, Matthew. "The Producer as Auteur." In *Auteurs and Authorship.* Malden, Mass.: Blackwell, 2008. 180–89.

Blair, Iain. "The World's Greatest Boss: John Lasseter." *Variety,* October 10, 2011; accessed May 27, 2015. http://variety.com/2011/digital/news/world-s-greatest-boss-john-Lasseter-1118044118/.

Blatter, Jane. "Roughing It: A Cognitive Look at Animation Storyboarding." *Animation Journal* 15 (2007): 4–23.

"Bob Peterson No Longer Directing *The Good Dinosaur* for Pixar." *Huffington Post,* August 30, 2013; accessed May 25, 2015. http://www.huffingtonpost.com/2013/08/30/bob-peterson-good-dinosaur_n_3843748.html.

Booth, Cathy. "The Wizard of Pixar." *Time,* December 14, 1998, 100.

Bordwell, David. *Poetics of Cinema.* New York: Routledge, 2008.

Bordwell, David, and Kristin Thompson. *Minding Movies: Observations on the Art, Craft, and Business of Filmmaking.* Chicago: University of Chicago Press, 2011.

Bradshaw, Peter. Rev. of *Cars 2. The Guardian,* July 21, 2011; accessed June 1, 2015. http://www.theguardian.com/film/2011/jul/21/cars-2-review.

Buchan, Suzanne. Introduction to *Pervasive Animation.* Ed. Suzanne Buchan. New York: Routledge, 2013. 1–21.

Capodagli, Bill, and Lynn Jackson. *Innovate the Pixar Way.* New York: McGraw-Hill, 2010.

Catmull, Ed. *Crativity Inc.: Overcoming the Unseen Forces That Stand in the Way of True Inspiration.* New York: Random House, 2014.

Chang, Justin. Rev. of *Cars 2. Variety,* June 19, 2011; accessed December 29, 2014. http://variety.com/2011/film/reviews/cars-2-1117945476/.

Christensen, Per H., Julian Fong, David M. Laur, and Dana Batali. "Ray Tracing for the Movie *Cars.*" IEEE Symposium. September 18, 2006; accessed July 7, 2014. http://www.cs.cmu.edu/afs/cs/academic/class/15869-f11/www/readings/christensen07_cars.pdf.

Ciment, Gilles. "*Cars*: Born in the USA (Route 66)." *Positif* 544 (June 2006): 13–15.

"Computer Animation: Golden Nica *Red's Dream.*" *Ars Electronica.* 1988; accessed August 7, 2015. http://90.146.8.18/en/archives/prix_archive/prix_projekt.asp?iProjectID=2411.

Cooper, Ann. "Two Ad Campaigns for Health and Beauty Aids Profiled." *Adweek,* April 12, 1993, 41.

Crafton, Donald. *Shadow of a Mouse: Performance, Belief, and World-Making in Animation.* Berkeley: University of California Press, 2013.

Crawford, Alice. "The Digital Turn: Animation in the Age of Information Technologies." In *Prime-Time Animation: Television Animation and American Culture.* Ed. Carol A. Stabile and Mark Harrison. London: Routledge, 2003. 110–30.

Daly, James. "Hollywood 2.0." *Wired* 5.11 (November 1997): 200–215.

Daly, Steve. "The Man Who Could Save Animation." *Entertainment Weekly,* April 21, 2006; accessed July 30, 2015. http://www.ew.com/article/2006/04/21/man-who-could-save-animation.

Darley, Andrew. *Visual Digital Culture: Surface Play and Spectacle in New Media Genres.* London: Routledge, 2000.

Davidson, Richard J., and Sharon Begley. *The Emotional Life of Your Brain.* New York: Hudson Street Press, 2012.

Day, Aubrey. "Interview: John Lasseter." *Total Film,* June 3, 2009; accessed July 30, 2015. http://www.gamesradar.com/interview-john-Lasseter/.

DeBruges, Peter. "John Lasseter: Empower Player." *Variety,* October 10, 2011; accessed May 27, 2015. http://variety.com/2011/digital/news/john-Lasseter -empower-player-1118044116/.

Denis, Sébastien. *Le Cinéma d'animation.* Paris: Armand Colin, 2011.

Deutschman, Alan. *The Second Coming of Steve Jobs.* New York: Broadway Books, 2000.

DiOrio, Carl. "*Toy* Touted as History-Maker." *Hollywood Reporter,* August 10, 1995, 1.

Duchovnay, Gerald. *Film Voices: Interviews from Post Script.* Albany: State University of New York Press, 2004.

Dumm, Thomas. "Toy Stories: Downsizing American Masculinity." *Cultural Values* 1.1 (1997): 81–100.

Ebert, Roger. "Interview with Tom Wilhite." *Chicago Sun-Times,* July 18, 1982; accessed August 6, 2015. http://www.rogerebert.com/interviews/interview -with-tom-Wilhite.

———. Rev. of *Cars. Chicago Sun-Times,* June 8, 2006; accessed December 22, 2014. http://www.rogerebert.com/reviews/cars-2006.

———. Rev. of *Cars 2. Chicago Sun-Times,* June 22, 2011; accessed December 24, 2014. http://www.rogerebert.com/reviews/cars-2–2011.

———. Rev. of *Toy Story. Chicago Sun-Times,* November 22, 1995; accessed May 20, 2014. http://www.rogerebert.com/reviews/toy-story-1995.

———. Rev. of *Toy Story 2. Chicago Sun-Times,* November 24, 1999; accessed September 12, 2014. http://www.rogerebert.com/reviews/toy-story-2-1999.

———. Rev. of *Young Sherlock Holmes. Chicago Sun-Times,* December 4, 1985; accessed July 7, 2013. http://www.rogerebert.com/reviews/young-sherlock -holmes-1985.

Elsaesser, Thomas. "The New New Hollywood: Cinema beyond Distance and Proximity." In *Moving Images, Culture, and the Mind.* Ed. Ib Bondebjerg. Luton: University of Luton Press, 2000. 187–203.

Elsaesser, Thomas, and Malte Hagener. *Film Theory: An Introduction through the Senses.* New York: Routledge, 2010.

Everett, Anna, and John T. Caldwell. *New Media: Theories and Practices of Digitextuality.* New York: Routledge, 2003.

Faber, Liz, and Helen Walters. *Animation Unlimited: Innovative Short Films since 1940.* London: Laurence King, 2003.

Field, Syd. *Screenplay: The Foundations of Screenwriting.* New York: Delacorte, 1982.

French, Lawrence. "*Toy Story*: Walt Disney and Pixar Team Up to Launch the First Computer- Animated Movie." *Cinefantastique* 27.2 (1995): 17–37.

French, Philip. Rev. of *Cars 2*. *The Guardian,* July 23, 2011; accessed June 1, 2015. http://www.theguardian.com/film/2011/jul/24/cars2-review.

Furniss, Maureen. *Animation: Art and Industry.* New Barnet, U.K.: John Libbey, 2009.

———. *The Animation Bible.* New York: Abrams, 2008.

———. *Art in Motion: Animation Aesthetics.* Eastleigh, U.K.: John Libbey, 2007.

Gillam, Ken, and Shannon R. Wooden. "Post-Princess Models of Gender: The New Man in Disney/Pixar." *Journal of Popular Film and Television* 36.1 (2008): 2–8.

Gillespie, Tareleton. "The Stories Digital Tools Tell." In *New Media: Theories and Practices of Digitextuality.* Ed. Anna Everett and John T. Caldwell. New York: Routledge, 2003. 107–23.

Goldfisher, Alastair. "Pixar Goes Commercial." *Silicon Valley Business Journal,* November 24, 1996; accessed August 8, 2015. http://www.bizjournals.com/sanjose/stories/1996/11/25/newscolumn2.html.

Goldmark, Daniel, and Yuval Taylor, eds. *The Cartoon Music Book.* Chicago: A Cappella Books, 2002.

Goldrich, Robert. "Pixar Gives Conceptual CGI Fit to Levi's Mannequin." *Shoot* 35.33 (September 19, 1994): 12.

Grant, Catherine. "www.auteur.com?" *Screen* 41.1 (Spring 2000): 101–8.

Griffin, Sean. *Tinker Belles and Evil Queens: The Walt Disney Company from the Inside Out.* New York: New York University, 2000.

Grodal, Torben. *Embodied Visions: Evolution, Emotion, Culture, and Film.* New York: Oxford University Press, 2009.

Gunning, Tom. "'We Are Here and Not Here': Late Nineteenth-Century Stage Magic and the Roots of Cinema in the Appearance (and Disappearance) of the Virtual Image." In *A Companion to Early Cinema.* Ed. André Gaudreault, Nicolas Dulac, and Santiago Hidalgo. Malden, Mass.: Wiley-Blackwell, 2012. 52–63.

Gurevitch, Leon. "Computer Generated Animation as Product Design Engineered Culture, or Buzz Lightyear to the Sales Floor, to the Checkout and Beyond!" *Animation: An Interdisciplinary Journal* 7.2 (July 2012): 131–50.

Halberstam, Judith. *The Queer Art of Failure.* Durham, N.C.: Duke University Press, 2011.

Hearn, Marcus. *The Cinema of George Lucas.* New York: Harry N. Abrams, 2005.

Henne, Mark, Hal Hickel, Ewan Johnson, and Sonoko Konisi. "The Making of *Toy Story.*" *Proceedings of the COMPCON* (Spring 1996): 463–68.

Herhuth, Eric. "Life, Love, and Programming: The Culture and Politics of *Wall-E* and Pixar Computer Animation." *Cinema Journal* 53.4 (2014): 53–75.

Hilditch, Nick. Rev. of *Toy Story 2. BBC.* December 5, 2001; accessed August 22, 2014. http://www.bbc.co.uk/films/2001/12/05/toy_story_2_1999_review.shtml.

Hooks, Ed. *Acting for Animators.* New York: Routledge, 2011.
———. *Acting Strategies for the Cyber Age.* Portsmouth, N.H.: Heinemann, 2001.
"Inspiration for *Cars.*" *Cars.* DVD. Disney-Pixar, 2006. DVD.
Isaacson, Walter. *Steve Jobs.* New York: Simon and Schuster, 2011.
Johnson, Mark. *The Meaning of the Body: Aesthetics of Human Understanding.* Chicago: University of Chicago Press, 2007.
Jones, Catherine. *Introduction to the Chansons de Geste.* Gainesville: University of Florida Press, 2014.
Jones, Kent. "Beyond Disbelief." *Film Comment* 44.4 (July–August 2008): 22–26.
Kalmus, Herbert. "Technicolor Adventures in Cinemaland." *Journal of the Society of Motion Picture Engineers* 31.6 (December 1938): 564–84.
Kanfer, Stefan. *Serious Business: The Art and Commerce of Animation in America from Betty Boop to Toy Story.* New York: Da Capo, 2000.
Kanner, Bernice. "Imitation of Life." *New York,* September 10, 1990, 22–23.
Kaplan, David A. "High Tech in Toon Town." *Newsweek,* December 4, 1995, 54–56.
Kapur, Jyotsna. "Obsolescence and Other Playroom Anxieties: Childhood in the Shadows of Late Capitalism." *Rethinking Marxism* 17.2 (2005): 237–55.
Kempley, Rita. "Close Encounters of the 'Antz' Kind." *Washington Post,* October 2, 1998; accessed August 2, 2014. http://www.washingtonpost.com/wp-srv/style/movies/reviews/antzkempley.htm.
Kilner, James M., and Chris D. Frith. "Action Observation: Inferring Intentions without Mirror Neurons." *Current Biology* 18.1 (January 8, 2008): R32–33.
Klady, Leonard. Rev. of *Toy Story. Village Voice,* November 19, 1995, 48.
Kurtti, Jeff. *A Bug's Life: The Art and Making of an Epic of Miniature Proportions.* New York: Hyperion, 1998.
LaSalle, Mick. "*Cars* Looks Cool. But Take It Out for a Spin for 2 Hours and It Runs Out of Gas." *San Francisco Chronicle,* June 9, 2006; accessed December 24, 2014. http://www.sfgate.com/movies/article/Cars-looks-cool-But-take-it-out-for-a-spin-for-2495072.php.
———. "*Cars 2* Review: Spy Plot Revs Up Sequel." *San Francisco Chronicle,* June 24, 2011; accessed June 1, 2015. http://www.sfgate.com/movies/article/Cars-2-review-Spy-plot-revs-up-sequel-2367009.php.
Lasseter, John. "Principles of Traditional Animation Applied to 3D Computer Animation." *Computer Graphics* 21.4 (July 1987): 35–44.
———. "A Tribute to Frank Thomas." *Animation World Network,* November 24, 2004; accessed February 14, 2013. http://www.awn.com/articles/people/tribute-frank-thomas.
———. "Tricks to Animating Characters in a Computer." *Computer Graphics* 34.2 (May 2001): 45–47.
Lasseter, John, and Steve Daly. Toy Story: *The Art and Making of the Animated Film.* New York: Disney Editions, 1995.

Laybourne, Kit. *The Animation Book.* New York: Three Rivers Press, 1998.

Lee, Nora. "Computer Animation Comes of Age." *American Cinematographer* 70.10 (October 1989): 78–87.

————. "Computer Animation Demystified." *American Cinematographer* 70.11 (November 1989): 98–106.

Lemieux, Philippe. *L'Image numérique au cinéma.* Paris: L'Harmattan, 2012.

Lenburg, Jeff. *John Lasseter: The Whiz Who Made Pixar King.* New York: Chelsea House, 2012.

Leslie, Esther. *Hollywood Flatlands.* London: Verso, 2004.

Lewis, Jon. "Disney after Disney: Family Business and the Business of Family." In *Disney Discourse: Producing the Magic Kingdom.* Ed. Eric Smoodin. New York: Routledge, 1994. 87–105.

LoBrutto, Vincent. *Sound-on-Film: Interviews with Creators of Film Sound.* Westport, Conn.: Praeger, 1994.

"The Look of *Cars*: Pixar's Production Designers Go to the Races and Get Their Kicks on Route 66." The Writing Studio. Accessed June 3, 2015. http://www.writingstudio.co.za/page1213.html.

Lucci, Gabriele. *Le Cinéma d'animation.* Trans. Claire Mulkai. Paris: Hazan, 2006.

Lyons, Mike. "Toon Story: John Lasseter's Animated Life." *Animation World Magazine* 3.8 (November 1998); accessed July 30, 2014. http://www.awn.com/mag/issue3.8/3.8pages/3.8lyonsLasseter.

Malandrin, Stéphane. Rev. of *Toy Story. Cahiers du Cinéma* 501 (April 1996): 79.

Malausa, Vincent. Rev. of *Cars 2. Cahiers du Cinéma* 669 (July–August 2011): 55–56.

Maltin, Leonard. *The Disney Films.* New York: Disney Editions, 2000.

————. *Of Mice and Men: A History of American Animated Cartoons.* New York: Penguin, 1987.

Mandell, Paul. "*Young Sherlock Holmes,* a 'What If?' Tale." *American Cinematographer* (March 1986): 58–69.

Manovich, Lev. *The Language of New Media.* Cambridge: Massachusetts Institute of Technology Press, 2001.

————. "What Is Digital Cinema?" In *Critical Visions in Film Theory.* Ed. Timothy Corrigan, Patricia White, and Meta Mazaj. Boston: Bedford/St. Martin's, 2011. 1060–70.

Martin, Adrian. "Possessory Credit." *Framework* 45.1 (Spring 2004): 95–99.

Maslin, Janet. "Out-of-Step Ant Sails Out to Save the Hill." *New York Times,* November 25, 1998; accessed August 5, 2014. http://www.nytimes.com/movie/review?res=9C02E7DA1639F936A15752C1A96E958260.

————. "Toy Story." *New York Times,* November 22, 1995; C9:3.

————. "*Toy Story 2*: Animated Sequel Finds New Level of Imagination." *New York Times,* November 24, 1999; accessed August 22, 2014. http://www.nytimes.com/library/film/112499toy-film-review.html.

MC206. "A *Bug's Life* Falls Short, but Demonstrates Potential for Proletarian Art." *Maoist Internationalist Movement.* Accessed August 20, 2014. http://www.prisoncensorship.info/archive/etext/movies/review.php?f=long/bugslife.txt.

McCarthy, Todd. Rev. of *A Bug's Life. Variety,* November 29, 1998; accessed August 6, 2014. http://variety.com/1998/film/reviews/a-bug-s-life-1200455803/.

McCracken, Harry. "Luxo Sr.: An Interview with John Lasseter." *Animato* (Winter 1990); accessed April 3, 2013. http://www.harrymccracken.com/luxo.htm.

McKee, Robert. *Story: Substance, Structure, Style, and the Principles of Screenwriting.* New York: Regan Books, 1997.

Merritt, Russell, and J. B. Kaufman. *Walt Disney's Silly Symphonies.* Udine, Italy: Le Cineteca del Friuli, 2006.

Morgenstern, Joe. "Oy Story: *Cars 2* Is a Dollar-Driven Edsel." *Wall Street Journal,* June 24, 2011; accessed June 1, 2015. http://www.wsj.com/articles/SB10001424052702303339904576403323317657598.

Naccache, Lionel. *Le Nouvel inconscient.* Paris: Odile Jacob, 2006.

Neupert, Richard. *French Animation History.* Malden, Mass.: Wiley-Blackwell, 2011.

———. "Kirikou and the Animated Figure/Body." *Studies in French Cinema* 8.1 (2008): 41–56.

Niogret, Hubert. "Faisons juste le film que nous avons envie de faire." *Positif* 544 (June 2006): 16–20.

Noyer, Jérémie. *Entretiens avec un empire: Rencontres avec les artistes Disney.* Vol. 2: *De Dinosaure à Toy Story 3.* Paris: L'Harmattan, 2011.

O'Connor, Stuart. "How to Tell a Great Toy Story." *The Guardian,* February 11, 2009; accessed June 20, 2013. http://www.guardian.co.uk/technology/2009/feb/12/interview-john-Lasseter-pixar.

Osmond, Andrew. Rev. of *Cars 2. Sight and Sound* (September 2011): 57.

Paik, Karen. *To Infinity and Beyond: The Story of Pixar Animation Studios.* San Francisco: Chronicle Books, 2007.

Pallant, Chris. *Demystifying Disney: A History of Disney Feature Animation.* New York: Continuum, 2011.

Petroff, B. Z. Telephone interview with the author, June 23, 2013.

Pintoff, Ernest. *Animation 101.* Studio City, Calif.: Michael Wiese Productions, 1998.

"Pixar's *Cars* Stalls with Reviewers." *The Guardian* June 7, 2006; accessed June 22, 2015. http://www.theguardian.com/film/2006/jun/07/news.

Plantinga, Carl, and Greg M. Smith, eds. *Passionate Views: Film Cognition and Emotion.* Baltimore: Johns Hopkins University Press, 1999.

Polan, Dana. "Auteur Desire." *Screening the Past* 12 (March 1, 2001): 1–16.

Porter, Tom, and Galyn Susman. "Creating Lifelike Characters in Pixar Movies." *Communications of the ACM* 43.1 (January 2000): 25–29.

Pourriol, Ollivier. *Vertiges du désir: Comprendre le désir au cinéma.* Paris: NiL, 2011.

Power, Patrick. "Character Animation and the Embodied Mind-Brain." *Animation: An Interdisciplinary Journal* 3.1 (March 2008): 25–48.

Price, David A. *The Pixar Touch: The Making of a Company.* New York: Knopf, 2008.

Prince, Stephen. *Digital Visual Effects in Cinema.* New Brunswick, N.J.: Rutgers University Press, 2012.

————. "True Lies: Perceptual Realism, Digital Images, and Film Theory." *Film Quarterly* 49.3 (Spring 1996): 27–37.

Robertson, Barbara. "*Toy Story*: A Triumph of Animation." *Computer Graphics World* (August 1995); accessed May 14, 2014. https://design.osu.edu/carlson/history/tree/related%20materials/08stry1.html.

Rodowick, D. N. *The Virtual Life of Film.* Cambridge, Mass.: Harvard University Press, 2007.

Roth, Laurent. "L'enfant et les sortilèges." *Cahiers du Cinéma* 501 (April 1996): 12.

Rouyer, Philippe. "*Toy Story*: De la vie des jouets." *Positif* 422 (April 1996): 32–33.

Rowley, Stephen. "Life Reproduced in Drawings: Preliminary Comments upon Realism in Animation." *Animation Journal* 13 (2005): 65–85.

Russett, Robert, and Cecile Starr. *Experimental Animation: Origins of a New Art.* New York: Da Capo Press, 1976.

Sarafian, Katherine. "Flashing Digital Animations: Pixar's Digital Aesthetic." In *New Media: Theories and Practices of Digitextuality.* Ed. Anna Everett and John T. Caldwell. New York: Routledge, 2003. 209–23.

Schaffer, William. "The Importance of Being Plastic: The Feel of Pixar." *Animation Journal* 12 (2004): 72–95.

Schager, Nick. "Lightning McQueen's European Vacation in *Cars 2.*" *Village Voice,* June 22, 2011; accessed July 30, 2015. http://www.villagevoice.com/film/lightning-mcqueens-european-vacation-in-cars-2-6431538.

Schlender, Brent, and Christopher Tkacyzk. "Pixar's Magic Man." *Fortune,* May 29, 2006, 138–49.

Schlender, Brent, and Jane Furth. "Steve Jobs' Amazing Movie Adventure." *Fortune,* September 18, 1995, 154–72.

Shay, Estelle. "Company File: Pixar." *Cinefex* 55 (August 1993): 23–24.

Shay, Jodi Duncan. "*Young Sherlock Holmes*: Anything but Elementary." *Cinefex* 26 (May 1986): 36–67.

Sims, Peter. *Little Bets: How Breakthrough Ideas Emerge from Small Discoveries.* New York: Free Press, 2011.

Sito, Tom. "Disney's *The Fox and the Hound*: The Coming of the Next Generation." *Animation World Magazine* 3.8 (November 1998); accessed June 19, 2013. http://www.awn.com/mag/issue3.8/3.8pages/3.8sitofox.html.

————. *Moving Innovation: A History of Computer Animation.* Cambridge: Massachusetts Institute of Technology Press, 2013.

Smith, Alvy Ray. "The Adventures of André and Wally B." Unpublished draft. July 20, 1984.

————. "Re: Questions about Early Pixar Style." Email message to the author, July 11, 2014.

Smith, Jeff. "Movie Music as Moving Music." In *Passionate Views: Film Cognition and Emotion.* Ed. Carl Plantinga and Greg M. Smith. Baltimore: Johns Hopkins University Press, 1999. 146–67.

Smith, Thomas G. *Industrial Light and Magic: The Art of Special Effects.* New York: Ballantine Books, 1986.

Snider, Burr. "The *Toy Story* Story: How John Lasseter Came to Make the First 100 Percent Computer-Generated Theatrical Motion Picture." *Wired* 3.12 (December 1995): 146–50.

Solomon, Charles. *Enchanted Drawings: The History of Animation.* New York: Knopf, 1989.

Spark, Nick T. "Working Out the Bugs: Interview with Pixar's Lee Unkrich." *Motion Picture Editors Guild Newsletter* (January/February 1999); accessed July 30, 2015. https://www.editorsguild.com/magazine.cfm?ArticleID=502.

Sragow, Michael. "How the Techies and Toonies Brought *Toy Story* to Life." *New York Times* 19 Nov. 1995, Arts & Leisure: 17, 28–29.

Stack, Peter. "'Bugs' Has Legs." *San Francisco Chronicle,* November 25, 1998; accessed January 11, 2015. http://www.sfgate.com/movies/article/Bug-s-Has-Legs-Cute-insect-adventure-a-visual-2976395.php.

————. "Computers 'Toy' with Us: Pixar-Animated Dazzler for All Ages." *San Francisco Chronicle,* November 22, 1995; accessed May 20, 2014. http://www.sfgate.com/movies/article/Computers-Toy-With-Us-Pixar-animated-dazzler-3018933.php.

————. "Fantasy Worlds: Clever 'Antz' Is Like a Remake of a Woody Allen Movie." *San Francisco Chronicle,* October 2, 1998; accessed August 5, 2014. http://www.sfgate.com/movies/article/Fantasy-Worlds-Clever-Antz-is-like-an-2987565.php.

————. "Toy-ing with Emotions: Funny, Action-Packed and Heart-Warming Sequel Draws Viewers into the Lives of Woody and the Gang." *San Francisco Chronicle,* November 24, 1999; accessed September 12, 2014. http://www.sfgate.com/movies/article/Toy-ing-With-Emotions-Funny-action-packed-2894661.php.

Stanton, Andrew. "*Wall-E* Teaser." July 5, 2007; accessed June 22, 2015. https://www.youtube.com/watch?v=nuAGE5_fglA.

Stewart, James B. *Disney War.* New York: Simon and Schuster, 2005.

"Story Tells Tale of O'seas Hit." *Variety,* April 1, 1996, 15.

Street, Rita. "Toys Will Be Toys." *Cinefex* 64 (December 1995): 76–91.

Swain, Bob. Rev. of *Knick Knack.* *Sight and Sound* (September 1992): 65.

Tan, Ed S. *Emotion and the Structure of Narrative Film*. New York: Routledge, 2011.

Tan, Ed and Nico Frijda. "Sentiment in Film Viewing." In *Passionate Views: Film, Cognition, and Emotion*. Baltimore: Johns Hopkins University Press, 1999. 48–64

Telotte, J. P. *Animating Space: From Mickey to Wall-E*. Lexington: University Press of Kentucky, 2010.

————. *The Mouse Machine: Disney and Technology*. Urbana: University of Illinois Press, 2008.

Tesson, Charles. "Les jouets meurent aussi." *Cahiers du Cinéma* 543 (February 2000): 40–42.

Thomas, Bob. *Disney's Art of Animation*. New York: Hyperion, 1991.

Thomas, Frank. "Can Classic Disney Animation Be Duplicated on the Computer?" *Computer Pictures* (July/August 1984): 20–26.

Thomas, Frank, and Ollie Johnston. *Disney Animation: The Illusion of Life*. New York: Abbeville, 1981.

Thompson, Kristin. "Reflections on *Cars*." David Bordwell's Website on Cinema, October 8, 2006; accessed July 30, 2015. http://www.davidbordwell.net/blog/2006/10/08/reflections-on-cars/.

————. *Storytelling in the New Hollywood: Understanding Classical Narrative Technique*. Cambridge, Mass.: Harvard University Press, 1999.

Thompson, Kristin, and David Bordwell. "A Glimpse into the Pixar Kitchen." David Bordwell's Website on Cinema, April 10, 2008; accessed July 30, 2015. http://www.davidbordwell.net/blog/2008/04/10/a-glimpse-into-the-pixar-kitchen/.

Torre, Dan. "Cognitive Animation Theory: A Process-Based Reading of Animation and Human Cognition." *Animation: An Interdisciplinary Journal* 9.1 (March 2014): 47–64.

"*Toy Story* Animated in O'seas B.O." *Variety*, April 8, 1996, 10.

Tyler, Dennis. "Home Is Where the Heart Is: Pixar's *Up*." In *Diversity in Disney Films*. Ed. Johnson Cheu. Jefferson, N.C.: McFarland, 2013. 268–83.

Vaz, Mark Cotta. *Industrial Light and Magic: Into the Digital Realm*. New York: Ballantine Books, 1996.

Venkatasawmy, Rama. *The Digitization of Cinematic Visual Effects*. Lanham, Mass.: Lexington Books, 2013.

Vercauteren, Gert, and Pilar Orero. "Describing Facial Expressions: Much More Than Meets the Eye!" *Quaderns Revista de Traduccio* 20 (June 2013): 187–99.

Waters, Keith. "A Muscle Model for Animating Three-Dimensional Facial Expression." SIGGRAPH *Computer Graphics* 21, 4 (July 1987): 17–24.

Watts, Steven. *The Magic Kingdom: Walt Disney and the American Way of Life*. Boston: Houghton Mifflin, 1997.

Wells, Paul. *Animation and America*. New Brunswick, N.J.: Rutgers University Press, 2002.

————. *The Fundamentals of Animation.* Lausanne: AVA Publishing, 2006.

————. "To Sonicity and Beyond! Gary Rydstrom and Quilting the Pixar Sound." *Animation Journal* 17 (2009): 23–35.

Wells, Paul, and Johnny Hardstaff. *Re-Imagining Animation: The Changing Face of the Moving Image.* Lausanne: AVA Publishing, 2008.

Whissel, Kristen. *Spectacular Digital Effects: CGI and Contemporary Cinema.* Durham, N.C.: Duke University Press, 2014.

White, Tim. "From Disney to Warner Bros.: The Critical Shift." In *Reading the Rabbit: Explorations in Warner Bros. Animation.* Ed. Kevin S. Sandler. New Brunswick, N.J.: Rutgers University Press, 1998. 38–66.

Wiedemann, Julius. "Pixar." In *Animation Now!* Koln: Taschen, 2004. 402.

Willats, John. *Art and Representation: New Principles in the Analysis of Pictures.* Princeton, N.J.: Princeton University Press, 1997.

Wilonsky, Robert. "Running on Fumes." *Village Voice,* May 30, 2006; accessed December 26, 2014. http://www.villagevoice.com/2006–05–30/film/running-on-fumes/.

Wuillème, Tanguy. "Hervé Aubron, *Génie de Pixar.*" *Questions de Communication* 20 (2011): 381–82.

Yabroff, Jennie. "The *Newsweek* 50: Lasseter, Pixar Animation Guru." *Newsweek,* December 19, 2008; accessed July 28, 2014. http://www.newsweek.com/newsweek-50-Lasseter-pixar-animation-guru-83115.

Young, John. "John Lasseter on Pixar's Early Days—and How 'Toy Story' Couldn't Have Happened without Tim Burton." *Entertainment Weekly,* June 16, 2011; accessed July 30, 2015. http://www.ew.com/article/2011/06/16/pixar-john-Lasseter-burton.

Thompson, Kristin, 4, 110, 155
Tin Toy, 72–80, 75, 76, 83, 89, 92, 98, 102, 133, 147, 178
Tin Toy Christmas, A, 89
Tkacyzk, Christopher, 5, 7, 9, 13, 23, 31, 56–57, 95, 101, 119
Tony de Peltrie, 54, 78
Toppan Printing, 86
Toronto Animation Festival, 44
Torre, Dan, 62
Toy Story, 1, 3, 5, 35, 49, 78, 85, 86, 89–120, 123, 124 126–29, 135–38, 143–50, 153, 158–61, 169–71, 174, 175, color plates 3–6; box office and reception, 112–16, 119, 142, 151; commercialism, 118–19; nostalgia, 116–18; plot structure, 106–10; production budget, 89, 101; script, 92–99; sound strategies, 97–98, 103, 111
Toy Story 2, 144–52, 163, 179, color plates 10–12; box office and reception, 149–51; end, 146; plot structure, 145–48; technical advances, 149, 151
Toy Story 3, 161, 162
Toy Story 4, 162
Triple-I, 24
Tron, 24–26, 33, 50
Tropicana, 86, 88
Trousdale, Gary, 143
Truffaut, François, 7, 65
Tuber's Two Step, 40
Turner and Hooch, 94
Turturro, John, 160
Tyler, Dennis, 117

Ugly Duckling, The, 98
Unkrich, Lee, 36, 99, 124, 135, 144, 152, 161, 165, 179–80
Up, 151
UPA Studios, 9

van Baerle, Susan, 43
van Tulden, Linda, 60
Variety reviews, 114, 142, 161, 164–65
VAX computers, 44
Vaz, Mark Cotta, 46
Venkatasawmy, Rama, 50, 151

Verbinski, Gore, 154
Vercauteren, Gert, 81

Wall-E, 121, 151, 152
Wall Street Journal, 162
Walt Disney Company, 1, 6, 21–28, 79, 89–96; aesthetic style, 5, 10–12, 16, 21, 24, 61, 70, 101–2, 137; and *A Bug's Life*, 124; purchase of Pixar, 2, 143, 164; and *Toy Story*, 89–96; and *Toy Story 2*, 143–44
Walter Lantz Productions, 8
Warin, Deirdre, 82, 178
Warner Bros., 8, 30–31, 61, 66, 82, 96, 170
Washington, Denzel, 118
Waters, Keith, 77
Watts, Steven, 10
Webb, Chris, 146, 180
Wedge, Chris, 25–26, 40
Welles, Orson, 150
Wells, Paul, 38, 60, 68, 76, 81, 115, 118, 119, 132, 167
Wenders, Wim, 154
Whedon, Joss, 93, 179
Where the Wild Things Are, 25–28
White, Tim, 9
Whitney, James, 4
Whitney, John, 4, 5
Who Framed Roger Rabbit, 80, 170
Who is Bud Luckey?, 119
Wiedemann, Julius, 63
Wilhite, Tom, 25–28, 32, 45
Williams, Chris, 164
Wilonsky, Robert, 153
Wilson, Owen, 156, 158
Wired, 3, 6, 101, 125
Wise, Kirk, 143
Wizard of Oz, 157
Wooden, Shannon R., 99, 118, 158
Woody Woodpecker, 8

Yabroff, Jennie, 165
Yates, Peter, 94
Young, John, 68
Young Sherlock Jr., 46–52, 50, 51, 54

Zaslove, Alan, 143
Zemeckis, Robert, 80

Richard Neupert is the Charles H. Wheatley
Professor of the Arts in the Department of Theatre
and Film Studies at the University of Georgia.
His books include *French Animation History*
and *A History of the French New Wave*.

Books in the series Contemporary Film Directors

Philip Kaufman
Annette Insdorf

Richard Linklater
David T. Johnson

David Lynch
Justus Nieland

John Sayles
David R. Shumway

Dario Argento
L. Andrew Cooper

Todd Haynes
Rob White

Christian Petzold
Jaimey Fisher

Spike Lee
Todd McGowan

Terence Davies
Michael Koresky

Francis Ford Coppola
Jeff Menne

Emir Kusturica
Giorgio Bertellini

Agnès Varda
Kelley Conway

John Lasseter
Richard Neupert

The University of Illinois Press
is a founding member of the
Association of American University Presses.

Composed in 10/13 New Caledonia
with Helvetica Neue display
by Kirsten Dennison
at the University of Illinois Press
Manufactured by Cushing-Malloy, Inc.

University of Illinois Press
1325 South Oak Street
Champaign, IL 61820-6903
www.press.uillinois.edu